"Richly engrossing, this is a multidimensional, multid memoir that reveals life-long, even intergenerational, elements embedded in the boarding schools' systems, easily surmise the author's preventive recommendations. Not only courageous in the revelations along its personal journey, but in challenging what has been considered a culturally desirable standard for the societal elites."

— **Yael Danieli, PhD**, Director, Group Project for Holocaust Survivors and their Children; founder, International Center for the Study, Prevention and Treatment of MultiGenerational Legacies of Trauma, New York

"In this brave and engaging book, Christine Jack offers a witness account of the life-long psychological consequences of sending children to boarding school. In a rare combination of academic research and personal testimony, Jack chooses Christopher Robin Milne as a travelling companion. The compelling narrative offers a searing indictment of the boarding school system. This book is a significant contribution to the history of education, as well as the literature on the hazards of leaving children in boarding schools. It will interest a wide range of readers including educational theorists, ex-boarders and psychotherapists."

— **Professor Joy Schaverien, PhD**, Jungian Psychoanalyst and author of *Boarding School Syndrome: The Psychological Trauma of the "Privileged" Child* (Routledge, 2015)

"This is a remarkable book that crosses the genres of memoir and historical and other forms of exposition. It needed to do so because its ambition was to describe and analyse the experience of children abandoned by their families to school boarding houses, from their point of view, and to understand the possible and probable impacts that the traumas involved might have on later lives. The range of theoretical reference the author brings to the work is astounding. This work marks a highly significant addition to the literature on the impact of school boarding on children and youth."

— **Craig Campbell**, Associate Professor, History of Education (Honorary), University of Sydney; co-author of *Jean Blackburn: Education, Feminism and Social Justice* (2019) and *A History of Australian Schooling* (2014)

"Christine Jack has presented us with a courageous, evocative and theoretically grounded memoir of the subtleness of attachment-related trauma. Although set in the boarding school experience, this trauma can be generalised to other childhood abandonments. As Christine explored her feelings of devastation and agony, she was able to reach a level of clarity about her trauma and find, in utilising her "undamaged part", a sense of hope towards the notion of recovery to an "earned secure attachment" and finally to self-acceptance. This beautifully written book will be a gift to my clients!"

— **Paulette Calabro, PsyD**, Clinical Psychologist and Relationship Psychotherapist, Mindcare Centre, Sydney, Australia

"This is a first-class piece of research using a novel way to get us to think about the horrors at Pooh Corner. In other words, Christine Jack argues tightly and cogently that we should take note of the peculiar and damaging attitude to children that results in normalised neglect, which the British spread to their colonies and which is now coming back to bite them in the form of a delusion politics, based in esprit de corps rather than empathy and creativity."

— **Nick Duffell**, psychotherapy trainer and author of *The Making of Them: The British Attitude to Children and the Boarding School System* (2000) and *Wounded Leaders: British Elitism and the Entitlement Illusion – a Psychohistory* (2014)

"A gripping and moving study that puts flesh on the dry bones of the terrible psychological disorder we know as "attachment-related trauma". Christine Jack juxtaposes vivid personal memoir with the true story of one of literature's most famous innocents to sum up the experience of neglect and abandonment that is for so many the reality of a boarding school education. The lessons drawn are important. Firstly, that this dominant culture of parenting, the one devised for and by the most privileged people in the world, was profoundly wrong. Second, that by shining the clean light of contemporary psychological understanding on this history we can find a way forward for the many who suffered and still suffer as a result of their time in industrialised residential care systems. Most important of all, this book takes a place among the essential literature that will guide us to giving children, whatever their circumstances, the love and protection they need and deserve."

— **Alex Renton**, author of *Stiff Upper Lip*: *Secrets, Crimes and the Schooling of a Ruling Class* (2017)

"Christine Jack has written a very thoughtful memoir documenting the traumatic effect of her own childhood boarding school experience interwoven with the story of Christopher Milne's parallel experience. It is not a memoir meant to shock the reader but to validate the survivors and to inform all those adults who influence the course of children's lives."

— **Janina Fisher, PhD**, international expert on the treatment of trauma, author of *Healing the Fragmented Selves of Trauma Survivors* (Routledge, 2017)

"Christine Jack brings together memoir and academic research with graceful ease as she explores the impact of boarding school on the lives of young children. The warmth and poignancy of her own experience gives powerful substance to the breadth and depth of her theoretical frameworks. It is a "must-read" for educators, parents and anyone who has been to boarding school."

> — **Patti Miller**, award-winning memoirist and author of *Writing True Stories: The Complete Guide to Writing Autobiography, Memoir, Personal Essay, Biography, Travel and Creative Nonfiction* (2017)

"As a young child I read British children's novels about boarding school, and fantasised about the delights of that adult-free world. Then, when my parents suggested I might like to go to such a school, I sensibly refused to go. I suspect children know intuitively that boarding school is always the wrong choice. This book explores these issues, in parallel narratives: one addresses Christopher Robin Milne's experience of boarding school, and its profound impacts on his life, speech and personality; the second is Christine Jack's own experiences of boarding school and its effects. Though her history is thirty-plus years later than Milne's, the stories are disturbingly similar. The language used refuses despair, and the stories are told in an inquisitive, tender voice that, says Jack, comes from 'a deep pool of hope that through it we may find fellowship with our imagined community of readers'. This book combines hope with the anguish of memory, in language that never swerves away from trauma, but throughout shows vividly how one can build resilience, and craft a life worth living."

> — **Professor Jen Webb**, Centre for Creative and Cultural Research, University of Canberra; co-author *Creativity in Context: How to Make a Poet* (2018)

"This insightful and well-written book is a most welcome addition to a growing body of work on the trauma that is inevitable when young children make the transition from family life to the institutional life of a boarding school. The effects of this trauma can be long-term and are often carried over, as baggage, into adult life. A major strength of this book is its breadth of perspective. The author examines the trauma, and indeed the path to recovery, through an educational and historical lens, in addition to highlighting psychological and social issues. She uses a narrative approach, courageously and sensitively exploring the effects of boarding school on both her own life and that of Christopher Robin Milne, as a companion on her journey to healing. Sending young children away to board is a particularly British habit and it is helpful that the author is able to shine a light on the practice in Australia and, in doing so, also illustrates clear links between the UK and Australia. This book is relevant to educationalists, teachers, historians, sociologists, psychotherapists, psychologists, mental health workers and indeed anybody who has had the experience of living in a boarding school."

> — **Thurstine Basset**, former Director of Boarding Concern and co-author of *Trauma Abandonment and Privilege: A Guide to Therapeutic Work with Boarding School Survivors* (Routledge, 2016)

Recovering Boarding School Trauma Narratives

Recovering Boarding School Trauma Narratives: Christopher Robin Milne as a Psychological Companion on the Journey to Healing is a unique, emotive and theorised narrative of a young girl's experience of boarding school in Australia. Christine Jack traces its impact on the emerging identity of the child, including sexual development and emotional capacity, the transmission of trauma into adulthood and the long process of recovery. Interweaving her story with the experiences of Christopher Robin Milne, she presents her memoir as an exemplar of how narrative writing can be employed in remembering and recovering from traumatic experiences.

Unique and powerfully written, Jack takes the reader on a journey into her childhood in Australian boarding school convents in the 1950s and 1960s. Comparing her experience with Christopher Robin Milne's, she interrogates his memoirs, illustrating that boarding school trauma knows no boundaries of time and place. She investigates their emerging individuality before being sent to live an institutional life and traces their feelings of longing and loneliness as well as the impact of the abuse each endured there. As an educational historian, Jack writes in a ground-breaking way from the perspective of an insider and outsider, revealing how trauma remains in the unconscious, wielding power over the life of the adult, until the traumatic memories are recovered, emotions released and associated dysfunctional behaviour changed, restoring well-being. Engaging the lenses of history, life-span and Jungian psychology, feminist and trauma theory and boarding school trauma research, this book positions narrative writing as a way of reducing the power of trauma over the lives of survivors.

Personal and accessible, this book will be essential reading for psychologists and educational historians, as well as students and academics of psychology, sociology, trauma studies, ex-boarders and those interested in the life of Christopher Robin Milne.

Christine Jack spent thirty-five years as an academic in the field of teacher education, including holding the position of Head of Primary Education at the University of Canberra. She is a respected and well-published Australian educational historian and is currently an honorary researcher at Charles Sturt University.

Recovering Boarding School Trauma Narratives

Christopher Robin Milne as a Psychological Companion on the Journey to Healing

Christine Jack

Routledge
Taylor & Francis Group

LONDON AND NEW YORK

First published 2020
by Routledge
2 Park Square, Milton Park, Abingdon, Oxon OX14 4RN

and by Routledge
52 Vanderbilt Avenue, New York, NY 10017

Routledge is an imprint of the Taylor & Francis Group, an informa business

British Library Cataloguing-in-Publication Data
A catalogue record for this book is available from the British Library

Library of Congress Cataloging-in-Publication Data
Names: Trimingham Jack, Christine, 1950- author.
Title: Recovering boarding school trauma narratives : Christopher Robin Milne as a psychological companion on the journey to healing / Christine Jack.
Description: Abingdon, Oxon ; New York, NY : Routledge, 2020. | Includes bibliographical references and index.
Identifiers: LCCN 2019059460 (print) | LCCN 2019059461 (ebook) |ISBN 9780367819507 (hardback) |
ISBN 9780367819521 (paperback) | ISBN 9781003010982 (ebook)
Subjects: LCSH: Trimingham Jack, Christine, 1950—Childhood and youth. | Milne, Christopher, 1920-1996. | School violence–Australia. | School violence–Psychological aspects. | Boarding schools–Australia. | Psychic trauma in adolescence. | Violence in adolescence. | Teenage girls–Australia–Biography.
Classification: LCC LB3013.34.A8 T75 2020 (print) | LCC LB3013.34.A8 (ebook) | DDC 371.7/82–dc23
LC record available at https://lccn.loc.gov/2019059460
LC ebook record available at https://lccn.loc.gov/2019059461

ISBN: 978-0-367-81950-7 (hbk)
ISBN: 978-0-367-81952-1 (pbk)
ISBN: 978-1-003-01098-2 (ebk)

Typeset in Times New Roman
by Swales & Willis, Exeter, Devon, UK

For all the children ...

Contents

Acknowledgements

I wish to acknowledge all Aboriginal and Torres Strait Islander people who are the traditional custodians of the land on which I write. I also pay my respects to the Elders past and present. Aboriginal and Torres Strait Islander people have suffered greatly from the forcible removal of their children.

I am beholden to many who have acted variously as critical readers and supporters: Linda Devereux, Mary Macken Horarik, David Watson, Susie Edwards, Marion Bearup, Craig Campbell, Helen Proctor, members of the Australian and New Zealand History of Education Society, Joy Schaverien, Thurstine Basset, attendees of the Brighton Mini Conference, 1 June 2019, who affirmed the value of the project, Jen Webb, Yael Danieli, Nick Duffell, Nikki Simpson, Elizabeth Smyth, Janina Fisher, Alex Renton, Paulette Corry Calabro, Camille Farrell, Sherri Gates, members of my book club, the Routledge team especially Vilija Stephens and Heather Evans and the four anonymous reviewers of my original proposal. I am indebted to my children and grandchildren for so many reasons but mainly because they enrich my life beyond words. I am grateful for having parents who believed in the power of education and wanted only the best for me. Above all, I have been blessed to have Neill Ustick as my partner, my beloved "other" psychological companion, research assistant, critical reader and faithful believer.

Introduction

This book is partly memoir and partly biography. It is an account of my experience of being sent to boarding school as a seven-year-old child in rural Australia in 1957. It is also the story of Christopher Robin Milne (1920–1996), son of the famous author Alan Alexander Milne, who was sent to British boarding schools in the 1930s at the age of nine. Our stories reveal the immediate and long-term impact on many children when they are separated from their parents and required to live an institutional life.

My relationship with Christopher Milne began at the movies. I had heard that the 2017 children's film *Christopher Robin* begins with a farewell party held when he is about to go to boarding school.[1] So I went to see it, thinking it might provide me with an introduction to the book I was writing on boarding school trauma. In my mind, it would just be a short paragraph aimed at capturing the reader's attention by linking to something of current interest. What I discovered was that the whole film could be read as the story of what often happens to a child when he or she is sent away to board: the trauma of leaving parents, home and all that is familiar; the need to suppress the associated grief ("homesickness") and the long-term consequences of dissociating from these emotions; the demands of finding a way of fitting in, which leads to the development of a false personality; the long-term impact on adult life, including difficulties with intimate and family relationships; the process of reconnecting with childhood and integrating traumatic memories into adult understandings; and the intergenerational pattern of young children being sent away to board, based on the entrenched belief that it is for their own good.

The movie is a fictionalised account of Christopher Robin, star of the Winnie-the-Pooh books written by A. A. Milne. It triggered my interest in the real Christopher Milne and I learnt that he had written three memoirs: *The Enchanted Places* (1974),[2] *The Path Through the Trees* (1979)[3] and *The Hollow on the Hill* (1982).[4] When I read them, I became enthralled because so much of his story mirrored my experience of being sent away to board as a young child and the long journey of adult recovery from childhood trauma. I was particularly fascinated by the passion he developed for the New Education Movement, which was popular in the UK in the 1960s. I too had become enamoured by Progressive Education, as it is more commonly known, when I went to university in the 1970s. The key ideas of the movement led both of us to reflect on, and to analyse, our school experience.

After reading Christopher's memoir, I turned to two biographies written by Ann Thwaite, centred on his father. The first was published in 1990 and in the introduction Thwaite establishes that she wrote it with Christopher's blessing.[5] It reassured me that I could use it with the confidence that her representation was close to how Christopher understood aspects of his early life. The second book, *Goodbye Christopher Robin* (2017), is a reworking of the first and its publication was tied to the release of the film under the same title.[6] Both books are a gold mine of well-researched information about the Milne family. I have drawn on Thwaite's books in my writing, although my story follows Christopher across his adulthood as a person in his own right, with a focus on the ramifications of his boarding school experience. My work is informed by recent research on boarding school trauma, which was not included in either of the biographies. The inclusion adds significantly to understanding his life.

After reading Thwaite's books and Christopher's memoirs, the intersections in some aspects of our experiences were so strong that I decided I wanted to interweave his story into my memoir. Initially, I assigned him the role of "companion writer", so that the book would be an interplay between our two stories. However, not long after I began writing, I discovered it was a two-way street. Reflecting on his experiences led me to think more deeply about my own, evoking memories and insights that might easily have been overlooked. In turn, my memories led me to notice pertinent aspects of his life. Yet there was even more at work here; it took me some time to realise the substantial nature of his role. Revisiting traumatic events involves allowing the mind to return to dark places in which one feels very much alone. Having Christopher beside me meant I had a "psychological companion"—one who had shared similar experiences, had faced them and now supported me in doing my own memory work. It became an essential companionship, knowing that I was not by myself in facing the trauma of my childhood.

There are three aims in writing this book. The first is to add to the body of literature on the emotional consequences for children whose parents choose to send them away to boarding schools. It exposes the long road to recalling and understanding those experiences—I refer to this as the *recovering* process— and the impact it has on adulthood. The second aim is to offer this memoir as an exemplar of the way in which narrative writing can be employed in recovering traumatic experiences and integrating them into autobiographical memory. The third aim is to offer an extensive narrative from the perspective of an Australian boarding school girl in the 1950s and 1960s. An outcome of this aim is that it provides evidence of the transcontinental movement of British boarding school practice based on a belief that children are best educated in living arrangements away from their families. The study, therefore, makes a contribution not only to educational history but also to transnational history: "the study of movements and forces that cut across national boundaries".[7]

This is the second book I have written about a boarding school, although, in my previous book, the experience of "boarding" was not a central focus. My doctoral thesis was a history of the small Catholic girls' preparatory boarding school I attended as a child.[8] It was later reworked and published as *Growing Good Catholic Girls: Education and Convent Life in Australia* (2003).[9] I conducted interviews with seven nuns, two of whom also attended the school as children, and seven other ex-students. I was interested in the interaction between ex-students' "construction" of their experience (how they put together their narratives) and school ideology (espoused beliefs and practices). However, when I now look back on the narratives I assembled from the interviews, I see that, although I often used the word "traumatic", I didn't theorise it. I simply didn't have the language (knowledge) to go further and perhaps I was not psychologically ready to look at it. In writing the current book I have returned to the narratives (which use pseudonyms), exploring them for signs of the impact of boarding school on those women.

The notion of "experience" has always been central in my writing. It is something we construct through our engagement in the world: an ongoing process that is continuous, interactive, sometimes contradictory, and formative of a sense of who we are.[10] French philosopher Michel Foucault has been key in showing us that when we "engage in the world" we construct our experience according to the "discourses" available to us at the time. An interpretation of "discourse" that I find helpful, one that draws on Foucault's work, is that engagement in the world is a process of interaction with a "preconceptual, anonymous, socially sanctioned body of rules that govern one's manner of perceiving, judging, imagining, and acting".[11] Our interactions in the world are significantly about making meaning and, in turn, the world in which we live informs, controls, limits and expands the understandings we come to about our experiences and, ultimately, about our lives.

While some of the discourses we interact with can enhance our lives, bringing new perspectives to our understanding of them, others are so powerful that they suppress the stories we want to tell. Yet thinking about how we construct experience from the perspective of "discourse" allows us, indeed calls out for us, to revisit later in life the stories we tell about ourselves. We can go back armed with new understandings that offer a wider but still incomplete perspective, accepting that final truth is hoped for but never fully realised—insight is always partial.[12] Recent research on boarding school trauma undertaken by UK researchers has propelled me into re-examining both the history I wrote about my preparatory school, my personal story and Christopher's story.

The content of this book is also a piece of educational history. Boarding schools are set in an educational context in a particular historical period, a matter which I will cover in Chapter 2. My school story is embedded in the narrative of the history of Australian education, which at that time was deeply influenced by British practices. There is a longstanding recognition of the problems associated with private boarding schools. In the eighteenth century, Scottish economist and philosopher Adam Smith wrote that the education of boys and girls away from their homes had done "crucial harm to domestic morals and thus to domestic happiness, both in France and England".[13] In 1861, The Clarendon Commission, a UK royal commission, discovered not only illegal financial transactions conducted by headmasters but also widespread brutal treatment of younger students. However, they still condoned the schools as fostering a discourse of "manliness and independence".[14]

It was only during the First World War that the psychological link was made between boarding experience and the repression of emotions. Psychiatrist William Halse Rivers noticed the connection between the way the army officers expressed being "shell shocked" and their boarding education. He concluded that officers who had been educated in elite boarding schools had been trained to suppress any expression of fear and this made their treatment difficult.[15] Further studies across the decades have continued the discussion of the problems associated with these schools.[16] Yet, in spite of such challenges, British parents have continued to send their children to these institutions. Until recently, much of the research into boarding schools has focussed on males, including experiential literature.[17] My aim is to add to the emerging literature on girls' experience, one which indicates that for many students the experience was traumatic.[18]

Australian educational historians are just beginning to make the "boarding" aspect of schools central in their work.[19] However, little attention has been given by educational historians to the long-term impact of boarding school experience on those students whose parents opted to send their children away to board. Recent government enquiries in Australia and Canada have led the way in bringing into public awareness alarming evidence of the abuse suffered by students in these settings.[20] The 2013–2017 Australian Royal Commission into Institutional Responses to Child Sexual Abuse reveals that, of the 8,000 survivors who testified to the Commission and an additional 1,000 individuals who offered written accounts, 31.6 per cent were abused in schools; 61.4 per cent reported abuse in Catholic schools and 14.8 per cent in Anglican schools.[21] Many of these institutions were boarding schools and, although a number of histories of these schools have been written, the experiences of abuse have not been included. An explanation for this silence may lie partly in the fact that school histories are celebratory (often commissioned by the school) and they focus on those in positions of power and on chronologically ordered events. Where personal experiences of staff and students are included, they are used to offer support to the hegemonic view of the school, that is, the view that those in positions of power have, or wish to express, about the school.[22] Even when historians seek to provide a wider picture, participants may be reluctant to engage with the process for reasons associated with trauma, including memory loss[23] and shame.[24] The outcome is that significant traumatic incidents are left out of official histories,[25] perhaps to avoid the damaging effect of such inclusions on the reputation of the school.

What we call "history" is a project with a powerful agenda of handing on tradition. It does so by examining progression and relationships between things, thereby telling us how we arrived at where we are. Underlying it is a claim of "universal authority". However, we also quietly know that history is a "reconstruction, always problematic and incomplete" because there is always more to add. Additions may arise from elusive, unincorporated memories, and yet many historians are "suspicious of memory".[26] They protect themselves from worry about unreliability by adopting a "scientific approach" that looks for commonality of experience at the cost of suppressing antithetical individual experience. It is an approach that I have been confronted with when I have told people I am writing a book about boarding school trauma and have been asked: *But what percentage of people experienced it that way?* It is a question I have interpreted as a form of suppression and silencing, but for questioners it may simply be adoption of scientific discourse—demanding proof that the number who experienced it in that way is sizeable. The outcome of such thinking is that the experiences of the *majority* of people are seen as the entire truth or the truth that matters. In writing this book, it is important to acknowledge that some people who went to boarding school enjoyed and benefited from the experience. For some children, it was "a relief from an intolerable situation at home", with boarding school being more predictable.[27] This book is about those who found it to be traumatic.

In the past, individual memory has found its legitimacy in literature, especially memoir. Writing memoir may be thought of as "the method of articulating and attempting to communicate the essence of one's existence to oneself".[28] Joan Didion expresses it powerfully and succinctly: we "tell ourselves stories in order to live".[29] In 1989, French historian Pierre Nora argued that the boundary between "memory-history" and "memory-fiction" was blurring as we allow the historical imagination a freer rein, creating *lieux de memoire* (sites of memory) which were moving to the centre of history.[30] I am writing out of a "site of memory", both as an insider (someone who went to boarding school) and as an outsider (an educational historian).

Christopher Milne used the analogy of writing a memoir as being like an "archaeologist who, not content with excavating a handful of pottery fragments, goes on to deduce how the completed vase must have looked".[31] Memories are like artefacts because they don't come with labels attached—interpretations must be made, and then remade, as new knowledge becomes available, giving rise to new perspectives. When we look back on past times, we are seeking to give meaning to particular experiences so that we can understand how we got from there to here.[32] When writing memoir, there is a need to approach it with an understanding that "memory is a new construction that always changes to reflect one's previous selves and experiences, and therefore, while *like* a past event, it is always a new event".[33] So memoirs are never final; they are a narrative constructed at a particular time, interpreted by the understandings we bring to them over a period of time. Christopher Milne wrote three memoirs to make meaning of his life. I explore them as artefacts, seeking to understand how he came to terms with his life, what shaped his narrative and what remained unsaid.

Pierre Nora argues that with the merging of history and memoir, history is no longer solely the work of the professional historian. "The task of remembering" makes everyone a historian, especially those who have been marginalised in traditional history, as they seek to "recover their buried pasts".[34] This is the work that a number of contemporary UK writers on boarding school experience and myself are engaged in—the interplay between memory and meaning to arrive at an understanding of our identity and history—the story of the boarding school child. It is not an easy process. The project must be firmly based in "a will to remember".[35] It is also an uncomfortable activity of diving deeply into the past, recovering memories, interrogating them and having the courage to publicly expose them.[36]

An essential part of the work of *lieux de memoire* (sites of memory) is what Nora refers to as "the involvement of the historian in his or her subject" which I see as making the thinking of the historian transparent in the writing.[37] Historians have been reluctant to reveal themselves in the text. Many adopt the position of the objective researcher, removed, scientific and seeking ultimate truth. Yet privately we know that all knowledge is constructed through the consciousness of the writer and hence is partial and problematic. I have found that, when I engage in what is termed "the reflexive movement" (examination of my own thoughts, feelings and unconscious), I am likely to deepen my analysis. This involves reflecting on my thinking and trusting that what may seem at first to be irrelevant memories or thoughts have something to offer me. This reflection is then incorporated explicitly into the text, so that the reader can follow the path of arriving at a conclusion.[38]

At times I have turned to my dreams as part of the material. The writings of Carl Jung have been ground-breaking in providing the world with insight into the importance of dreams. He argues that there are events in our lives "of which we have not consciously taken note", so that they remain "below the threshold of consciousness".[39] The attached emotional content may be of vital importance in understanding our lives, but it is difficult to get back to it. When we have ignored the importance of an event, it may well up from the unconscious in the form of a dream "where it appears not as a rational thought but as a symbolic image".[40] He argues that a dream should be considered as "a fact", although one should approach it with no previous assumptions, except that it "somehow makes sense".[41] Dreams offer us a wider, deeper perception of our lives, although, Jung argues, we can never perceive or comprehend anything completely.[42] I have found that, at times, paying attention to dreams has been critical in alerting me to emotional content around traumatic events I have been trying to understand. Sometimes they have warned me that I have not fully explored the content of an experience. Taking them seriously has pushed me into a more complex analysis.

It would have been possible (and therapeutic) to write the narrative of my boarding school experience purely for myself. Taking it that step further, making the work public, requires another level of commitment that is not unproblematic. Life writer Kate Holden notes that writing memoir requires a measure of "self-absorption" and "conceit".[43] However, she justifies the ego-centric memoir project with the argument that we write "because we believe our specific experience also fingers the universal".[44] Surely she is right and those who engage in such writing do so from a deep pool of hope that through it we may find fellowship with our imagined community of readers.

Historians of education have also been caught up in the argument that "truth is a debated concept".[45] British historian Richard Aldrich writes that "history is a narrative discourse which is as much invented or imagined as found".[46] Yet in spite of a recognition of the conditional outcomes of the historical project, he concludes that:

> Words, whether spoken or written, will never be able to recapture the events of the past in their entirety, but the search for as accurate a representation as possible is as important for the historian in the lecture hall or journal article as for the judge and jury in the courtroom.[47]

It is a challenge I have accepted. At times I have completed one version and moved on, only to be confronted by the tough researcher part of myself to include memories that I would rather avoid.

The last 30 years have seen significant research published about boarding school trauma. The context of the research has been the United Kingdom due to the long-standing tradition of sending children away to board in that country. Nick Duffell, ex-boarder and psychotherapist, has been a foundational leader in the field. For three decades he has argued that these schools are a mid-Victorian practice in which normal "child development is interrupted by a dramatic and drastic change in which family attachments are deliberately broken".[48] In his first book, *The Making of Them: The British Attitude to Children and the Boarding School System* (2000),[49] he sets out the effects on adults of being sent to board as children and the psychological process that many adults, including himself, must face in recovering from the experience. In his second book, *Wounded Leaders: British Elitism and the Entitlement Illusion* (2014),[50] he widens the discussion to include the "disservice" done not only to individuals raised in boarding schools but also to the whole of society. He argues that many of the men who have emerged from these schools have an "Entitled Brain": "one that is over-trained in rationality, has turned away from empathy and has mastered and normalised dissociation in its most severe dimensions".[51] This occurs because, in order to survive, the child must "cut off parts of himself that get him into trouble or are unwanted ... his feelings, his vulnerability, his childishness, his trust in others, his innocence, his sexuality". He reinvents himself as someone who does not require love and cannot be betrayed.[52]

British psychotherapist Joy Schaverien has made a significant contribution to the growing body of literature. In 2002 *The Dying Patient in Psychotherapy: Desire, Dreams and Individuation* was published.[53] The intention was to offer professionals working with dying patients insight into the process of therapy at that stage of life. It is based on a case study of therapy she offered to a man in his 40s. Sadly, James is diagnosed with cancer after three months which leads to his death two and a half years later. When James begins therapy, his life is in chaos with a broken marriage, nowhere to live and problems in maintaining work. What soon becomes obvious is that being sent away to boarding school when eight has had "catastrophic psychological consequences" leaving "a wound" that "was still fresh". It seemed to Schaverien that "he had been waiting to tell his story since that time".[54] Some aspects of James's story (hereafter referred to as James X) are interwoven into the following chapters.

In 2015, Schaverien provided the first in-depth analysis of the enduring psychological impact on men *and* women sent to boarding school as children: *Boarding School Syndrome: The Psychological Trauma of the "Privileged" Child*.[55] Her work comes from 20 years of research based on working with clients who are ex-boarders. A key understanding is that sending the child to live away from home ruptures the child's primary attachments and this strongly impacts on their adult lives, especially in their significant relationships.[56] She defines "boarding school syndrome" as an "identifiable cluster of learned behaviours and emotional states" that may follow growing up in the inflexible boarding school regime, which leads children to bury their emotions and struggle with intimacy in their adult relationships.[57] Her work is underpinned by her understanding of the importance of attachment to one or more carers for the child and the trauma of the young child when these relationships are broken.[58] While she states that some children have reported that they enjoyed their time at boarding school, for others it is traumatic. The trauma occurs because boarding is a form of captivity where a child is "held against his or her will and subjected to the will of the other" and to a "harsh regime".[59]

In 2016, Duffell co-authored a third book with social worker, mental health trainer and boarding school survivor Thurstine Basset: *Trauma, Abandonment and Privilege: A Guide to Therapeutic Work with Boarding School Survivors*.[60] It is aimed at psychotherapists and based on clinical evidence for the challenges facing those working with ex-boarders. It contains detailed information about the ways in which the child adapts and survives in a setting typically devoid of love and security. In particular, they argue that, generally, the child responds by adopting one of three Strategic Survival Personality types: those who comply or conform, those who rebel and those who become "casualties" of the system, being "crushed" by it.[61] The adopted persona is difficult to shed because it is so closely connected to personal identity.[62]

Two books written by English journalists and ex-boarders, Ysenda Maxtone Graham, *Terms and Conditions: Life in Girls' Boarding Schools 1939–1979* (2016) and Alex Renton, *Stiff Upper Lip: Secrets, Crimes and the Schooling of a Ruling Class* (2017), have also been sources of valuable material. Renton's book arose from an article he wrote in the *Observer* about a group of his fellow ex-boarders bringing a civil case against two teachers who had perpetrated "horrific attacks" against them. The newspaper encouraged readers to send in their stories and the response was overwhelming, with only 12 of over 800 accounts recounting a positive experience. Nearly a quarter of the contributors were women and over a quarter of them recounted stories of physical and psychological abuse. For many of these people school was traumatic and he includes cases of people who can't drive past their old schools without suffering panic attacks.[63]

Ysenda Maxtone Graham focussed on the experience of women at boarding schools between 1939 and 1979. She travelled across England, interviewing women from all kinds of boarding schools, including convent schools. She discovered that the women interviewed live with "flashbacks both joyous and nightmarish".[64] At the end of her book she sums up the many narratives she compiled from ex-boarding school women in the following words:

> The very vividness and rawness of the memories seemed proof to me that the experiences were traumatic: it's the traumatic memories from our childhoods that remain the strongest. The very fact of being torn away from home at a young age and sent to live in the bracing air of an institution made the memories indelible.[65]

She considers that "some of them were traumatised for life".[66]

A final important publication is a series of short autobiographical memoirs of English women edited by ex-boarder Nikki Simpson. The title of the book, *Finding Our Way Home: Women's Accounts of Being Sent to Boarding School*,[67] is poignant, as are the narratives. In her foreword to the book, Joy Schaverien refers to the narratives as evidencing the "psychological wounding" that arises from "the enduring loneliness of the school years" and the lifelong consequences of "living without love at such a formative time".[68] In addition to these books, there are other articles that have also been helpful in writing this book, including those by Jane Barclay[69] and Simon Partridge.[70]

My writing is also informed by trauma research, attachment theory and research into narrative therapy. There are a variety of explanations of trauma and many books written about it. I have found the work of Bessel van der Kolk and Peter Levine to be helpful. Van der Kolk argues that, by definition, trauma is "unbearable and intolerable".[71] We try to push it out of our minds, to move on, but the memory persists in our unconscious, the "imprint" of the experience left on "the mind, brain and body".[72] It is not sufficient for the traumatised person to tell the story of what happened: "The body needs to learn that the danger has passed and to live in the reality of the present".[73] He distinguishes between "ordinary memories (stories that change and that fade with time) and traumatic memories (recurring sensations and movements that are accompanied by intense negative emotions of fear, shame, rage, and collapse)".[74] Trauma results in breakdown in the part of the brain that is responsible for creating autobiographical memories.[75] Therefore, the event/s cannot be smoothly integrated into the chronological narrative that we tell about our lives. The danger is that the person gets caught in the past, often repeating the trauma in their subsequent life. As Peter Levine writes, the challenge facing traumatised people is to identify and revisit traumatic experiences, to process them and finally to integrate them into "coherent narratives" of their lives.[76]

A key understanding that underlies recent boarding school research is that sending young children away to board disrupts the attachment bond between parent and child and has traumatic consequences.[77] The history of the development of Attachment Theory begins in the 1940s and 1950s with the work of John Bowlby.[78] His research led to recognition that in order to grow into mentally healthy adults "the infant and young child should experience a warm, intimate, and continuous relationship with his mother (or permanent mother substitute) in which both find satisfaction and enjoyment".[79] Bowlby revolutionised thinking about a child's tie to the parent and about its disruption through separation, deprivation and bereavement.

Recent research has linked "trauma" and "attachment" via the concept of "attachment-related traumas". These occur where "a frightening experience is accompanied by, or results from, the appraisal of loss, rejection, or abandonment by an attachment figure".[80] One type of attachment-related trauma occurs when there is a disruption in the relationship involving an "unanticipated and/or prolonged" separation with "very little communication" and "no common plan for reunion".[81] This is exactly what happens to the young child sent away to board. The decision may arrive unexpectedly (as in my case) and, as will be evidenced by Christopher's story, even expectation of the fact is not synonymous with an understanding of what is entailed. The young child may be told that they will come home at the end of the term; perhaps the number of weeks is even given. However, due to lack of experience, he or she does not have a well formed schema for time and hence such explanations are not properly understood and cannot protect against the shock of separation. Children who have suffered from attachment trauma are likely to develop "avoidant" (rejecting of intimacy) attachment or "preoccupied" (anxiety about close relationships) attachment behaviour in adulthood.[82]

Judith Lewis Herman is a foundational leader in the field of trauma and recovery. She has found that, for those who suffer from childhood trauma, it may only be in the "third or fourth decade of life" that the "defensive structure may begin to break down", leading to conscious recognition of the traumatic experience.[83] Her findings offer an explanation as to why traumatic experiences have not surfaced when ex-students were interviewed as part of school histories. It also explains what happened to Christopher and myself in our late 20s.

She argues that the process of recovery from trauma involves three stages. The first involves the establishment of a safe place from which the person can courageously face the trauma. I have found the support of my partner, close friends and a therapist have been essential. The second stage is "remembrance and mourning" which is "inherently turbulent and complex".[84] It involves not only remembering the event, but also reconnecting with all the associated thoughts and feelings. Herman, drawing on the work of Suzanne Sgroi, states that recovery is "a spiral, in which earlier versions are continually revisited on a higher level of integration".[85] For me, and for Christopher, iterations of the traumatic events have been both a sporadic and an ongoing spiral of revelation across many years. The third stage of recovery is "reconnection with ordinary life".[86] Certainly I have found that writing this book has initially been a movement away from much of ordinary life, resulting in experiences that needed to be interpreted and negotiated.

Both Herman and van der Kolk discuss the value of groups for providing a safe space in which a person can be both validated and supported in the stages of recovering.[87] In the UK, the specialised groups for ex-boarders who have been traumatised by the experience have been operating for a number of years. It wasn't possible for me to join a group as there are none offered in Australia. In this country, we are in our infancy in recognising the trauma that experiences can evoke. However, when ex-boarders have discovered the focus of my writing, they have wanted to tell me their traumatic stories, including the ongoing difficulties experienced in adult life. Their stories have supported my belief in the project. I have also had a small number tell me (often adamantly) that they enjoyed boarding school. It would indeed be horrifying to think that it was a traumatic experience for all students! However, as the work of many researchers whose work I draw upon in this book attest, many children and young people found it to be a harrowing experience.

Herman's stages of recovery have influenced an approach that is referred to in the field as "narrative therapy". It involves accessing traumatic memories and deconstructing the story by bringing into focus the meanings they have drawn on previously to understand what happened. This allows space for a "re-authoring" of the experience.[88] Psychologist Marie-Nathalie Beaudoin has found that some clients can remember the actions they took in the situation but which subsequently they discount, judging them as "ineffective". She argues that these actions need to be re-thought as "valuable" and incorporated into their narratives, providing a sense of agency.[89] This is particularly important in knitting together the schism that trauma can create in autobiographical memory—the story people tell about themselves across time, including their sense of self, values and identity.[90]

Beaudoin has also found that exposure to the stories of others about similar events is helpful in challenging current understandings and developing "more realistic perspectives".[91] In reading their stories, the traumatised person discovers that she or he is not alone in the complexity of emotional responses. They are affirmed that others responded, thought and acted similarly, thereby normalising their reactions and revealing a common humanity. The key processes in narrative therapy involve reflecting on and deconstructing events by bringing different understandings to bear on them, especially those provided by research and the experience of others. These ideas are at the very heart of this book. In turn, it is my hope that my experience resonates with ex-boarder readers who also found the experience to be traumatic.

A trope that dominates the genre of memoir is the triumphant one of "the resilient writer who has overcome adversity".[92] It is not a stance I wish to take. I am not *beyond* trauma. What happened to me at boarding school needs to be an *integrated* part of who I am. It is an essential part of my identity, but there is no point of final arrival and there are legacies from it that must be carried for the rest of my life. Herman states: "Resolution of the trauma is never final; recovery is never complete".[93] The word "recovering", used in the title, builds on this understanding.

Memory theorists argue that the events we remember, the ones that are "paramount in our memories", are ones we have not fully explored for meaning.[94] This can be seen at work in the person who tells the same story over and over until someone finally asks them why *that particular story* seems so important. The question can often lead to profound insights. This interrogation is a process I have used in my writing: *Why is that memory so important and what does it mean?* We also have a propensity to "forget" those memories which are highly problematic for us because they are too painful, too threatening, but these memories are usually retrievable.[95] The recovering process must be entered into in order to process the trauma. It is also important to reflect on the silences, the memories that cannot be recovered. Any absence indicates the traumatic nature of the event and, even if it cannot be recalled, witnessing the silence is a way of honouring the absence. It may be that making space for the memory gives it freedom to surface in the future. I am not alone in using writing as a form of narrative therapy for dealing with traumatic experiences[96] and there is research indicating it has long-term benefits.[97] An outcome of this approach is that it restores our sense of who we are and what we value, ultimately providing "the foundation" for a "richer story" about the development of our lives.[98]

My work as a university teacher educator involved teaching developmental psychology for many years. Erik Erikson is a foundational theorist in the field. In 1950 he published *Childhood and Society*, which included what he termed the "Eight Stages of Man".[99] A limitation of Erikson's theory is that originally it focussed on a male development, although recent research has found that gender differences are not as disparate as first imagined.[100] In the writing,

I draw on Erikson's stages, particularly those relating to adolescence and young adulthood because they offer insight into Christopher's and my life.

A counterbalance to Erikson's research, which has been important to me since I first read it when I was in my 30s, is that by Mary Belenky and her colleagues, *Women's Ways of Knowing: The Development of Self, Voice, and Mind*.[101] They studied the ways in which 135 women of diverse backgrounds, ranging in age from mid-adolescence to 60, "struggled to claim the power of their own minds" in relationship to "truth, knowledge, and authority".[102] As a result of listening to the women talk about their experience of changes in their lives, they identified five stages of development which begin with "Silence" characterised by seeing oneself as "voiceless and subject to the whims of external authority".[103] The women then proceed through four other stages, which I draw upon as I write, finally arriving at a stage in which they view themselves as "creators of knowledge".[104] The researchers found that for women there is a significant relationship between self-concept and their "struggle to claim the power of their own minds".[105] I have seen this in my own life as my boarding school experience thwarted my engagement with knowledge. In adulthood, it was my involvement in education that fostered it.

My approach to writing involves taking ideas from each of these research sites and using them as lenses to interrogate Christopher's and my experience. Educational history provides a wider context beyond our immediate settings. Developmental psychology allows for exploration of expectations for normal development, including gender differences, and contrasting it with the impact of boarding school. Trauma research, including that related to boarding school experience, is used to explain both the long-term effects and the process of memory recovery. Depth psychology, especially the work of Carl Jung, is used to explain my experiences in regard to the remembering and writing process. I have also used other research projects, including educational psychology, in my analysis of particular experiences.

An important principle in developmental psychology is recognition of the importance of culture and context in the way in which a person advances across their lives. We are all born into a particular family, in a particular culture, at a point of historical time. The task is to understand ourselves by understanding the context in which we live and have lived and how it has shaped us. We are also people of individual differences: biologically, cognitively and psycho-emotionally. Our individuality impacts on the way in which we respond to our environment. Additionally, there are idiosyncratic events that influence who we become.

Christopher Milne was the son of a famous children's author, bringing with it fame which he enjoyed as a child but which caused him suffering as an adolescent. Yet to some degree, every person leads an idiosyncratic life. Events that happened to us but not to others shape our lives, sometimes fostering, sometimes hindering, development. All must be integrated into a coherent understanding of one's life. Christopher was sent to two British boarding schools in the late 1920s and 1930s. I was sent to board in Catholic convents in Australia in the 1950s and 1960s. These are historical and cultural settings against which our experiences must be examined. We came to them not as a blank slate but as individuals with capacity and potential, as well as being caught up in a particular family trajectory (parental aspirations of a social, cultural and economic pathway through life). We came to them as children who had already lived some years of life, with a life history that had already taught us much about ourselves and the world and which shaped how we responded to boarding school life. Judith Herman, like Marie-Nathalie Beaudoin, stresses that, in order to recover traumatic memories, it is important for the person to seek a life-affirming aspect of themselves that was present *before* the experience.[106] The following Prelude contains childhood stories, from Christopher and myself, that reveal expression of our individual drive to express who we were before we went to boarding school. They also shaped who we were to become in adulthood.

References

1 Forster, M. (Director) (2018) *Christopher Robin* (Motion Picture), Walt Disney, USA.
2 Milne, C. (1974) *The Enchanted Places: A Childhood Memoir*, London: Pan Books.
3 Milne, C. (1979) *The Path Through the Trees*, London: Eyre Methuen.
4 Milne, C. (1982) *The Hollow on the Hill: The Search for a Personal Philosophy*, London: Eyre Methuen.
5 Thwaite, A. (1990) *A. A. Milne: His Life*, London: Bello Pan Macmillan, p. xv.
6 Thwaite, A. (2017) *Goodbye Christopher Robin: A. A. Milne and the Making of Winnie-the-Pooh*, London: Pan Books.
7 Iriye, A. (2004) "Transnational history", *Contemporary European History*, 13 (2), p. 213.
8 Trimingham Jack, C. (1997) "Kerever Park: A History of the Experience of Teachers and Children in a Catholic Girls' Preparatory Boarding School 1944–1965". Thesis submitted in fulfilment of the requirements of Doctor of Philosophy, University of Sydney, School of Social and Policy Studies in Education.
9 Trimingham Jack, C. (2003) *Growing Good Catholic Girls: Education and Convent Life in Australia*, Melbourne, Vic: Melbourne University Press.
10 Weedon, C. (1987) *Feminist Practice and Poststructuralist Theory*, Oxford: Basil Blackwell, p. 34.
11 Flynn, T. (1994) "Foucault's mapping of history", in G. Gutting (ed.), *The Cambridge Companion to Foucault*, Cambridge: Cambridge University Press, p. 24.
12 Haraway, D. (2003) "Situated knowledges: The science question in feminism and the privilege of partial perspective", in N. K. Denzin & Y. S. Lincoln (eds), *Turning Points in Qualitative Research: Tying Knots in a Handkerchief*, Walnut Creek, CA: AltaMira, pp. 21–46.
13 Smith, A. (1759), cited in Duffell, N. & Basset, T. (2016) *Trauma, Abandonment and Privilege: A Guide to Therapeutic Work with Boarding School Survivors*, Abingdon: Routledge, p. 5.
14 Schaverien, J. (2015) *Boarding School Syndrome: The Psychological Trauma of the "Privileged" Child*, Abingdon: Routledge, p. 27.

15 Rivers, W. H. (1918), cited in Duffell & Basset (2016), op. cit., p. 6.
16 Lambert, R. (1968) *The Hothouse Society*, London: Weidenfeld & Nicolson; Gathorne-Hardy, J. (1977) *The Public School Phenomenon, 597–1977*, London: Hodder & Stoughton; De Symons Honey, J. R. (1977) *Tom Brown's Universe: The Development of the Public School in the Nineteenth Century*, London: Millington Books Ltd.; Heward, C. (1988) *Making a Man of Him: Parents and Their Sons' Education at an English Public School 1929–1950*, Abingdon: Routledge; Duffell, N. (2000) *The Making of Them: The British Attitude to Children and the Boarding School System*, London: Lone Arrow Press; Schaverien (2015) op. cit.; Duffell & Basset (2016) op. cit.; Renton, A. (2017) *Stiff Upper Lip: Secrets, Crimes and the Schooling of a Ruling Class*, London: Weidenfeld & Nicolson.
17 Corrigan, P. D. R. (1988) "The making of a boy: Meditations on what grammar school did to and for, my body", *Journal of Education* 170 (3), pp. 142–161; Duffell (2000), op. cit.; Renton (2017), op. cit.
18 Trimingham Jack, C. (2003), op. cit.; Schaverien, J. (2015), op. cit.; Maxtone Graham, Y. (2017) *Life in Girls' Boarding Schools 1939–1979: Terms and Conditions*, St Ives, Cornwall: Abacus; Simpson, N. (ed.) (2019) *Finding Our Way Home: Women's Accounts of Being Sent to Boarding School*, Abingdon: Routledge.
19 Downs, J. (2002) "Adapting to secondary and boarding school: Self concept, place identity and homesickness". Self-concept research [electronic resource]: driving international research agendas: proceedings of the 2nd International Biennial Conference, University of Western Sydney, Sydney 6–8 August 2002, edited by R. G. Craven, H. W. Marsh & K. B. Simpson; White, M. A. (2004) "An Australian co-educational boarding school: A sociological study of Anglo-Australian and overseas students' attitudes from their own memoirs", *International Education Journal* 5 (1), pp. 65–78; Mander, D. J. (2012) "The transition experience to boarding school for male Aboriginal secondary school students from regional and remote communities across Western Australia", retrieved from: https://ro.ecu.edu.au/theses/521 (accessed 3 November 2018); Hodges, J., Sheffield, J., & Ralph, A. (2013) "Home away from home? Boarding in Australian schools", *Australian Journal of Education* 57 (1), pp. 32–47; Martin, A. J., Papworth, B., Ginns, P., & Liem, G. A. D. (2014) "Boarding school, academic motivation and engagement, and psychological well-being: A large-scale investigation", *American Educational Research Journal* 51 (5), pp. 1007–1049; Mander, D. J. & Lester, L. (2015) "A longitudinal study into indicators of mental health, strengths and difficulties reported by boarding students as they transition from primary school to secondary boarding schools in Perth, Western Australia", *Journal of Psychologists and Counsellors in Schools* 27 (2), pp. 139–152.
20 *Report of the National Inquiry into the Separation of Aboriginal and Torres Strait Islander Children from Their Families* (1997), Commonwealth of Australia, available at: www.humanrights.gov.au/sites/default/files/content/pdf/social_justice/bringing_them_home_report.pdf (accessed 5 July 2018); Truth and Reconciliation Commission of Canada (2015) *Honouring the Truth, Reconciling for the Future: Summary of the Final Report of the Truth and Reconciliation Commission of Canada*, available at: http://publications.gc.ca/site/eng/9.800288/publication.html (accessed 20 June 2018); Australian Royal Commission into Institutional Responses to Child Sexual Abuse (2017) *Final Report of Royal Commission into Institutional Responses to Child Sexual Abuse*, available at: www.childabuseroyalcommission.gov.au/sites/default/files/final_information_update.pdf (accessed 20 June 2018).
21 Australian Royal Commission into Institutional Responses to Child Sexual Abuse (2017), op. cit.

22 Trimingham Jack, C. (1997b) "School history: Reconstructing the lived experience", *History of Education Review* 26 (1), pp. 42–55.
23 Schaverien (2015), op. cit., p. 113.
24 Renton (2017), op. cit., p. 80.
25 Ibid., p. 88.
26 Nora, P. (1989) "Between memory and history: *Les lieux de mémoire*", *Representations* 26, Spring Issue, p. 9, available at http://rep.ucpress.edu/content/26/7 (accessed 28 May 2018).
27 Schaverien, J. (2004), "Boarding school: The trauma of the 'privileged' child", *Journal of Analytical Psychology* 49 (5), p. 695.
28 Maftei, M. (2013) *The Fiction of Autobiography: Reading and Writing Identity*, London: Bloomsbury Publishing, p. 62.
29 Didion, J. (2006), cited in Maftei (2013), op. cit., p. 127.
30 Nora (1989), op. cit., p. 24.
31 Milne (1979), op. cit., p. 265.
32 Maftei (2013), op. cit, p. 137.
33 Ibid., p. 124.
34 Nora (1989), op. cit., p. 15.
35 Ibid., p. 19.
36 Ibid., p. 19.
37 Ibid., p. 24.
38 Trimingham Jack, C. (2018) "Lucky or privileged: Working with memory and reflexivity", *History of Education Review* 47 (2), pp. 208–216.
39 Jung, C. (1964) "Approaching the unconscious", in C. Jung (ed.), *Man and His Symbols*, New York: Dell Books, p. 18.
40 Ibid., p. 5.
41 Ibid., p. 18.
42 Ibid., pp. 4–20.
43 Holden, K. (2011) "After the words: Writing and living a memoir", *Griffith Review*, Ed 33: Such is Life, pp. 80–81, available at:https://griffithreview.com/articles/after-the-words/ (accessed 21 June 2018).
44 Ibid.
45 Sköld, J. & Vehkalahti, K. (2016) "Marginalised children—methodological and ethical issues in the history of education and childhood", *History of Education* 45 (4), p. 408.
46 Aldrich, R. (2003), cited in Sköld & Vehkalahti (2016), op. cit., p. 408.
47 Ibid.
48 Duffell & Basset (2016), op. cit., pp. 4–5.
49 Duffell (2000), op. cit.
50 Duffell (2014), op. cit.
51 Ibid., pp. iii–xi.
52 Ibid., p. 108.
53 Schaverien, J. (2002) *The Dying Patient in Psychotherapy: Desire, Dreams and Individuation*, New York: Palgrave Macmillan, p. 1.
54 Ibid., pp. 22–25.
55 Schaverien (2015), op. cit.
56 Ibid., p. 2.
57 Ibid., p. 2.
58 Ibid., p. 8.
59 Ibid., p. 50.
60 Duffell & Basset (2016), op. cit.
61 Ibid., p. 45.

62 Ibid., pp. 6–8.
63 Renton (2017), op. cit., p. 382.
64 Maxtone Graham (2016), op. cit., p. 12.
65 Ibid., p. 283.
66 Ibid.
67 Simpson (2019), op. cit.
68 Schaverien, in Simpson (2019), op. cit., p. xiv.
69 Barclay, J. (2011) "The trauma of boarding school", *Self and Society* 38 (3), pp. 27–34.
70 Partridge, S. (2013) "Boarding school syndrome: Disguised attachment-deficit and dissociation reinforced by institutional neglect and abuse", *Attachment: New Directions in Psychotherapy and Relational Psychoanalysis* 7, pp. 202–213.
71 Van der Kolk, B. (2014) *The Body Keeps the Score: Mind, Brain and Body in the Transformation of Trauma*, London: Penguin Random House, p. 1.
72 Ibid., p. 21.
73 Ibid.
74 Ibid., pp. 175–176.
75 Ibid., p. 180.
76 Levine, P. A. (2015) *Trauma and Memory: Brain and Body in a Search for the Living Past*, Berkeley, CA: North Atlantic Books, pp. 7–8.
77 Schaverien (2015), op. cit.; Duffell & Basset (2016), op. cit.
78 Bowlby, J. (1969) *Attachment and Loss, 1: Attachment*, New York: Basic Books; Bowlby, J. (1973) *Attachment and Loss, 2: Separation*, New York: Basic Books.
79 Bowlby, J. (1951), cited in Bretherton, I. (1992) "The origins of attachment theory: John Bowlby and Mary Ainsworth", *Developmental Psychology* 28 (5), p. 765.
80 Erozkan, A. (2016) "The link between types of attachment and childhood trauma", *Universal Journal of Educational Research* 4 (5), p. 1076, available at:www.hrpub.org, DOI: 10.13189/ujer.2016.040517.
81 Kobak, R., Cassidy, J., & Zir, Y. (2004), cited in Erozkan (2016), op. cit., p. 1076.
82 Erozkan (2016), op. cit., p. 1076.
83 Herman, J. L. (1992, 2001) *Trauma and Recovery: From Domestic Abuse to Political Terror*, London: Pandora, p. 114.
84 Ibid., p. 155.
85 Sgroi, S. M. (1989) "Mechanisms of injury to child victims of sexual abuse", *Pediatric Emergency Care* 5 (4), p. 295, in Herman (1992), op. cit., p. 155.
86 Herman (1992), op. cit., p. 155.
87 Ibid., pp. 214–236; van der Kolk (2014), op. cit., p. 244.
88 Beaudoin, M. N. (2005) "Agency and choice in the face of trauma: A narrative therapy map", *Journal of Systematic Therapies* 24 (4), pp. 32–50.
89 Ibid., p. 33.
90 Ibid., p. 37.
91 Ibid., p. 44.
92 Douglas, K. (2002) "The universal autobiographer: The politics of normative readings", *Journal of Australian Studies* 26 (72), p. 179, https://doi.org/10.1080/14443050209387750.
93 Herman (1992), op. cit., p. 211.
94 Crawford, J., Kippax, S., Obyx, J., Gault, U., & Benton, P. (1992) *Emotion and Gender: Constructing Meaning from Memory*, London: Sage, p. 38.
95 Ibid., pp. 155–158.
96 Penn, P. (2001) "Chronic illness: Trauma, language, and writing: Breaking the silence", *Family Processes* 40 (1), pp. 33–52; Tamas, S. (2012) "Writing trauma:

Collisions at the corner of art and scholarship", *Theatre Topics* 22 (1), pp. 39–48; Spear, R. (2014) "'Let me tell you a story': On teaching trauma narratives, writing and healing", *Pedagogy* 14 (1), pp. 53–79.

97 Pennebaker, J. W. (1997) "Writing about emotional experiences as a therapeutic process", *Psychological Science* 8 (3), pp. 162–166.

98 White, M. (2004) "Working with people who are suffering the consequences of multiple trauma: A narrative perspective", *International Journal of Narrative Therapy & Community Work* 2004 (1), p. 46.

99 Erikson, E. H. (1950) *Childhood and Society*, New York: Norton.

100 Lytle, L. J., Bakken, L., & Romig, C. (1997) "Adolescent female identity development", *Sex Roles* 37 (3–4), pp. 175–185; Sandhu, D. & Tung, S. (2006) "Gender differences in adolescent identity formation", *Pakistan Journal of Psychological Research*, 21 (1 & 2), pp. 29–40; Côté, J. E. & Levine, C. (2016) *Identity Formation, Youth and Development: A Simplified Approach*, New York: Psychology Press.

101 Belenky, M. F., Clinchy, B. McV., Goldberger, N. R., & Tarule, J. M. (1986) *Women's Ways of Knowing: The Development of Self, Voice and Mind*, New York: Basic Books.

102 Ibid., p. 3.

103 Ibid., p. 15.

104 Ibid.

105 Ibid., p. 3.

106 Herman (1992), op. cit., p. 202.

Prelude

One impact of trauma is a loss in continuity with the life that came before. For the child, it breaks the thread of an emerging individuality. Commonly, the narratives of boarding school trauma begin with the experience of being sent away as if nothing occurred prior to that event. Yael Danieli is an American clinical psychologist who has worked extensively with trauma victims, including Holocaust survivors and their children. She believes that in the recovery process it is essential for the person to "re-create the flow" of life before the event.[1] This has led me to think about what was emerging for Christopher and myself, our individual selves, *before* boarding school. In the following sections I draw upon significant memories and stories about both of us that act as a prelude to our narratives about boarding school life. The memories offer insight into our evolving selves, as well as being precursors to what was to come later in our lives.

Christopher

Christopher was born on 21 August 1920. Alan Milne (hereafter Milne) married Dorothy "Daphne" de Sélincourt in 1913 and so the birth of their only child was "long in coming".[2] So unprepared was Daphne as to what giving birth entailed that she decided never to repeat it.[3] When Christopher was born, his father was writing plays, novels, verse and humorous stories for *Punch* magazine. Milne then turned to children's literature and his poem "Vespers" is one of his most famous poems. It was based on seeing his young son saying his evening prayers beside his bed.[4] He gave the poem to Daphne who sold it to *Vanity Fair* magazine in New York, which published it in 1923.[5] In 1924, Milne published his first book of children's verse, *When We Were Very Young*, dedicating it: "To Christopher Robin Milne or, as he prefers to call himself, Billy Moon, this book which owes so much to him is now humbly offered".[6] The book was an enormous success and, by 1927, 260,000 copies had been sold.[7] The first *Winnie-the-Pooh* book was published in 1926,[8] a second book of children's poems, *Now We Are Six*, in 1927[9] and *The House at Pooh Corner* in 1928.[10] The four books introduced Christopher to the world as

Christopher Robin and, in the minds of the adoring public, the real child and the fictional child became synonymous.

Christopher was four when the first book was published and he became the focus of an immense amount of media attention. Photographs of him appeared in newspapers in the United Kingdom and America. At four years of age, his father reported with pride that his young son had publicly autographed a copy of *When We Were Very Young*, claiming ownership by referring to it as "my book".[11] So celebrated was Christopher that, at one stage, he was declared one of the "five most famous children in the world".[12] At home he was known as Billy Moon, the first name *Billy* one his parents preferred, the second *Moon* adopted because it was how Christopher pronounced "Milne" when he was learning to speak. It is likely that the difference in names afforded Christopher a degree of separation between the real and fictional child, but not in the mind of the public. Milne saw no need to protect his son from the publicity and his mother actively encouraged it.[13] However, while this was happening, Christopher was busy adopting another persona. By the time he was five, he had developed a fascination for the legend of St George and the Dragon. So much so that on his fifth birthday his parents gave him a "shining suit of armour", which he wore all through the day "at the prospect of being unstrapped from it".[14]

Milne was besotted with cricket and hoped that his son would become a successful cricketer, perhaps even playing for England. He spent much of his time with the child teaching him to play the game. In one of his letters to his brother Ken, Milne wrote about one of these efforts, beginning with reference to Christopher's passion for St George and the Dragon. He then told Ken that he had been trying to teach Christopher to catch but the child was not doing well. So he decided to give his son a little talk about why he needed to learn to be a good catcher, telling him that when he turned nine or ten he would "think of nothing but cricket". In response, the child "opened his eyes very wide and said: Nothing but cricket? Not armour?" Milne concluded that "a dreary prospect" had opened up before his son.[15] Christopher also recounts the event in his 1974 memoir, stating how "aghast" he felt about the prospect of abandoning his armour, especially the helmet with the red plume that "he could pull down when danger threatened".[16]

In another letter to his brother, Milne reflected that his son had a "passion for drawing and painting" and that in 1925 he produced his "masterpiece", which he told his father was of St George and the Dragon. His parents admired it in front of him, but privately talked about the details of the drawing, trying to decipher how it worked. While they were doing this, Milne overheard his son conclude his lunch with the following prayer: "Thank God for my good lunch—and let those people understand the dragon".[17] A play therapist would be interested in why the child was so taken with the legend and what he hoped his parents might understand about it.

Child-centred play therapy has its origins in the person-centred work of psychologist Carl Rogers, which was then adapted for children by Virginia

Axline.[18] A central belief is that the child is always striving towards improvement, independence, maturity and self-realisation and that play contributes towards this goal.[19] By observing the child at play, the therapist is able to identify "feelings and attitudes that have been pushing to get out into the open".[20] Careful analysis of it provides an understanding of "the internal frame of reference of the child".[21] Christopher's interest in the story of St George and the Dragon and his play around it provides insight into his inner efforts to cope with the pressure of being enmeshed with the fictional Christopher Robin. This is further exemplified in the following story.

The most significant account in regards to Christopher's passion for the legend comes from an encounter children's author Enid Blyton had with him when she was a young reporter. It is a story that caught my attention and puzzled me when I first read it. Eventually, it started to make sense to me as I followed the course of Christopher's life through childhood, adolescence and into adulthood. She had been granted an interview with Milne and, when she arrived, Milne took the opportunity to show off his son's prowess with mathematics by setting the child some problems to solve. However, what struck Blyton was not Christopher's mathematical skills but his behaviour. He moved between pretending to *be* a dragon and then being *pursued* by it. First, Christopher stared "fiercely" and "blew tremendously hard" at her. Then he looked around "for something to devour" and his "bright eyes fell upon his father's fountain-pen which he took up and pulled into as many pieces as possible".[22] Thwaite, who includes this interaction in her book, offers no analysis of the child's behaviour beyond expressing a belief that he would have been able to put it together again because "he was already very good with his hands".[23] However, there is no indication that he *did* put the pen together again, so it is likely that showing off how good he was mechanically was not the goal. There was another message at play here and it was tied up with his passion for an ancient legend. Blyton also noticed that the child had tied paper around his legs, so she curiously asked him why? He responded: "So the dragons won't bite me".[24]

The "golden legend" of St George and the Dragon dates back to the 1260s. It is set in a city in Libya, which is threatened by a dragon that spews poison and lives in a nearby pond. The citizens appease it by giving it a daily offering, starting with two sheep and then, when the sheep become scarce, one sheep and a man. Finally, they offer it their children and young people selected by lottery. One day, the king's daughter's name is drawn and, although the king offers the people his treasure to save her, they insist she take her place. So she sets out for the pond dressed as a bride. It is at this time that St George arrives and, seeing her plight, vows to save her. He goes with her to the pond and, while she is trying to convince him to leave her to her fate, the dragon emerges. St George charges on horseback, wounding but not killing the dragon. He calls to the princess to throw him her girdle (belt), which is a symbol of chastity and protection. He takes the belt and throws it around the dragon's neck and it immediately becomes tamed, allowing itself to be led back to the city on a leash. But the people are terrified of it and St George offers to kill it if they become Christians, which they agree to do and so the dragon is slain.[25]

Play offers the child a "first experience in creating metaphors".[26] French philosopher Paul Ricoeur defines metaphor as a "split reference" in which we take one thing for another, maintaining a tensive quality between two symbols, an "is–is not" tension, employing it to describe reality.[27] Blyton's description of Christopher's play, as he moves from being the dragon who blows his fiery breath to being pursued by the dragon, is a kind of metaphor, an attempt to describe his experience: "Please let them understand the dragon". He both wanted to be the powerful dragon while at the same time he was frightened by it.

Christopher's behaviour around the legend reveals some aspects of his inner frame of reference. A reading of his actions is that, subconsciously, he is imagining he has the power to remove yet another visitor who had come to see him as the fictional Christopher Robin. It seems that Blyton picked up on his enactment when she described him as looking around the room for "something to devour". What he chose to destroy was his father's writing pen, perhaps signalling his desire to put an end to both his father's writing and the boy he had created with it. Yet he also feared the dragon and had to wear protective armour against it. The dragon may also represent his father's idealised child, Christopher Robin, who was threatening to devour him.

The legend belongs to the genre of hero myths and is a common trope across many different historical periods and cultures: Sun Wukong (Chinese); Beowulf (Norse); Karna (Hindu); and Hercules (Greco-Roman).[28] Jung argues that the myth has a special function "in the development of the individual's ego consciousness—his awareness of his own strengths and weaknesses—in a manner that will equip him for the arduous tasks with which life confronts him".[29] The battle between the hero and the dragon is a process of the person coming to terms with their shadow (the dragon): "the hidden, repressed and unfavourable (or nefarious) aspects of the personality". Overcoming the dragon includes the capacity to "master and assimilate the shadow".[30] In summary, he writes: "The hero-dragon battle is the symbolic expression of the process of 'growing up'".[31]

Joy Schaverien uses the metaphor of an "armoured ... personality" as being one which is drawn upon by some ex-boarders to disguise "the distressed child within the adult".[32] The personality keeps "encapsulated the unconscious emotional life of the person" which "might include the love, hate, sadness, and erotic sexuality, elements that were rejected as belonging to the feminine in society".[33] She argues that this personality is a product of the masculine construction of boarding schools where the child must learn to hide their feelings creating "the first split ... between thought and deed, between feeling and action, between inner world and outer world".[34] It seems that this split occurred for Christopher before he went to boarding school. He both enjoyed the attention of being associated with the fictional Christopher Robin but he was also frightened by it and had no words to express his ambivalence. He had learned how to protect his vulnerable self before he went to boarding school and this repression was both reinforced and called upon in order to survive in that setting.

Christopher's passion for the heroic legend no doubt provided him with fun and engagement in imaginary play that young children so enjoy. But it also allowed him to "act out" the psychological dilemma that faced him in separating himself from Christopher Robin and finding his own sense of personhood. The notion of being a hero arose in Christopher's early childhood but was submerged throughout his school years. It surfaced again in early adulthood until eventually he was able to establish himself as a person in his own right separate from the fictional Christopher Robin. Eventually he did blow Enid Blyton away by championing a new form of education and eventually he did save a town. It was this story that led me to understand Yael Danieli's imperative of the need to reconnect with the life-force before trauma, leading me into my own *before* story.

Christine

Like Christopher, I was an only child until I was almost five and I too was a long time coming. My parents had been married five years before I was born in 1950. My father was a medical doctor before and during the war, but immediately afterwards he trained in the specialty of ophthalmology. His medical practice was located in a section of our home on a busy street in the not so salubrious suburb of Campsie in Sydney. We lived a quiet life and I was a solitary child with no neighbouring children. I remember being rather stunned when a new baby arrived just before I turned five, with my parents expecting me to be thrilled. I wasn't.

My father was an intellectual. His interests, apart from ophthalmology, included astronomy, mathematics, music (he played the piano well), chess and carpentry. I was taught to play chess, draughts and darts at an early age. He loved astronomy and built a large equatorial mounting (a column of cement to achieve stability) in the backyard for a telescope he bought from an observatory when they were updating. I remember many nights waiting up so that I could climb the wooden stairs he had built to take me up to the telescope. There I could look out to see the rings of Saturn, the Southern Cross constellation, or a planet that had moved into our sky. He also took me on visits to the Natural History museum and enjoyed showing me the geological rock display, but I really liked the diorama exhibition on the development of prehistoric "man". My parents also took me to symphony concerts, the ballet and opera.

I was never terribly interested in toys. Books are my key memory from childhood. We subscribed to *National Geographic* and I loved looking at the pictures of other lands. I was especially fascinated by depiction of traditional cultures such as Tibetan and African tribal life. We had a large encyclopaedia of natural history and I enjoyed looking through it, but it was all in black and white so not as interesting as the glossy pages of the *National Geographic* magazine. I didn't learn to read until I was six. My mother read me classical children's stories: *Peter Pan*, *Alice in Wonderland* and *The Water Babies: A Fairy Tale for a Land Baby* (1862–1863) by Charles Kingsley (my favourite). Now children would be given little books that introduce them to text but that wasn't the practice when I was growing up.

The most significant memory for me is of a series of art books that were kept in a big cedar bookcase in the dining room. They were large, thick books that covered the history of art from its earliest expression, chronologically moving into the field of modern art. They had glossy removable covers with an image that represented the style of that period. Inside were beautiful reproductions of further paintings that could be lifted almost from the page, as they were attached only by glue at the top. I liked all the art books and understood that it was a history of art from the beginning of time. However, the one that fascinated me was the first in the series, a book on the prehistoric artwork in the Lascaux Caves. It mesmerised me: the scenes of large dark caves with black and ochre images of prehistoric horses and bulls/bison with long horns. The pictures in the other books, many of which were religious images, were familiar to me because we were practising Catholics and the church we attended was full of them. The cave paintings were so different, so ancient, they evoked a mysterious, strange world.

While I was at boarding school, my parents bought the property next door to our home and moved the medical practice there, so that my father's old surgery became another bedroom. The waiting room became a study, with books lining the shelves and a large desk and swivelling leather chair in the corner. I loved the room. It was quiet, almost cave-like, and when I came home from boarding school I often retreated there. I loved the books that lined the shelves, a world waiting for me, but my eyes always turned to the book on the Lascaux Caves. The caves are located near the French town of Montignac and were rediscovered in 1940. It is an enormous complex of passages leading from one cave to the next and contains nearly 6,000 paintings. The images are not simply painted onto the walls. The walls themselves—the rock formations—are integrated to form a three-dimensional image, with some of the animals seeming to emerge from them. They are between 10,000 and 50,000 years old and date back to the Upper Palaeolithic or Old Stone Age.

In 2010 while in France, I visited the reconstruction, an accurate replication of two parts of the caves, that has been in use since 1983 to protect the originals from deterioration due to the large crowds that visit them. While there, I bought David Lewis-Williams' book, *The Mind in the Cave: Consciousness and the Origins of Art*.[35] Even the title pleased me, because the formation of consciousness in educational settings is the very thing that has fascinated me for many years, forming the focus of my historical research. There is also synchronicity at work when I discovered what drove Lewis-Williams' research. His approach involves an exploration of the way in which the caves were understood by, interacted with and shaped the world of the community who used them. In his words, there was an "interaction of mental activity and social context".[36] Similarly, my approach to educational history is about the ways in which students and teachers interact with the context of an educational setting, including the physical structures, iconography and settings and how that, in turn, shapes consciousness.

The largest of the caves was accessed by the general community. It was the shamans who went into the smaller caves where they acted out a pact between the "spirit world" and the community. Lewis-Williams argues that "physical entry into these subterranean passages was probably seen as equivalent to psychic entry into deeply altered states of consciousness".[37] The people believed that powerful animals lay immediately behind the walls and it was the role of the shamans to courageously face those animals in their spiritual quests on behalf of the community.[38] Those who took on the role of shaman were "said to die" to themselves as they had been before, then "to be resurrected with a new persona and social role".[39]

The subterranean passages of the caves represented entrance to the psychic, spirit world, which was "malleable", able to be shaped by the people who used them and, in turn, that shaped their consciousness: "There was thus a fecund interaction between the given topography of the caves, mercurial mental imagery, and image-fixing by individuals and groups".[40] Across time, they "built up and modified the spiritual world both materially (in the caves) and conceptually (in people's minds)".[41] This description of the interaction between the topography of the cave, the deep spaces that represented the unconscious world and the meanings the people drew from these interactions well describes my approach to "doing" history.

The metaphors and images that the shamans worked with in their interactions within the caves were complex and served different community needs. My approach to history involves exploration of memory, including if possible the subterranean passages of the unconscious that are often expressed through metaphor. Memory is a complex construction formed and re-formed across time. Often when recalling events it is not at all clear to us what they really meant; we only know that they were important. Metaphor provides an expression of understandings we have yet to realise. What interests me is exploration of memories relating to educational experience, how the experiences shaped the person recalling them and how, in turn, I (the historian) shape them as I integrate them into my writing.

This book is an exploration of my boarding school experiences, their impact on my consciousness and on the decisions I made across my life. My metaphor for the process is one of "deep diving and re-surfacing"—a journey into the subterranean recesses of memory. At times, like the ancient shamans, it has taken courage to proceed with the project and, like them, facing the memories that lie buried in the unconscious has reshaped the essence of how I understand my "self", leading to a new persona. However, well before my understanding of that aspect of the cave metaphor came into my consciousness (like Christopher's suit of armour), I constructed another inner cave that I escaped into as protection of my vulnerable self at boarding school.

References

1   Danieli, Y. (1988), cited in Herman, J. L. (1992, 2001) *Trauma and Recovery: From Domestic Abuse to Political Terror*, London: Pandora, p. 176.
2   Thwaite, A. (1990) *A. A. Milne: His Life*, London: Bello Pan Macmillan, p. 254.
3   Ibid.
4   Milne, A. A. (1924, 1984) *When We Were Very Young*, London: Methuen Children's Books.
5   Milne, A. A. (1923) "Vespers", *Vanity Fair*, January, available at: https://archive. vanityfair.com/article/1923/1/vespers (accessed 5 November 2019).
6   Milne (1924), op. cit.
7   Thwaite, A. (2017) *Goodbye Christopher Robin: A. A. Milne and the Making of Winnie-the-Pooh*, London: Pan Books, p. 92.
8   Milne, A. A. (1926) *Winnie-the-Pooh*, London: Methuen.
9   Milne, A. A. (1927) *Now We Are Six*, London: Methuen.
10   Milne, A. A. (1928) *The House at Pooh Corner*, London: Methuen.
11   Thwaite (1990), op. cit., p. 113.
12   Ibid., p. 24.
13   Ibid., p. 183.
14   Milne, C. (1974) *The Enchanted Places: A Childhood Memoir*, London: Pan Books, p. 40.
15   Thwaite (2017), op. cit., p. 115.
16   Milne (1974), op. cit., p. 40.
17   Thwaite (1990), op. cit., p. 333.
18   Rogers, C. (1951) *Client-Centered Therapy*, Boston, MA: Houghton-Mifflin.
19   Axline, V. M. (1989) *Play Therapy*, Edinburgh: Churchill Livingstone, p. 13.
20   Ibid., p. 22.
21   Landreth, G. L. & Sweeney, D. S. (1997) "Child-centred play therapy", in K. O'Connor & L. M. Braverman (eds), *Play Therapy Theory and Practice: A Comparative Presentation*, Hoboken, NJ: John Wiley & Sons, pp. 17–18.
22   Blyton, E., cited in Thwaite (2017), op. cit., pp. 179–181.
23   Thwaite (2017), op. cit., p. 179–181.
24   Ibid., p. 180.
25   Wikipedia (2018) "St George and the Dragon", 18 October, available at: https://en. wikipedia.org/wiki/St_George_and_the_Dragon (accessed on 29 October 2018).
26   Belenky, M. F., Clinchy, B. McV., Goldberger, N. R., & Tarule, J. M. (1986) *Women's Ways of Knowing: The Development of Self, Voice and Mind*, New York, NY: Basic Books, p. 33.
27   Ricoeur, P. (1978) *The Rule of Metaphor: Multidisciplinary Studies of the Creation of Meaning and Language*, translated by R. Czerny with K. McLaughlin & J. Costello, London: Routledge & Kegan Paul, pp. 21–22.
28   Wikipedia (2019) "List of culture heroes", Wikipedia: The free encyclopedia, available at: https://en.wikipedia.org/wiki/List_of_culture_heroes (accessed 20 September 2019).
29   Jung, C. (1964) "Approaching the unconscious", in C. Jung (ed.), *Man and His Symbols*, New York: Dell Books, p. 100.

30 Jung (1964), op. cit., pp. 110–112.
31 Ibid., p. 118.
32 Schaverien, J. (2004), "Boarding school: The trauma of the 'privileged' child", *Journal of Analytical Psychology* 49 (5), p. 696.
33 Ibid.
34 Ibid., p. 697. See also Duffell, N. (2000) *The Making of Them: The British Attitude to Children and the Boarding School System*, London: Lone Arrow Press, p. 286.
35 Lewis-Williams, D. (2002) *The Mind in the Cave: Consciousness and the Origins of Art*, London: Thames & Hudson.
36 Ibid., p. 9.
37 Ibid., p. 252.
38 Ibid., pp. 259–260.
39 Eliade, M. (1972), cited in Lewis-Williams (2002), op. cit., p. 265.
40 Lewis-Williams (2002), op. cit., p. 210.
41 Ibid., p. 211.

Going somewhere

In 1956, when I was six, my parents took me on a lengthy drive away from urban Sydney and into the countryside. I have no recollection of being told where we were going or why. We often went on drives so I probably assumed that it was just one of our occasional outings. It was a long way out of the city and we travelled up over steep green hills, plunging down again to wind our way through small villages. After some hours, we turned off the main road and drove down a short lane with a polo field on the corner, past pretty wooden houses with big gardens. Finally, we passed through open gates attached to stone structures and along a gravel drive. Tall dark fir trees dominated the surrounding gardens.

The drive finished by turning back on itself around a circular garden with a stone sundial in the middle. We parked the car, got out and looked around. It was a silent, empty place broken only by the occasional cawing of a crow. What I saw was an imposing two-storey house with white stucco walls, deep red windows and steep angular roofs topped with tall chimneys. We climbed the few steps up and across the wide wooden veranda to the large deep red door where my father pressed the bell button. After a short wait, the door opened and we were greeted by an elderly nun who ushered us inside. I was familiar with nuns who taught me in the day school I attended so I wasn't surprised by her appearance.

It was gloomy inside the house, with high ceilings and a lot of dark wood including the imposing staircase at the back of the foyer. However, I liked the pretty flowered chintz wallpaper and I noticed the large painting of a nun with a halo around her head showing an open book to two smiling children, with Jesus looking on in the background. I have little memory of any talk between the adults but I followed dutifully as the elderly nun with big glasses showed us over the building. We ascended the ornate dark wooden stairs to a landing with several rooms running off it where we were shown some small bedrooms with three or four beds in them plus a large long room with a row of many beds on each side. I liked the small bedrooms because each had a tiny balcony overlooking the front garden. Next we went into a large chapel filled with familiar religious paraphernalia and an altar at the far end. Then we descended the stairs, peeping into an empty dining room before being taken through various rooms at the back of the building. Finally, we crossed a large room full of empty desks and out into a concrete area where children wearing a blue school uniform were playing.

It was at this point that I realised, with a degree of surprise, that we were visiting a school. Some of the children stopped their play and we stared at each other but there was no exchange between us. Then our little party turned back into the building, walking through to the front foyer and into a small parlour with a window seat looking out over the drive where our car was parked. I sat at the window looking out at the garden while my parents each took a large chair and the elderly nun sat in front of them. I didn't pay any attention to their talk, although I turned back to them when there was a knock at the door and another nun entered, bringing afternoon tea. It was over this cup of tea that one of the three adults, I don't remember which one, perhaps it was the nun, perhaps it was one of my parents, turned to me and asked a deceptively simple question: *Would you like to go to this school?*

It is important to say that I had been brought up to be a polite child and, because I was the eldest child by almost five years, I was used to being in the company of adults. So I assumed that this question was one of those (rhetorical) ones that adults often asked me, when they included me in their conversation: *Would you like to go for a holiday to the beach? Would you like to be a doctor when you grow up? Would you like to learn ballet when you are older? Would you like to visit France one day?* I was often asked questions that required a "Yes" response, with an implicit knowledge attached to them that the suggestion may come to fruition in the fullness of time, or it may not. It was just one more of those type of questions and I saw no danger. Such a *simple* question luring me in, with a total lack of understanding that peril was lurking. Some parents prime children to agree to being sent away by telling them their own happy memories of boarding school.[1] James X was told that "he alone had been chosen for this exciting event whilst his sisters were to stay at home".[2] Initially, it led him to feel "special" until he arrived and the "appalling realisation" hit him including the "utter loneliness and abandonment". The reality was that he went from being a "special" only son to being "an insignificant boy in a vast male institution".[3]

It is unlikely that I was primed. I have never heard my father, at any stage in my life, talk about any happy memories of his boarding school days and my mother went to day school. My surprise to discover it was a school indicates that I was unprepared for where we were going. I was certainly not provided with any explanation of what agreement would entail: being physically removed from my family and all that was familiar; seeing them only occasionally for a few hours two or three times a term; growing up removed from my younger sisters; having no one to turn to when I was in trouble or distressed; and the strict demands of a boarding school regime. So when I was asked if *I would like to go to this school*, I pleased the expectant adults, as I always did when they asked me these general sorts of questions, with an immediate response: *Yes.* Why would I think that it would *actually* happen? After all, for the past two years I had attended a day school in Sydney a short drive from my home and, although I found the nuns to be harsh with their occasional caning, I did have friends there. I had never complained about the school, never even had such thoughts, and I don't remember any talk about my leaving it.

Christopher was also surprised when he discovered that he would be sent away to boarding school. One afternoon, when his nanny and mother were out, his father told him that they needed to have a serious talk about the future. Milne then proceeded to tell his son that the next year, when Christopher turned nine, he would be going to boarding school. His son's wistful reply was: "Do I ever come back to you after that?"[4] His question reveals the lack of understanding that many children have about what is going to happen to them when they are sent away to board. The parents may have a fully developed understanding of what this entails but often this knowledge is not conveyed to the child. This lack of understanding is implicit in Christopher's question: *Will it be forever?* Does the parent realise that the child does not know all that he or she knows as an adult from their accumulated experience?

The discussion Christopher had with his father that day was doubly significant for him. Not only was he going to be sent away from his parents but, more importantly, he was going to lose his nanny, Olive Brockwell. She arrived when he was 18 months old. There had been other nannies but, for unclear reasons, they hadn't stayed. He writes that his first memory is of lying on a rug, looking up and seeing her kind, smiling face. He believed she was the one he "had been waiting for".[5] They lived together in the large nursery on the top floor of the family's London home, spending almost the entire day in each other's company, eating together, playing together and sleeping in adjacent rooms. It was Olive who took him downstairs after breakfast and afternoon tea, then finally in the evening to the dining room for visits with his parents—those "occasional encounters" that stood out as events of the day rather than the norm.[6]

When Christopher came to write his first memoir in 1974, he dedicated the book to Olive. He remembered that it was she who explored the countryside with him when the Milnes bought their country home, Cotchford Farm, in 1925 when he was five years old. The property became the setting for the famous Winnie-the-Pooh books. Together, nanny and child discovered and named Dragon's Bridge, because they both agreed there was something in the water, a fallen, rotting tree, that certainly looked like parts of a dragon.[7] Together they explored Posingford Wood, which includes a bridge that later became Poohstick's Bridge from which Winnie-the-Pooh and the fictional Christopher Robin threw sticks into the running water below.

Hannah Symons, then a young child and daughter of a local chicken farmer, remembered that it was Christopher's nanny who called at their farm one day and asked her mother if she could play with her charge. The two children came to spend a good deal of time together, although only in the countryside, never visiting each other's homes no doubt due to the different class status of the families.[8] However, it would have been the Milnes who established and condoned the relationship between their son and Anne Dartington. She was the daughter of family friends, eight months older and, like him, an only child who was entrusted to the care of a nanny. The children's nannies facilitated the close relationship between them by taking them on visits to Kensington Gardens, the Embankment or Battersea Gardens with their hoops or skipping ropes. The children attended day school together, sitting next to each other in class for three years until Christopher was sent to another boys' day school, Gibbs, before later being sent away to a preparatory boarding school. It was also Olive's job to take him to day school and pick him up at the end of the day. When she went on her annual two-week holiday, Christopher stayed with Anne and her family on the Kent coast. The two children spent Christmas together and Anne often stayed with the Milne family at Cotchford Farm. They drifted apart as they got older, probably a causality of boarding school—another loss for him.[9]

Olive was the adult who wrapped her hands around his when he said his bedtime prayers. Hearing her moving in the next room reassured him when alone in bed in the night nursery. Her absence caused him anxiety when she left him alone in his nursery bed to run an errand in another part of the house.[10] Christopher considered that as a child he might have missed his mother if she had disappeared, and would not have missed his father, but would "have missed Nanny—most desolately".[11] She was to him, as he expressed it, "almost a part" of himself.[12]

It is highly likely that Christopher's mother, Daphne, was brought up by a nanny, with the resultant distancing from her own mother. She was a child in Victorian times, so she would have been educated at home by a governess (who took over from the nanny as she grew older), while her brothers would have been sent to boarding school. Christopher recalled that he enjoyed spending "the occasional half hour" playing games with his mother in the afternoon, as long as Olive was "at hand in case of difficulty".[13] If Daphne was brought up by a nanny (who ranged from responsive, to benign, to cruel[14]), leading to a distant relationship with her parents, it explains her struggle to play easily with her son without the presence of Olive. She did not push herself to develop a mental schema, an understanding of how to manage a child, because that was the job of the nanny, as it had been in her upbringing. Researchers have found that the loss of an early primary surrogate mother in childhood resulted in an "inordinate fear of separation and avoidance of intimate contact" in adulthood.[15] I suspect this accounts for much of Daphne's behaviour with her son. She avoided emotional connection for fear of loss which, in a self-perpetuating circle, leads to avoidance of intimacy and close connection.

Christopher wrote that his mother had not been taught any aspects of housework. He and his father knew that she had been sent to a finishing school somewhere in France but that was all they knew about her upbringing.[16] He believed that she was not clever but that there was much she "could have learnt" in the right setting, perhaps referring to a more effective form of education than the one she received.[17] It is a reference to the limited opportunities for women's education in that period.[18] He was right. Daphne was born in 1890 when educational opportunities for upper- and middle-class women were improving. However, some parents were worried that educating their daughters might make them '*socially* handicapped – that men would not marry such women'. It seems that Daphne was the recipient of this concern and was not educated beyond finishing school, preparing her for marriage.[19]

It is surprising that they knew so little about her, that she talked so little about her upbringing. It suggests it was problematic. Christopher recalls that his mother seemed to be the most happy when she was alone. She liked to go for long walks in the country but resisted him accompanying her. Instead, she encouraged him to meet up with her as she returned because that was what she most enjoyed.[20] So father and son would go out to join her as she returned from her walks. However, Christopher was allowed to accompany her during her night walks: "It was different in the dark. You could be with someone and they would be there if you felt you wanted them, and if you didn't you could forget them". When a car came past with its bright head-lights, catching them up in its windy vortex as it rushed past, they would both back into the hedge that typically lined those small country lanes, holding tightly to each other until the car had passed.[21] I find the description of these events so poignant, so moving. She seems to be enacting with her son and husband a childhood drama of separation, aloneness and rapprochement.

I was unaware of the history lying behind Olive's position until I read Jonathan Gathorne-Hardy's *The Rise and Fall of the British Nanny*.[22] His analysis is helpful in understanding why British parents subscribed to the tradition of sending young children away to board. It also provided me with a proper response to the typical statement or question put to me when I mentioned that I was writing a book about sending children away to boarding school: *I can't imagine how parents could send their children away to boarding school! Why do people have children and then send them away?* It was similar thinking that led Gathorne-Hardy to ask himself why "hundreds of thousands" of mothers from the middle classes, as well as those from the upper ranks, put aside "all loving and disciplining and company of their little children, sometimes almost from birth, to the absolute care of other women, total strangers, nearly always uneducated?"[23] No doubt it was the answer to his question about nannies that led him to follow up his research into nannies with an exploration of the rise of the elite public school system, *The Public School Phenomenon 597–1977*,[24] following the trajectory of those who cared for the children when they left the hands of their substitute parents. First, they are cared for by a nanny, then they are cared for by others in a boarding school.

Harry Hardin (who refers to Gathorne-Hardy's work) spent 20 years at the end of the twentieth century exploring the impact on adult patients who were under the care of surrogate mothers early in life. A significant finding arising from the research, published with co-author Daniel Hardin, is that changes for the young child from one significant carer to another (from the mother to a surrogate or changes in surrogates) lead to feelings of significant loss which the researchers categorise as a "catastrophic" event. Yet the mourning that is required for this loss is not completed because the separation is only significant to the child, not to the parents. They remain unaware of the child's suffering.[25] The research signals what a loss it would have been for Christopher when Olive left. He wrote that he "was all hers" until he went away to boarding school. There were "other people" who moved around the edges of his life but his "total loyalty" was to his nanny.[26] It is likely that this would have been the case for many other English children who were cared for by nannies until they went away to boarding school. One of the English women interviewed by Ysenda Maxtone Graham remembered that she "desperately" missed her home and sought out places to hide so she could cry. What she found "especially difficult" was hearing someone singing a song her nanny used to sing, bringing on "a wave of homesickness".[27]

The fact that a nanny was the de facto mother to many children for the first five to ten years gave her "a fundamental emotional foothold that was never lost".[28] Olive certainly had such a hold on Christopher. In his first memoir, he summarises his life with her and what he was about to lose by being sent away to board in May 1930. She had been his constant daily companion for eight years until he was almost ten years of age. Now he was leaving his day school and her to spend "the next three months in a strange place amongst strange people".[29]

For many young children, being sent away at such a young age is a "rupture" of the connection they have to their primary attachment figures and their homes with all the security it holds for them.[30] That is how it was for both of us, an event that became an ongoing and traumatic memory across our lives.

References

1 Renton, A. (2017) *Stiff Upper Lip: Secrets, Crimes and the Schooling of a Ruling Class*, London: Weidenfeld & Nicolson, p. 37.
2 Schaverien, J. (2002) *The Dying Patient in Psychotherapy: Desire, Dreams and Individuation*, New York: Palgrave Macmillan, p. 24.
3 Ibid.
4 Thwaite, A. (2017) *Goodbye Christopher Robin: A. A. Milne and the Making of Winnie-the-Pooh*, London: Pan Books, p. 177.

5   Milne, C. (1974) *The Enchanted Places: A Childhood Memoir*, London: Pan Books, p. 16.
6   Ibid., p. 17.
7   Ibid., p. 50.
8   Harrison, S. (2011) *The Life and Times of the Real Winnie-the-Pooh: The Teddy Bear Who Inspired A. A. Milne*, Barnsley: Pen & Sword Books Ltd.
9   Milne (1974), op. cit., p. 18.
10 Ibid., p. 20.
11 Ibid., p. 22.
12 Ibid., pp. 16–17.
13 Ibid., p. 17.
14 Gathorne-Hardy, J. (1972) *The Rise and Fall of the British Nanny*, London: Faber & Faber, pp. 229–230.
15 Hardin, H. T. & Hardin, D. H. (2000) "On the vicissitudes of early primary surrogate mothering II: Loss of the surrogate and arrest of mourning", *Journal of the American Psychoanalytic Association* 48 (4), p. 1230.
16 Milne (1974), op. cit., p. 97.
17 Ibid.
18 Ibid., p. 17.
19 Delamont, S. (1989) *Knowledgeable Women: Structuralism and the Reproduction of the Elites*, Abingdon: Routledge, p. 70.
20 Milne (1974), op. cit., p. 38.
21 Ibid., p. 38.
22 Gathorne-Hardy (1972), op. cit.
23 Ibid., p. 19.
24 Gathorne-Hardy, J. (1977) *The Public School Phenomenon, 597–1977*, London: Hodder & Stoughton.
25 Hardin & Hardin (2000), op. cit., p. 1246.
26 Milne (1974), op. cit., p. 26.
27 Maxtone Graham, Y. (2017) *Life in Girls' Boarding Schools 1939–1979: Terms and Conditions*, London: Abacus, p. 83.
28 Gathorne-Hardy (1972), op. cit., p. 129.
29 Milne (1974), op. cit., p. 86.
30 Schaverien, J. (2015) *Boarding School Syndrome: The Psychological Trauma of the "Privileged" Child*, Abingdon: Routledge, p. 3.

Chapter 2

The lure of boarding schools

When I was a child, I loved Milne's book *When We Were Very Young*.[1] My parents read it to me and I can still recite lines from many of the poems. Anglo-Australians, like the family I was born into in the 1950s, were oriented towards England. We read English literature and ate English-style food. School children were educated in classrooms where a picture of newly crowned Queen Elizabeth II was proudly displayed. I was taken by my parents a few days before I turned four to stand in the crowds and wave at her when she visited Australia in 1954—the first English monarch to do so. We called England "the Mother Country".

When the English arrived in 1788, they came with their minds skewed by a belief that their race and culture gave them a God-given "innate superiority", leading them to ignore a culture that dated back for at least 60,000 years.[2] They put Aboriginal people into the "hunter-gatherer" category, allowing Australia to be declared "terra nullius", "nobody's land", facilitating easy appropriation into the Empire. It wasn't true. Indigenous man Bruce Pascoe, in his award-winning book *Dark Emu*, has systematically unrolled evidence that Aboriginal people lived a largely sedentary lifestyle. They cropped and stored significant volumes of grain, built large villages and permanent fishery systems across the country, preserved food and maintained grasslands to attract animals.[3] They traded, shared their resources with other clans and engaged in cultural and social exchange that was a "civilising glue", reducing the risks of war.[4] When early settlers came they destroyed the houses, let their sheep and cattle take over the cultivated fields and grasslands and usurped the wells.[5] There has been a long silence about, and deliberate underestimation of, the achievements of Aboriginal and Torres Strait Islander people. This was a "tactic" of British colonialism practiced not only in Australia but also in North America and South Africa.[6] It is a legacy that has lasted well into contemporary times.[7] When I was a child I saw drawings in our school textbooks of the "primitive" people who populated Australia before we brought our superior culture. We were taught that history began with white settlement and was oriented towards England.

My preparatory school was located in the Southern Highlands of New South Wales (we adopted British names for places), approximately a two-hour drive south of Sydney. When Lachlan Macquarie (1761–1824), Scottish-born governor of New South Wales in 1809 (replacing the infamous William Bligh of the Mutiny on the Bounty), first saw the area, he remarked that it "was particularly beautiful and rich, resembling a fine extensive pleasure ground in England".[8] I now realise that what he saw was the cultivated grassland that explorer Thomas Mitchell described as a "shining verdure".[9] It didn't just "happen"; it was the result of careful land management by the original custodians of the land: the Gundungarra and Tharawal people.

The similarity of the climate of the Southern Highlands to that in England led many wealthy Sydneysiders to build large second homes there, based on English "country house" designs in the 1880s. In 1865, English writer Robert Kerr outlined the requirements for such homes: privacy, comfort, convenience, elegance and spaciousness; they should be light and airy, conveying a sense of importance with a good aspect.[10] Australian "country houses", following this tradition, were usually two storey and based on what we called the Queen Anne style. The school I attended was built in this manner and surrounded by an extensive English-style garden. It was originally built for a wealthy newspaper magnate who lived in Sydney. The country home, Cotchford, in which Christopher spent much of his childhood and which became so central in his life and that of the fictional Christopher Robin, was built in the same style.[11] It is another commonality I share with him—spending much of my childhood in a picturesque country house and being shaped by British cultural sensibility.

My preparatory school announced its English orientation in the first article published about it in the school magazine:

> Start off the garden path with its borders of daffodils, freesias and grape hyacinths; turn to the right where it branches, and find yourself in view of the country home-like gables, its broad verandahs and the lovely English trees that shelter it.[12]

The school was originally established in the area because of the evacuation of city school children to safe country retreats during the war. The nun, who decided when the war was over to make a permanent school in the area for the country children, argued that the children "should not be taken from their great outdoors". She knew about loss because her parents had died when she was a child.[13]

In 1957, the year after I had been taken to visit the school, I was put on a train in Sydney, joining students who would be dispersed to the many boarding schools that were located in the rural setting of the area. Seven or eight years of age was the usual age that most English children were sent off to board but some of the children at my school started when they were five or six.[14] Many of the 55 or so children who attended the school had parents who were "on the land" as it was termed, meaning they owned large rural farms.

Australian rural properties are usually well out of town and consist of thousands of acres—the size required to make a viable living. Many are so far removed from local settlements that children have to receive their initial education via the School of the Air (via two-way radio) which began in 1951, although education by "correspondence" (through the post) dates back to the 1900s.[15] The system is still in operation. Each term, packs of books and exercises are sent to enrolled students and an adult, usually the mother but occasionally a nanny or governess (often a young girl just out of school and not always easy to obtain in such remote settings), supervises the work. Once or perhaps twice a week, an interaction occurs via two-way radio between the teacher and the student. Some of my fellow students were taught by this system before they were sent away to board.

My school followed the tradition of the English preparatory boarding schools which grew out of the tradition of English public schools. They owe their origins to monastic times when the Catholic Church was establishing itself in England at the end of the sixth and beginning of the seventh century. The Church set up schools to recruit new members who would eventually become clergy. They took students as young as possible, when they were easily trained, especially those of the poor, because the wealthier families organised the education of their own children. Initially, young boys were used as choir boys and, as they grew older, a custom was built up of offering them some elementary education in the grammar school.[16] It was a tradition that continued into the seventeenth century, although by the sixteenth century there were more fee-paying students than poor ones.[17]

Students were offered a classical education (Greek and Latin) by methods that involved learning grammar, the skill of parsing (analysing sentence structure) and translating and memorisation of slabs of classical literature.[18] It continued well into the eighteenth century because it gave a feeling of continuity: "safety in its ideals, its achievements, its discipline; the past had in some way the secret of eternal life".[19] Originally, boys boarded in private homes near the school but by the nineteenth century they were almost exclusively boarding schools.[20] Eventually, the younger boys were taken out of city schools and sent to smaller schools in the country, leading to the establishment of preparatory schools that fed into the secondary schools that had established them. Their initial purpose was to remove the young boys from both the bullying of older boys and exposure to disease. A fundamental belief inherent in English preparatory school philosophy was that they provided a place where young children could grow up in the healthy climes of a rural life.[21] It was a similar desire that drove the nun who instigated the establishment of my school.

From 1750 to 1890, if girls were educated, it was at home by governesses.[22] In the eighteenth century, private schools, later known as Ladies Academies, were opened, offering girls a small amount of general education, including languages (French, German and Italian), some mathematics and geography, but the majority of the curriculum focussed on the "accomplishments": dancing, needlework, painting, music and manners. The goal of this education was preparation for marriage.[23] Small private Ladies Academies were also established in Australia.[24] The rise of the suffragettes in the late 1800s assisted in the establishment of schools that offered girls a more substantial education, in keeping with that offered to their brothers. It was the "rich class-obsessed middle class markets" that made boys' public schools profitable, and this was extended to aspirations for girls.[25]

The establishment of elite girls' boarding schools which offered an academic education began in the 1850s. In the UK, America and Australasia it was a fraught project in which pioneering women had to deal with anxiety about the possible loss of a woman's reputation by being "polluted" through being educated.[26] Alongside this was the fear that educated women would be "*socially* handicapped", with men rejecting them as suitable wives.[27] In order to deal with the problem, those in control of these early schools engaged in what sociologist Sara Delamont refers to as "double conformity".[28] They ensured that their students conformed highly to the demands of being a lady, while at the same time adopting the same practices that governed male education with its focus on the classics, although some "separatists" included "modern languages and literature in their 'women's curricula'".[29] Australian girls' schools followed the pattern.[30] The vigilance included restrictions on what places students could be seen in and on their always wearing hats, gloves and behaving with the greatest of decorum.[31] It is a practice that has lasted well beyond the early need for it in those pioneering days. When day schools were established admitting students from the lower echelons of society, girls' boarding schools prevented the mixing of classes by admitting only students from upper-class families.[32]

The success of the pioneers included charting a future for their graduates into one of two lifestyles: "the celibate career woman and the wife who was an intellectual partner to her husband".[33] The second category was a way of selling to men that educated women could still be "good" wives who were both "beautiful and learned".[34] They managed to obtain an education for women but not challenge the Victorian domestic ideal of the family. Of course, not all parents were convinced and did not want their daughters educated in this way.[35] The resistance lasted into the twentieth century. The parents of many of my boarding school friends at an elite Catholic boarding convent had little interest in their daughters being prepared for any other career than that of wife to a successful man.

In late-nineteenth-century Britain there were 700 preparatory schools established to feed into the private secondary schools, although only 11 were for girls.[36] At the beginning of the twentieth century, sending young children away to boarding school had moved beyond necessity and become a well-entrenched part of British upper-class culture. Winston Churchill referred to the practice as an "irresistible tide"—not one to be challenged.[37] Parents saw these schools as a path for upward social mobility[38] and the schools reinforced themselves as an important part of a boy's development through removal from the "softening influence" of their mothers.[39] In 1967 there were over 60,000 young children in English boarding schools, with a quarter of these being girls.[40] In 2019 there are almost 70,000 students in boarding school in the UK.[41] The number of students in boarding schools in Australia is currently on the increase after two decades in decline, the numbers estimated at 27,430 in 2016.[42]

The removal of children from their parents to be "educated" was a practice adopted early in the history of white Australia. In 1849, Australian explorer Charles Sturt wrote that Aboriginal children should have "complete separation" from their parents. The goal was to bring them up "in total ignorance of their forefathers".[43] A similar approach was adopted in relation to Canada's first people.[44] The history of removal of children from their families in the Australian context has been well documented in the 1997 *Report of the National Inquiry into the Separation of Aboriginal and Torres Strait Islander Children from Their Families*.[45] It began when Governor Macquarie established a school for Aboriginal children in 1814. Aboriginal parents were at first attracted to the idea until they discovered that the intent "was to distance the children from their families and communities". In 1839 the colonial government established a "Native Location" School for Aboriginal children, followed by several more such schools in the 1840s. All became boarding schools so as to maximise control over the children.[46]

In the 1950s and 1960s, the years when I was a boarder, greater numbers of Aboriginal and Torres Strait Islander children were forcibly removed from their families to advance the cause of assimilation: the merging of Aboriginal people into white culture. Some were removed for "alleged neglect", to be adopted out at birth or to attend school in distant places far from the influence of their families. Many of these children were then put into service in white families. It is noted in the *Report of the National Inquiry* that this was happening at the same time as John Bowlby was undertaking his pioneering research on child attachment. He reported to the World Health Organization, leading to a 1951 United Nations report "which stressed that child welfare services should be focussed on assisting families to keep their children with them".[47] Many Aboriginal children suffered from neglect and abuse. Many never saw their parents again, some being lied to by being told that their parents were dead.[48] Later research revealed that in fact the "removed" children were no more likely to be employed than those who weren't, nor were they more likely to earn a higher income or undertake post-secondary-school education. They were, however, twice as likely to be arrested than those who remained with their families.[49] The report states that this tallied with "the very damaging effects of institutionalisation on personal emotional development and on the individual's sense of self-worth" as well as on health outcomes. A conclusion reached by the Commissioners of the Enquiry was that the practice "constituted a crime against humanity".[50]

While Aboriginal people resisted having their children removed to be educated, Anglo-Australians embraced the British discourse of teaching a child independence and developing a particular form of "character" by sending them away to boarding schools. In 1907, a well-known Australian newspaper published a report taken from an English newspaper advocating that "the entirely home-reared girl, particularly if she is the only girl or one of a very small family, is very liable to become self-centred and selfish". The dangers of home-rearing included "unlimited self-indulgence" by the over-anxious and self-sacrificial mother, thereby negating the development of "a strong and noble character".[51] Students took on the discourse, as 15-year-old Jennifer Brown wrote in a letter to a Melbourne newspaper: "I think being away from home teaches young people some independence—and avoids some being spoilt by their parents!"[52]

British parents sent their sons away to board in order to offer them an education that would lead to financial and social success in adulthood, largely based on the connections they formed there. Similar ideas were promoted in Australian newspaper advertisements. For example, it was claimed that choosing a particular school would lead to the attainment of an "advanced and truly liberal education" that would result in the development of a "young gentleman" who is then likely to enter university or be successful in business.[53] The promotion of boarding school for girls at the beginning of the twentieth century had more emphasis on preparation for the role of an active wife. However, as time passed, more emphasis was placed on an academic education for girls, as in England, although the "double conformity" continued. An example is a school being opened in Sydney by Miss Allanby. She is described in a country newspaper note about her establishment of a new school as one of the "best educators in the State and does more than polish a girl's manners or teach her how to use a fan. Miss Allanby educates girls, and brings out the best that is in them".[54]

My parents were part of a social group that had high educational aspirations for their children, especially as both my parents had encountered financial hardship as they grew up. My father's father had an aneurism at the age of 34 which left him bed-ridden for the rest of his life. My mother's father suffered a horrific saw mill accident. In both cases, the men were unable to earn a living and the burden fell on their uneducated wives. My parents knew the hardship of worrying about money and they wanted their four girls to have a good education in case they ever needed to earn a living. They were also Catholic and at that time it was imperative in those circles that their children be educated in the faith at Catholic schools—a private Catholic boarding convent met all desired criteria. The early establishment of British girls' boarding schools included a religious divide, such as the foundation of Catholic boarding schools, so that students would not be "polluted" by those of the "'wrong' religious tendency".[55] Sometimes Catholic children were sent to a particular school because they had relatives who were members of the religious congregation or because their mothers or fathers had attended it. I was sent to the school that my mother's sister recommended. Her daughter, who was 12 years older than me, boarded at the Sydney secondary school run by the same order and to where it was assumed I would move on after finishing at the preparatory school.

A number of the children at my school were from Sydney or towns where they could have easily attended the local Catholic school. The school register reveals that over the years of its operation the majority came from rural towns, but 34.7 per cent came from Sydney.[56] I had three best friends at the school, two from country areas and one, like me, from Sydney. My close friend Judith lived on a rural property outside a town but attended the local Catholic school until she was sent to board. In her rural area it was expected that the children of well-to-do families would be sent away to school. Judith's brother went to a boys' Catholic school in the Southern Highlands. The same practice was followed by other families. While the siblings were in close proximity, there were no visits between schools, so that they did not see each other unless parents came to take the siblings out together from their respective schools. The nearness of the schools simply provided ease for the parents in terms of transporting the children to the school and for occasional visits. Many children from the same family were sent away at the same time. Emily aged seven and her younger sister Michelle aged five arrived at the school in 1944 and were sent together so that they could provide company for each other. Their parents wanted a better standard of education than the local school could provide and they were worried by the large class sizes.[57]

After the war, the explosion of migration from Europe meant that many schools, especially Catholic schools, were swamped. The post-war baby boom and increased migration also added to schools being crowded. Teachers and appropriate buildings were in short supply.[58] Classes were large and I remember the day school I attended for the first two years of my education having so many students in one year that I couldn't see the teacher at the front. Frances, who was at my preparatory school in the 1940s, was sent to the school for similar reasons, although it was intended that she would not be sent away to attend the school her mother went to until secondary school. Her parents changed their minds because of the large classes and corporal punishment in the local Catholic convent school.[59]

Some children were sent away because it was thought that being in a country area would be beneficial to their health. Boarding school advertisements virtually always alluded to the advantages of a country environment. For example, an 1894 newspaper article about a girls' private country boarding school run by Miss Pennie referred to its having the "best climatic advantages of Toowoomba".[60] A boarding school 12 miles from Sydney, Highfield Hall in Guildford, stated first on the list of features in a newspaper advertisement the "excellent climate".[61] In the period before the advent of antibiotics, many children died of what would now be considered simple infections. Parents thought that sending their children away from cities might keep them safe, as had been part of the original intention behind English preparatory schools. My mother was born into a house of grief because her two older siblings died of diphtheria. When she contracted the disease, she spent weeks in hospital lying still in bed and not being allowed to see her parents. When she returned home, her parents seemed like strangers to her.

At the beginning of the twentieth century, although high schools were being opened in rural towns, the belief that secondary education of any kind belonged to the middle classes persisted.[62] Elite private girls' schools employed single women who were well educated and had a disposition to encourage girls into the professions. Yet even in these schools, and the new public state schools, there was still a belief that most girls would marry and not pursue a career.[63] State secondary schools took on a new agenda around technical and vocational training for a skilled workforce, but there was still opposition to them, with boarding schools promoted amongst the middle classes as being superior. A journalist in the *Nowra* newspaper quoted from an education journal where it was argued that parents were being "tempted" to send their children to these local high schools or to send their children to board for only a year or so at the end of their education. The writer argues that state-run high schools are "an excellent thing for people who find the expense [of boarding] ... more than they can afford". However, he or she saw this as "a great pity", because "boarding-school is an education in itself and equips a child for life in a way nothing else can".[64] Nick Duffell would argue that this claim is based on a misconstrued belief that "interrupting the child's dependence on the family will help him become a healthily independent adult".[65] This is a belief in direct contradiction to the recognition by developmental theorists that "dependence" is "an inevitable, necessary and healthy stage of human growth" including in middle childhood.[66]

Some children, and perhaps their parents, were seduced by tales of boarding school life being full of adventures. Midnight feasts became part of boarding-school mythology. Australian school girl Joyce Cartel won a blue certificate from the local paper for her story of a boarding school feast involving the purchase of "two dozen meringues, 18 lobster patties, one dozen eclairs, two dozen chocolate biscuits" which they devoured as an indoor picnic. However, one girl drank a bottle of quinine instead of lemonade, but because she felt no after-effects all was well.[67] Children's story books, especially those by Enid Blyton, also promoted this myth, with stories of fun and adventure enticing prospective students.[68] There were a few special feast days at our school when classes were put aside, exciting group games were played and we participated with relish. The day often included picnics down near the river where we consumed sandwiches and cakes. However, although this was not the reality of daily life, there was little public discourse to provide an alternative view. If

I had been enamoured by stories of adventures and fun at boarding school, reality would soon teach me it was not the case. Many students left home for boarding school not at all clear about what was in front of them but "full of hope", only to discover that what they had been told about "homeliness" there was indeed "a con".[69] Ex-boarder Alex Renton sums up the trend to send children away to board, arguing that an entire class of British people "decided that its children need to suffer in order to become useful citizens".[70]

References

1 Milne, A. A. (1924, 1984) *When We Were Very Young*, London: Methuen Children's Books.
2 Pascoe, B. (2014) *Dark Emu*, Djugun, WA: Magabala Books, pp. 3–4.
3 Ibid., p. 49.
4 Ibid., pp. 197–198.
5 Ibid., p. 55.
6 Ibid., p. 132.
7 Ibid., p. 105.
8 Trimingham Jack, C. (2003) *Growing Good Catholic Girls: Education and Convent Life in Australia*, Melbourne: Melbourne University Press, p. 2.
9 Mitchell (1939), cited in Pascoe (2014), op. cit., p. 25.
10 Kerr, R. (1865) *The Gentleman's House: How to Plan English Country Residences from Parsonages to the Palace*, 2nd edition, London: John Murray, p. 67.
11 Milne, C. (1974) *The Enchanted Places: A Childhood Memoir*, London: Pan Books, pp. 36–37.
12 Anon (1945–1946), cited in Trimingham Jack (2003), op. cit., p. 13.
13 Trimingham Jack (2003), op. cit., p. 3.
14 Renton, A. (2017) *Stiff Upper Lip: Secrets, Crimes and the Schooling of a Ruling Class*, London: Weidenfeld & Nicolson, p. 7.
15 NSW Department of Education and Training (2019) "School of the Air Broken Hill and Hay: parted but united", available at: https://schoolair-p.schools.nsw.gov.au/history.html (accessed 5 November 2019).
16 Gathorne-Hardy, J. (1977) *The Public School Phenomenon, 597–1977*, London: Hodder & Stoughton, pp. 22–24.
17 Ibid., p. 27.
18 Ibid., p. 31.
19 Ibid., p. 33.
20 Ibid., p. 29.
21 Leinster-Mackay, D. (1984) *The Rise of the English Preparatory School*, East Sussex: Falmer Press, p. 12.
22 Gathorne-Hardy, J. (1972) *The Rise and Fall of the British Nanny*, London: Faber & Faber, p. 235.
23 Gathorne-Hardy (1977), op. cit., pp. 231–233.
24 Theobald, M. R. (1996) *Knowing Women: Origins of Women's Education in Nineteenth-Century Australia*, Cambridge: Cambridge University Press.
25 Gathorne-Hardy (1977), op. cit., p. 239.
26 Delamont, S. (1989) *Knowledgeable Women: Structuralism and the Reproduction of the Elites*, Abingdon: Routledge, pp. 73–74.
27 Ibid., p. 70.
28 Ibid., p. 72.

29 Ibid., p. 115.
30 Ibid., p. 108.
31 Ibid., p. 88.
32 Ibid., p. 98.
33 Ibid., p. 145.
34 Ibid., p. 144.
35 Ibid., pp. 142–146.
36 Renton (2017), op. cit., p. 26.
37 Churchill (1947), cited in de Symons Honey, J. R. (1977) *Tom Brown's Universe: The Development of the Public School in the Nineteenth Century*, London: Millington Books Ltd., p. xi.
38 de Symons Honey (1977), op. cit., p. 152.
39 Renton (2017), op. cit., pp. 25–27.
40 Ibid., p. 29.
41 Boarding School Concern (2019), "Spring 2019 Update".
42 Parkinson, Emily (2016) "Boarding schools appealing to the city as much as to the country", *Financial Review*, 6 May 2016, available at: www.afr.com/news/special-reports/boarding-schools-appealing-to-the-city-as-much-as-the-country-20160503-golmnt (accessed 15 October 2017).
43 Sturt (1849), cited in Pascoe 2014, op. cit., pp. 202–203.
44 Rose, H. A. (2018) "'I didn't get to say goodbye … didn't get to pet my dogs or nothing': Bioecological theory and the Indian Residential School experience in Canada", *Journal of Family Theory and Review* 10, pp. 348–366.
45 Commonwealth of Australia (1997) *Report of the National Inquiry into the Separation of Aboriginal and Torres Strait Islander Children from Their Families*, Human Rights and Equal Opportunity Commission, Commonwealth of Australia, available at: www.humanrights.gov.au/sites/default/files/content/pdf/social_justice/bringing_them_home_report.pdf (accessed 5 July 2018).
46 Ibid.
47 Bowlby, J. & World Health Organization (1952) *Maternal Care and Mental Health: A report prepared on behalf of the World Health Organization as a contribution to the United Nations programme for the welfare of homeless children*, 2nd ed., World Health Organization, available at: https://apps.who.int/iris/handle/10665/40724 (accessed 18 June 2019).
48 Commonwealth of Australia, *Report of the National Inquiry* (1997), op. cit.
49 Australian Bureau of Statistics (1995), cited in Commonwealth of Australia, *Report of the National Inquiry* (1997), op. cit.
50 Commonwealth of Australia, *Report of the National Inquiry* (1997), op. cit.
51 *Weekly Times*, Melbourne (1907) "Boarding School—or What?", Saturday 28 December, p. 11.
52 *The Age*, Melbourne (1954), "Boarding School", Friday 24 September, p. 17.
53 *Bacchus Marsh Express* (1872) "Landsberg House Boarding School", Saturday 28 December, p. 2, available at:https://trove.nla.gov.au/newspaper/title/246# (accessed 17 August 2018).
54 *The Sydney Stock and Station Journal* (1906) "A girls' boarding school", Tues 11 December, p. 2.
55 Delamont, op. cit., p. 98.
56 Trimingham Jack (2003), op. cit., p. 4.
57 Ibid., p. 42.
58 Campbell, C. & Proctor, H. (2018) *A History of Australian Schooling*, Sydney: Allen & Unwin, pp. 178–179.
59 Trimingham Jack (2003), op. cit., p. 49.

60 *Darling Downs Gazette*, Queensland (1894) "'Ivanhoe' Boarding School", Monday 24 December, p. 5.
61 *Western Champion*, Parkes (1932) "Boarding school", 18 August, p. 15.
62 Campbell & Proctor (2017), op. cit., p. 93.
63 Ibid., p. 131.
64 *The Nowra Leader* (1928) "Boarding school for girls", Friday 23 March, p. 7.
65 Duffell, N. (2000) *The Making of Them: The British Attitude to Children and the Boarding School System*, London, Lone Arrow Press, p. 99.
66 Kohn, H. (1978), cited in Duffell (2000), op. cit., pp. 98–99.
67 *The Sun* (1930) "Supplement to the Sunbeams boarding school", 28 December, p. 2.
68 Simpson, N. (ed.) (2019) *Finding Our Way Home: Women's Accounts of Being Sent to Boarding School*, Abingdon: Routledge, p. 18, 23, 37.
69 Maxtone Graham, Y. (2017) *Life in Girls' Boarding Schools 1939–1979: Terms and Conditions*, London: Abacus, pp. 39, 42.
70 Renton (2017), op. cit., pp. 7–9.

Chapter 3

Leaving rituals

I had no expectations about boarding school when I was put on the train at my local station in Sydney. I knew no one who had been to one and I don't remember any enticing tales of boarding school adventure contained in children's novels. I suppose there were discussions about it before I went away but I have no memory of them. I vaguely remember that uniforms were bought as well as sheets, blankets, a pink patterned mohair blanket, an eiderdown, a set of play clothes (jodhpurs and a jacket), brown school shoes and a pair of white sandshoes. Special tags with my name on them were stitched on to each item: all put into a suitcase. I suppose my mother or father handed it over when I boarded the train but I don't remember that happening. There were no personal items beyond clothing, bedlinen and toiletries. I don't remember who drove me to the station to put me on the train and I have no memories of saying goodbye. Anyway, there wouldn't have been time for an extended farewell because the train only stopped at the station for a few minutes.

The lack of memory about the first goodbye is common for ex-boarders. Six of the 16 narratives of British women in Nikki Simpson's book refer to having no memory of their parents leaving them. The absence is significant to them. Louise Sinclair writes: "My mother must have left me and I imagine I said goodbye, but I have no recall of that. Nothing at all. Not kissing her goodbye, not waving the car off. Nothing".[1] Similarly, Alex Renton doesn't remember saying goodbye to his mother who took him to the school: "My arrival story is ordinary, except that I don't remember saying goodbye".[2] In contrast, some of the women in Simpson's book did express their fear and grief at being left. Renton also refers to a few students having to be dragged from the car or running down the drive after it.[3] I made no fuss.

Attachment theory, which confirms the importance of the emotional connection of child and primary carer, may offer an explanation for the different responses of students: why some expressed distress while others do not. Most students are in middle childhood when they go away to board (seven to twelve years of age) and it is only recently that the research focus has moved from infancy and early childhood to exploration of attachment in these years.[4]

A study of the attachment patterns of 97 children between the ages of eight and twelve found that those who are poorly attached to their primary care-givers are less likely to report distress than their securely attached peers. The researchers concluded that securely attached children are "more accurate per-ceivers" of the distress they are experiencing and are "more comfortable expressing their distress compared to dismissing children".[5] Poorly attached children (referred to as 'dismissing children' by some researchers) have a "tendency to downplay the negative impact of adverse experiences" around separation.[6] So one possible explanation for some boarding school children such as myself not showing distress on being left is that we had poor attach-ment to our parents.

Another interesting finding is that poorly attached children rate their mothers and fathers as "significantly warmer and more caring", although the researchers point out that more research needs to be conducted to support the validity of these claims. They also found that children in the upper age brackets of middle childhood tend to idealise their parents more than younger children.[7] Perhaps older children who do not complain about being left want to see their parents as loving and hence believe that anything their parents might do, including sending them to boarding school, they do because they care. How-ever, Joy Schaverien has found in her work with ex-boarders that those who have "close maternal bonds" are "extremely vulnerable and exposed when the rupture occurs". She concludes that whether the children have close bonds or not, "few ... are prepared for the shock of finding themselves at 6 or 8 years of age in a totally alien and unloving environment".[8] The relationship between the level of attachment boarding school children have to their parents before they leave home is an area for further research that has also been alluded to in relationship to the Indian residential school experience in Canada.[9]

Another interesting research finding is that the ability to "downplay" distress is more likely to "elicit a positive response from the environment".[10] This is certainly true at boarding school where expressing distress ("homesickness") was something teachers believed children would "get over". As Renton sug-gests, this was "kindly meant" but resulted in the child hiding the emotion and "developing a mask that protects".[11] Schaverien simply and powerfully refers to this suppression as "unprocessed grief" and says that, even when home-life is not ideal, being sent away to boarding school still results in "a rupture in the continuity of the life of the child".[12] At my school, we looked down on the rare child who expressed any "homesickness".

Duffell and Basset refer to suppression of grief as key in triggering what they refer to as boarding school trauma.[13] Their argument is supported by recent research into "attachment-related traumas": events in which "a frighten-ing experience is accompanied by, or results from, the appraisal of loss, rejec-tion, or abandonment by an attachment figure".[14] These separations are particularly traumatic because they "pose a threat to survival, since the survival of the child is closely related to the presence of and protection provided by the parents".[15] Being sent away to board involves disruption of the bond between parent and child with the security it offers and the loss of the familiarity and safety of home. It has been argued that family relationships are never the same again.[16] Home becomes a place of "strangeness" where they don't fully belong anymore because there is always the return to boarding school where they spend the majority of their lives.[17]

I have only one memory from my childhood of expressing my distress at my parents leaving me. It happened when I was about four years of age and my grandfather had come to look after me while my parents went out. I liked him but I was furious at not being allowed to go with them, so I screamed, cried and thrashed when Poppy (as I called him) tried to console me. I kept it up until there was no hope of changing their minds and they were gone. Then I sat on the outside steps of the house, looking at the solid blue back gate through which they exited to get into the car and drive away. I had stopped crying and now I was trying to take in that they had not taken me with them in spite of my demands. I was amazed that, even though I had protested so vehemently, they had still left me. The memory of this event is so powerful that I believe I learnt from it that there was no use in complaining about being left. So to some degree I was somewhat prepared for the train trip to boarding school.

Another explanation is that I didn't know what was going to happen to me when I was put on that train. I had no understanding of what going to boarding school meant, so I didn't realise how significant that goodbye was. As I have been thinking back over my lack of memory, the idea that keeps coming into my mind is that it is like someone suddenly dying. When that happens, the thought that people in that situation often have is that they didn't get to say goodbye or, perhaps even more importantly, failed to somehow recognise that they needed to say goodbye. It may also be that for some boarders there is a degree of guilt, self-blame and shame in the quiet acquiescence with which many of us allowed ourselves to be left with no significant ritual around the event. A final possibility is that I had closed down emotionally as I tried to understand and cope with what was happening to me. On reflection, I believe that all three explanations are salient.

There are differences in the ways in which parents and children manage their goodbyes but most ex-boarders, when they are retrieving their memories, include stories about leaving home.[18] Although Christopher makes no mention of his first goodbye, he discusses in some depth the ritual around subsequent ones. The goodbye ritual would begin with the return of his parents and himself from the country home to their London house (probably a day or so before he was due back at school). On the morning of parting, his father would go to his club and Christopher would lunch alone with his mother, after which she would read aloud to him in the drawing room. His father would return about 3 p.m. Christopher would then change into his school clothes, an employee would place his trunk in the car and his mother would say goodbye to him there, as she never accompanied him to school. He and his father would then sit together to do *The Times* crossword, remaining quietly seated after its completion until it was time to leave. Father and son then drove to school together, finding it easier to say their goodbyes in the car while they were a mile or so out from the school.[19] The complex ritual Christopher and his family established reveals that all three of them were aware that the separation was difficult and it had to be managed.

I was the only child to get on the train at our local station, as the rest had boarded earlier at Central Station in Sydney where the train commenced its journey. Some of the other students would have come as part of a group travelling to the city on trains from country towns. Others would have been driven by their parents to be put on the school train, but I never saw that farewell ritual. If I had, I might have thought differently about how other children felt about being sent away. Judith, who was six and would become my best friend, had been looking forward to going to boarding school but, when she arrived at Central Station in the middle of Sydney with her father, she was amazed by what she saw. Another child who was about nine or ten years old had accompanied them on the long trip from their local area and Judith was surprised when the girl began to cry softly when they reached the train. When she looked along the platform, she saw that many other girls were crying and one girl had thrown herself down on to the concrete, with her legs in the air as she shrieked and screamed.[20] Somehow the children were bundled onto the train by the accompanying adults. Once on board, the nuns took over, walking up and down the train, using their wooden clickers to signal for attention while directing the students to get in their seats, be quiet and say the rosary. It was an early lesson for students that feelings of distress were to be suppressed.

My parents probably thought it was fortunate that one of the few stops the train made was close to where we lived, saving them the drive into the busy city centre. In contrast, I would have liked to have been on the train right from the start, becoming part of the group—fitting in. I also had no idea that other students were upset at being sent away because I didn't see any of them crying when I boarded. Getting on the train later resulted in me feeling different, which is precisely not what a boarding school child needs to feel—the great push is not to stand out but to belong, to be part of the group. The child is forced to fit in at "high speed, without any love and little support" and taking in what I saw and then fitting into the group was what filled my mind on that initial train journey.[21]

The carriages were the old-fashioned kind, broken into separate small cabins inside. The Reverend Mother, the same one whom I had met at the school, was at least a familiar but not a warm face and she guided me into one of the compartments, leaving me there with three or four other children. I don't remember being introduced to anyone—but perhaps I was. I was mesmerised by the dark wooden lining of the cabin, the two glasses suspended on the wall in a metal holder and an ornate silver oval shape in the middle of a wall. The children in my compartment had formed a group and they quickly showed me that they knew more than I did by opening up the silver oval to reveal that it turned into a sink held up by two chains on either side. I was surprised to see that it even had a tap inside it. They also told me that the compartment was a sleeping one and the leather-covered seat could be turned into a bed. I felt intimidated by their knowledge as they positioned themselves as "in the know" with me being a "newcomer" with little knowledge. At some stage, the Reverend Mother visited us again, offering us a biscuit from a large tin. I have no other memory of the trip or that I spoke to anyone at all until we arrived at the station where we were taken off to be met by taxis ferrying us the short distance to the school.

The lack of any feelings attached to leaving home, saying goodbye to my parents and the few memories about the first train ride indicates a closed down emotional state. However, it was an event that occurred many years later involving one of my grandchildren that helped me to recognise what had happened and reconnected me with the experience. My grandson was sent to day care when he was 18 months old. He was a clever, happy, active child who loved exploring the world. My partner and I had enjoyed spending the previous nine months looking after him one day a week while his mother slowly began working again. On his first day at childcare, we organised to pick him up early in the afternoon and take him home to look after him until his parents returned from work. We arrived about 3 p.m. and, as the centre was in the middle of the city, it was hard to find a legal parking space close by, so my partner waited outside in the car while I went up to get him.

I arrived not long after the children had been given afternoon tea following their daily nap. After introducing myself to the staff, I was told that my grandson had just been put into the playroom with the other children, so I walked into the large room to find him. It took some time to locate him amongst the other children but finally my eyes fell upon him moving away into the room with his back to me. He was walking slowly, his gait stiff, slow, tentative and heavy—most unlike his usual fast pace. He was also slowly turning his head slightly from side to side as if trying to take in what surrounded him. When he moved side on to me, I could see that his face was pale and the pupils of his eyes were dilated, with a dazed expression on his face. I immediately recognised his lost state (although at the time I didn't realise why) and, without a moment's hesitation, I grabbed him to me, pulling him close into my body, saying his name over and over, comforting myself as much as I was comforting him. I was shocked and horrified that my beautiful grandson, who had been so happy in our care and in the care of his parents, had been left alone to have such an experience.

After quickly gathering his things, I took him down to the car and he settled into his car seat, immediately regaining his usual animated happy self, gabbling the whole way home while pointing to various things outside the car. We picked him up a number of times from the centre after this and he never showed that lost state again. He had adapted and enjoyed his time with the other children, safe in the knowledge that he would be picked up each day by his parents or us. However, I knew that the event had triggered memories of my first train ride to boarding school.

I was shaken by what happened at the childcare centre, yet I never spoke to anyone about it, including my partner and my grandson's parents. When I was watching my grandson on that initial visit, it was as though I was frozen in time, looking back on myself as a young traumatised child and experiencing the stunned state again, while recognising that he was experiencing the same lost state. I was reacting as if my experience of being put on that train was happening in the present, a characteristic of unprocessed trauma.[22] When trauma occurs, the memories are split off from consciousness.[23] What exists are "frozen barely comprehensible fragments".[24] This explains why some ex-boarders, including myself, can remember small snippets of the initial "leaving our parents" experience but not all of it. On the train, I remember just looking at what was happening around me in the train, trying to take in what I was seeing in this strange new world.

It has been recognised that the experience of the young child sent to boarding school "could be literally unspeakable" because at this age the child "lacks the language to describe their emotional experience".[25] A way of thinking about it is that they are *stunned*, struck speechless because they have no words to explain to themselves or to others what has happened to them. That is the meaning of a "stunned state": to be semi-conscious; shocked or astonished so that one cannot react. It is the state I was in on the train and the reason I could not speak about the experience with my grandson—it was a flashback thrusting me back into the stunned psychological state I was in as a child. I believe I stayed in this dazed state throughout that initial train ride and for the first few weeks at the school. It would be another significant event that finally thrust me into consciousness and a realisation of what had happened to me.

References

1 Sinclair in N. Simpson (ed.) (2019) *Finding Our Way Home: Women's Accounts of Being Sent to Boarding School*, Abingdon: Routledge, p. 3.
2 Renton, A. (2017) *Stiff Upper Lip: Secrets, Crimes and the Schooling of a Ruling Class*, London: Weidenfeld & Nicolson, p. 15.
3 Ibid.
4 Borelli, J. L., David, D. H., Crowley, M. J., Snavely, J. E., & Mayes, L. C. (2013) "Dismissing children's perceptions of their emotional experience and parental care: Preliminary evidence of positive bias", *Child Psychiatry and Human Development* 44 (1), doi:10.1007/s10578-012-0310-5, p. 72.
5 Ibid., p. 81.
6 Ibid.
7 Ibid., p. 82.
8 Schaverien, J. (2004) "Boarding school: The trauma of the 'privileged' child", *Journal of Analytical Psychology* 49, p. 687.

 9 Rose, H. A. (2018) "'I didn't get to say goodbye … didn't get to pet my dogs or nothing': Bioecological theory and the Indian residential school experience in Canada", *Journal of Family Theory and Review* 10, p. 356.
10 Borelli et al. (2013), op. cit., p. 83.
11 Renton (2017), op. cit., p. 116.
12 Schaverien, J. (2015) *Boarding School Syndrome: The Psychological Trauma of the "Privileged" Child*, Abingdon: Routledge, pp. 164–165.
13 Duffell, N. & Basset, T. (2016) *Trauma, Abandonment and Privilege: A Guide to Therapeutic Work with Boarding School Survivors*, Abingdon: Routledge, p. 19.
14 Erozkan, A. (2016) "The link between types of attachment and childhood trauma", *Universal Journal of Educational Research* 4 (5), p. 1076.
15 Ibid.
16 Maxtone Graham, Y. (2017) *Life in Girls' Boarding Schools 1939–1979: Terms and Conditions*, London: Abacus, p. 79.
17 Barclay, J. (2011) "The trauma of boarding school", *Self and Society* 38 (3), p. 27.
18 Simpson (2019), op. cit.; Maxtone Graham (2017), op. cit.
19 Milne, C. (1974) *The Enchanted Places: A Childhood Memoir*, London: Pan Books, pp. 86–87.
20 Trimingham Jack, C. (2003) *Growing Good Catholic Girls: Education and Convent Life in Australia*, Melbourne, Vic: Melbourne University Press, p. 55.
21 Renton (2017), op. cit., p. 116.
22 Van der Kolk, B. (2014) *The Body Keeps the Score: Mind, Brain and Body in the Transformation of Trauma*, London: Penguin Random House, p. 45.
23 Ibid., p. 180.
24 Smith, S. & Watson, J. (2010) *Reading Autobiography: A Guide for Interpreting Life Narratives*, St Paul, MN: University of Minnesota Press, p. 21.
25 Schaverien (2015), op. cit., p. 6.

Chapter 4

The dormitory

Black taxis met the school train that had left Central Station in Sydney a few hours earlier. We had been put off at a little country station—no station building, just two short platforms. The trees were high around the narrow lanes that the cars drove along to get us the mile or so to the school. I don't remember arriving or what happened in the following days, except a sense that I was trying to understand what I had to do. I must have looked like I was coping because no one asked me how I was feeling. I certainly did not publicly express any distress, nor do I remember feeling it in the early period. My stunned state continued as I tried to work out how to follow the various strict requirements.

Like many other boarding school children, going was not my choice and I did not feel I had the "right to object", and so I entered into a process of survival and adaptation which in itself is traumatic.[1] The trauma is incurred because, in order to learn to cope with the new regime, the child must split off their emotional life. This process is well expressed in the narrative of British woman Susanna Hoare: "I am faced with no memory of coming to school, finding my dormitory and bed, nor of saying goodbye to my parents. I had shut down inside and knew that I would have to survive by relying on myself".[2] Another ex-boarder writes: "I cannot remember who led me away".[3] An outsider might think that it is what we *do* remember that is traumatic, and indeed there are examples of this being the case, but the trauma lies in what is *not* remembered. It is worrying to suffer from amnesia, bringing with it a sense of powerlessness and feelings of apprehension about a missing part of life.

The rupture for Christopher between home and school is exemplified by a story he tells that remained with him across the years.[4] It concerns his parents' first visit to him in his first term at Boxgrove, his preparatory boarding school. He recalls it was a Wednesday afternoon and he was playing cricket at the bottom of the field when a message came that his parents had arrived:

> I hurried back up the hill towards the school. And then I saw them, side by side, coming towards me. How strange and unfamiliar they looked, how out of place in these surroundings. How little I felt I knew them. How little they seemed to be mine.[5]

So deep was the rupture that he also wondered if they would like him: "Who is he? Are we going to like him?"[6]

The dormitory is one of the first memories I retrieve when I think about that early period. It was a long room broken into two parts. At the far end there were alcoves (small spaces that could fit a bed with a small cabinet beside it and a full-length curtain to give privacy), while beds lined either side of the open part of the room. I slept in the open section, probably because I was a new girl and the idea was to keep an eye on me. There was also an alcove just inside the room entrance where a nun slept. She would supervise us into bed, turn off the lights, then read by the light of a lamp almost covered with a black drape. We were forbidden to talk in the dormitory and there was certainly no scope for midnight feasts. A key learning was how to get dressed and undressed using your dressing gown as a shield. It was a skill I soon learned, sending me a strong message that my body was a thing of shame.[7] Some girls wet their beds and I remember feeling sorry for them as their beds were stripped by the nun each morning. I was thankful something so shameful didn't happen to me. I also remember later some of my friends telling me about special "bags" that were placed under certain girls' beds, indicating that they were having their "periods" (menstruating). I had no idea what this was about, but I do remember it being another thing to be glad about not happening to me, thereby avoiding another cause of shame. Joy Schaverien has also found that, for the boarding school girl, the early stages of puberty may become even more problematic than usual.[8] A difficult stage to go through and one which would be ameliorated by a mother.

The narratives of the 16 British ex-boarding school women contained in Nikki Simpson's book often include details about the dormitory, as expressed in the following statement by one of the women: "The memory of the dormitory is still so clear". This student describes it as a cold, barren place which was in strong contrast to her "comfortable bedroom" at home.[9] Another remembered trying "not to think about my bedroom at home".[10] The contrast between one's bed at home and the one at boarding school is reinforced by Christopher's memory of the lingering pleasure of being in one's own bed at home during the holidays.[11] Marianne Simpson has a similar memory: "To be in my own room, my own bed and have time to be my own person again and free to do what I wished, when I wished".[12]

While boarding school was difficult for Christopher, there was one benefit. At home he suffered from "night terrors" but when he went to boarding school his "one consolation" was that he didn't dream of dragons in the dormitory.[13] His memory of the association of dragons with home supports my explanation contained in the Prelude, that his childhood play around the St George and the Dragon legend was a working out of his childhood dilemma of being associated with the fictional Christopher Robin.

Christopher had developed two physical problems by the time he went away to preparatory school: he trembled and stammered. His father was very keen for him to be an outstanding cricketer but any illusions about him being a top cricketer were set straight by the preparatory school cricket master who pointed out that if he wanted to captain the first eleven in cricket then he "just ought not to tremble".[14] His speech problems emerged when he was eight and his voice started to get "knotted up".[15] He could cope with this at the preparatory school because he was valued for his singing voice but in adolescence, when his voice had broken, it became very difficult.[16]

"Cold" is a word that often surfaces in dormitory memories, including mine, and I wonder if the word fulfils a double meaning of both physical and emotional coldness. Some of the women in Simpson's book remember crying in bed at night.[17] Another shared a room with students who didn't want her,[18] while another was bullied there.[19] At home, a child's bedroom is usually a safe space that is theirs alone. They may have had a part in decorating it or at least feel valued that their parents were thoughtful about what went into it. Sometimes the child can forbid siblings to enter it—clarifying the power they have over the space. Even the direction—*Go to your room*—as a form of punishment is an acknowledgement of it as personal space. A bedroom may contain valued treasures, mementoes, favourite toys, special pillows and a bedspread, all of which are comforting in their familiarity. It is also an intimate place where children feel safe to undress and to explore all aspects of their own bodies. There they are free to play imaginative games, acting out scenarios that might assist them in working through issues that are problematic or puzzling to them.

It is a place of retreat when tired. Children can often be found lying on the bedroom floor or bed, seemingly doing nothing, daydreaming, deep in their own world. In my day, boarding school life was highly regimented into time periods: "Bells controlled our lives, from the moment we woke in the morning until the prayer bell went at night".[20] There was no place for lying on your bed because you were tired. Thus begins the process of denying the needs of one's body and there are long-term consequences for this denial. I am still prone to pushing myself well past tiredness into exhaustion, not even recognising that it is happening.

The bedroom is somewhere a child can go when overwrought by emotion. Children in middle childhood may not get angry as often as younger children, but they tend to "sulk" for longer periods when they do.[21] Their anger tends to be "reactive", in response to the hostility of another or to frustration from the physical environment.[22] In those situations, their bedroom can be a place of refuge as they learn to manage their emotions—an important learning in that stage of development. Adults can support them in this withdrawal, allowing them to calm their emotional responses with the possibility of talking about the incident at a later time. None of this was possible for the boarding school child in my day. I believe that ex-boarders often talk about the dormitory as one of their early memories because it signals that in this other world they are removed from their own bedrooms—a core aspect of the safety of their homes. Instead, they are placed in an institutional room shared with others, largely devoid of individuality, privacy and the possibility of safe emotional and physical space.

Dormitories are not benign. In some English boarding schools they were unheated and the windows were left open on winter nights, making it a freezing experience.[23] At home, showering and sleeping are experienced in a "relaxed manner", creating "a sense of security that is fundamental to health". The rituals foster a caring relationship with one's own body and ultimately with the bodies of others when they come to care for their own children and partner. In contrast, the boarding school child may adopt a position of vigilance around them.[24] This was so for me in the dressing and undressing ritual, learning to use my dressing gown so as not to reveal my body. Each week I endured having my hair washed by one of the lay sisters, the nuns who did the domestic work. It was painful because they were rough and pulled at your hair. Girls at other boarding schools were also forbidden from washing their own hair.[25] Perhaps the purpose was to stop nits but it was an unpleasant experience, adding to denial around care for one's body.

Schaverien also argues that the boarding school timetable around such activities can undermine the child's capacity to settle into their own rhythms of sleeping, dreaming and reverie.[26] I found sleeping difficult in the early stages of my boarding school years and I began to sleep-walk. It happened with a degree of consciousness. While knowing I was asleep, I would rise, put on my dressing gown and walk out into the open dormitory, only to turn around and go back to bed. I suspect a key aspect of the importance of the bedroom is also to do with safety in sleep, feeling that one can sink into the unconscious without worry about what might happen when one is in such a vulnerable state.

Dormitories can be dangerous places. *The Final Report of the Australian Royal Commission into Institutional Responses to Sexual Abuse* found that over one in ten of those who testified (11.7 per cent) were sexually abused by dormitory or house masters.[27] It became a fraught space for me a year or two into my early boarding school years. After students spent some time at the school, they were moved into sections of the dormitory that consisted of alcoves with a curtain at the front. It meant that each student had some privacy. Probably when I was eight or so, I was moved into one of these spaces. We were given no choice regarding where we slept, although students from other schools report that they could choose their bed in the assigned room. We arrived back at school each term to discover where we were to sleep, so that one term I must have discovered that I had been placed in an alcove. I don't remember when it happened but I do remember being there, largely because of what happened there.

One morning I dressed early and lay on my bed with the curtain drawn, waiting for the other students to finish so that I could join them for the communal procession to the study room. While I was lying on the bed, I started to rub my genitals. It was something I began to do when I went away to board. A few minutes later, a nun pulled aside the curtain and saw what I was doing. Nothing was said then or later but that day my things were moved out of the alcove into one of the open sections of the dormitory. I knew why I was being moved but, as was my way, I closed down my emotional reaction.

The area of childhood sexuality continues to be under-theorised.[28] The fact that childhood masturbation is not well researched may be explained by the fact that such investigation is problematic, given the vulnerability of children, and by continued anxiety surrounding the subject. As early as 1977, Gathorne-Hardy, in his history of *The Public School Phenomenon*, turned to the work of Alfred Kinsey (1953) to try and explore what might be happening with girls in schools in regard to sexuality. He found that Kinsey's research revealed that before adolescence the incidence of masturbation in girls and boys was roughly the same, with girls becoming less active than boys in adolescence. Kinsey also found that 58 per cent of girls discovered masturbation for themselves.[29] Gathorne-Hardy was also interested in the incidence of lesbian relationships between girls but found it "hard to pin down ... there is a greater reticence, things are less definite, inchoate, the atmosphere is tense and charged—but you are not quite sure what with". He is contrasting this with what he discovered in his research into boys' schools.[30] At my school, we were so closely supervised that there was no possibility of any such contact between students, indeed we were forbidden from touching each other. However, when I was in the open dormitory (before I was put into an alcove) I remember a student initiating "tickles". It involved putting your arm out towards the next bed and taking turns tickling the inside of it. It was a delicious feeling and was the only physical contact I had with another person.

A report of the first controlled study investigating the developmental features of childhood masturbation was published in 2000. A finding from the study was that the onset of masturbation is often associated with a "stressful life event" (85.2 per cent in 52 children), including "the birth of a sibling or separation from the parents". It was also associated with sleep problems.[31] In contrast, another study indicated that it is a "common and developmentally related behaviour", with the young child learning to explore their body and find places of pleasure. This study found that 10 per cent of children aged seven engage in masturbation, rising to 90 per cent aged 13. The same review found that it is also a "mechanism to cope with negative emotions".[32] Schaverien has argued that the loneliness of boarding school "may be expressed through addictive masturbation, in a vain attempt at self-soothing" and that if discovered it may "bring more censure and loneliness".[33] The research suggests that my behaviour fell somewhere between being developmentally normal and a response to the trauma I was experiencing from being in such a stressful setting.

Alex Renton remembers that, as a 13 year old in boarding school, masturbation "was normally private" but not considered "shameful" amongst his friends. In contrast, he reports that at Christopher Hitchens' school it was a "shared competitive sport". Renton concludes that for some ex-boarders masturbation was learnt early in prep schools, becoming a "comfort blanket", while for others it was an "expression of freedom and individuality in a world that demanded conformity".[34] It isn't clear to me if he includes girls in the statement but I suspect not. In an earlier chapter he concludes that for many girls "shame and stigma were attached to anything connected with sexuality", including menstruation.[35] That was certainly the case at my school.

The night I was moved into the open section of the dormitory, and for many subsequent nights, a nun sat praying on a chair placed at the end of my bed. My response was to crawl under the bedding and spend the night moving around the bed, entirely hidden by the covers. Looking back, I believe my behaviour was fuelled by resistance: *You can't see me under these covers and you can't see what I am doing!* Perhaps it also had something to do with a sense of shame. Nick Duffell had a similar experience when he was caught by a master engaging in sexual play with other boys. The chastising he received led him to develop new understandings around sexuality, replacing "innocence" with "shame" and "curiosity" with "fear".[36]

For children, the adults around them are the moral experts. Children engage in "social referencing", looking to trusted adults for emotional information about situations which lack certainty for them.[37] The information regarding sexuality that I picked up from the nuns who taught me at that time was deeply flawed. Marie Keenan, in her groundbreaking book on *Child Sexual Abuse and the Catholic Church*, writes that it is not always the experience that causes the greatest trauma but "the meaning of the experience and how victims make sense of what happened".[38] While my experience may not fully fall into the category of "abuse", it was an assault on my budding sexuality. It was made clear to me that masturbation was shameful. It is a view inherited across generations of Catholics and some students, including boys, in other boarding schools learnt the same lesson.

The development of what has been termed masturbation "insanity" began in Europe in the eighteenth century (although it was present in Roman Catholic moral theology since the Middle Ages), finding its way to England in the nineteenth century and becoming "fixed with medical orthodoxy" by the middle of the century.[39] This insanity lasted well into the twentieth century and some men who grew up in the 1950s and 1960s carried worry about the supposed detrimental effects of masturbation for decades as a result of lessons given to them at school.[40] Boys were warned to do nothing "when alone" that they would not want their mothers to know about.[41] In the case of girls in Catholic convents, we knew that God was everywhere. He might watch over us, providing us with some reassurance of safety, but the problem was that he was also watching when we did something wrong, leaving a residue of shame, especially about masturbation. Even in the 1970s, girls at a convent school were instructed to sleep with their hands outside the bed linen.[42]

In boys' schools it was thought that keeping students busy was a way of thwarting sexual urges. In some preparatory boarding schools, headmasters organised boys into "bands of purity", no doubt to reduce the incidence of masturbation.[43] In my preparatory school, every year we put on our white veils and made a procession to visit the statue of Mary, the mother of Jesus, in the grotto in the front garden where we would place a lily and declare: *Oh Mary I give you the lily of my heart, be thou its guardian for ever.* It was never explained to us what this was about but it was clear to me that it had something to do with sexuality.

The Catholic Church in Australia was established by Irish priests and nuns. Irish Catholic sexuality was based on the belief that sexuality was about "purity, chastity, virginity, modesty and piety" and involved a "deep sense of shame and embarrassment about sexual practices".[44] According to American feminist scholar and Catholic theologian Rosemary Radford Ruether, there was an ambivalence in the Catholic Church towards women. It consisted of both misogyny towards, and praise for, the virginal woman, who was considered to be the ideal woman.[45] Married Catholic women from the 1930s to the 1950s were cast as the "guardians" of the home and nation, especially in moral matters.[46] Sexuality was certainly not welcomed in the schools of the 1950s, including the one I attended. It wasn't only Catholic schools that practised sexual repression.

Renton writes that many of the women who reported to him told of head-mistresses "going to extraordinary lengths to hide and conquer sex".[47] He argues that boarding school regimes fostered "ignorance, prejudice, fear and guilt … often quite deliberately" in the students who attended the schools.[48] Many of the women who gave him accounts of their time at boarding school reported that headmistresses also suppressed any discussion of sex, with a view that it was "filthy" and "degrading".[49] Maxtone Graham found that the women she interviewed indicated that "there was such deep embarrassment about anything to do with sex" that the teachers at the girls' schools could "not bring themselves to tell pupils what really went on between consenting adults".[50] A practice undertaken at my school was to cover pictures in books of male genitalia on Roman and Greek statues with pieces of glued paper. At least we didn't have to bathe with "calico tent tunics" as did some girls at English schools, including the novelist Antonia White who went to a convent in England.[51]

When I went to boarding school I knew nothing about sex, but I was soon initiated into an understanding by my peers. Being country girls, many knew about the mating of animals and they were helpful (and scornful of my ignor-ance) when I asked them how people do it: *The same as animals do, the man mounts the woman at the back!* So now I knew and that was the understanding I lived with for many years. Looking back, I can also see that the occasional story I heard from girls about "learning about sex from their brothers" worried me at the time, as though they were doing something with their brothers, but I have no more specific details. Another woman also remembers hearing what she, from the informed perspective of an adult, called "strange stories" about sexuality.[52] Duffell argues that the devolution by parents of sex education to school staff or peers is a form of problematic "abrogation". Peer groups can share misinformation, staff may ignore the responsibility or, worse still, engage in "grooming" the child for their own purposes.[53] Some teachers may also have had little knowledge, including the nuns who educated me. Most of the women who taught me had grown up in boarding schools and became nuns soon after they left school, offering little chance to develop an understanding. They were also the recipients of the repressive view towards sexuality of the period, passed on "effortlessly and invisibly from one generation to another".[54]

Years later, as an adult, I went to a retreat run at our local Catholic church and it involved people sharing aspects of their lives that had been harmfully impacted by the Church. One brave single mother of a number of children stood in front of the group and, with tears streaming down her face, told her story. Her marriage had broken down, largely because she had difficulties with sex. At the end of her testimony she asked: *How are we to manage that aspect of our lives when for all of our school years we have been told to deny that part of our lives, and to say: No! No! No! Then when we marry to suddenly turn it around and say: Yes! Yes! Yes!* It wasn't just Catholic women who experienced problems later in life due to the repressed sexuality and negative messages they received in childhood. Alex Renton writes that many of those who participated in his research reported that it "took many years, and more than one marriage, to be at peace with their sexuality".[55] Joy Schaverien writes that some girls experimented with sexuality when they left boarding school, while others "were more conformists, marrying early sometimes into relationships that were lacking in intimacy".[56] Sometimes repressed sexuality surfaced in girls' schools with younger girls becoming besotted with older girls, although at our school it was not discussed. The most it ever amounted to was the giving of Holy Cards (usually with images of the saints) with passionate messages inscribed on the back.

Duffell references the continuing problematic attitudes towards sexuality in England, including in the field of psychotherapy, compared with countries such as Holland. His explanation, which seems a valid one, is that "the renowned British embarrassment about sexuality" has arisen because many theorists are themselves ex-boarders who do not want to stir up painful memories for themselves. He acknowledges that parents also continue to have difficulty in this area. He argues that best practice involves boys and girls being "*sexually mirrored*", a term coined by Dutch Sexual Grounding Therapist Willem Poppeliers.[57] The term refers to the "natural right" of the child to "have their parents' active support" reflecting (mirroring) back to them "that they are good, natural" and welcomed as a "sexual, genital being". This is particularly important between the ages of four and six, as well as in puberty.[58]

The narratives of British women ex-boarders in Simpson's recent book contain no discussion of emergent sexuality until puberty and then only in relation to shame around menstruation.[59] The silence perhaps reflects the continued moral panic around childhood sexuality, built on the socially constructed notion of "childhood innocence".[60] There has been significant recent debate in Australia around what is deemed to be "appropriate" sex education. Experts know that children need access to "open, well-informed honest discussions around sexual knowledge that take account of children's agency in order to build their resilience and competencies in this area".[61] Yet even today knowledge around sexuality for children and young people is obtained "most often in secrecy" in opposition to the adult desire to save children from sex.[62]

The "worry" around childhood sexuality can continue to be problematic for ex-boarders, including myself. I was ambivalent about including my sexual experience in the pages of this book. My concern was around the vulnerability that comes with such disclosure, arising from fear of judgement from others who still cast the subject of childhood sexuality as taboo. There was also left-over shame for me, perhaps arising from the internalisation of misogyny, as psychotherapist Nicola Miller argues from her work with ex-boarders: "many of us are terrorised by the internalised projection of the destructive, uncontrolled power of our sexuality".[63]

Ultimately, I realised that I had a choice between aligning myself with the suppression of sexuality, as I had been brought up to do, including the taboo subject of masturbation, or I could acknowledge myself as an embodied sexual person. As a child, I had the right to explore all aspects of my body and to be scaffolded into thinking positively and acting appropriately about it. This was denied to me, leading to shame and suppression. It is likely that self-censorship around that subject of sexuality happens in the minds of other ex-boarders. It makes it difficult, perhaps even impossible, to retrieve and work openly with memories around their childhood knowledge and experiences of sexuality in boarding school. Jane Barclay, who has worked with boarding school survivors, writes: "Telling how it really was, and having these truths received, is what releases the boarding school girl from her self-perpetuated exile of silence and encourages her home".[64]

References

1 Duffell, N. & Basset, T. (2016) *Trauma, Abandonment and Privilege: A Guide to Therapeutic Work with Boarding School Survivors*, Abingdon: Routledge, p. 4.
2 Hoare in N. Simpson (ed.) (2019) *Finding Our Way Home: Women's Accounts of Being Sent to Boarding School*, Abingdon: Routledge, p. 93.

3 Morris in N. Simpson (ed.) (2019), op. cit., p. 101.
4 Milne, C. (1974) *The Enchanted Places: A Childhood Memoir*, London: Pan Books, p. 87.
5 Ibid.
6 Ibid.
7 Schaverien, J. (2015) *Boarding School Syndrome: The Psychological Trauma of the "Privileged" Child*, Abingdon: Routledge, p. 39.
8 Ibid., p. 218.
9 Simpson (2019), op. cit., p. 38.
10 Trotter in N. Simpson (ed.) (2019), op. cit., p. 74.
11 Milne, C. (1979) *The Path Through the Trees*, London: Eyre Methuen, p. 100.
12 Simpson (2019), op. cit., p. 40.
13 Milne (1974), op. cit., p. 21.
14 Ibid., p. 120.
15 Ibid., p. 125.
16 Milne (1979), op. cit., pp. 271–272.
17 Sinclair in N. Simpson (ed.) (2019), op. cit., p. 4; Henderson in N. Simpson (ed.) (2019), op. cit., p. 65.
18 Wilson in N. Simpson (ed.) (2019), op. cit., p. 18.
19 Trotter in N. Simpson (ed.) (2019), op. cit., p. 73.
20 Simpson (2019), op. cit., p. 38.
21 Peterson, C. (2004) *Looking Forward Through the Lifespan: Developmental Psychology*, Sydney, NSW: Pearson, p. 293.
22 Rotenberg (1985), cited in Peterson (2004), op. cit., p. 294.
23 Maxtone Graham, Y. (2017) *Life in Girls' Boarding Schools 1939–1979: Terms and Conditions*, London: Abacus, pp. 198–199.
24 Schaverien (2015), op. cit., p. 218.
25 Maxtone Graham (2017), op. cit., p. 46.
26 Schaverien (2015), op. cit., p. 218.
27 Royal Commission into Institutional Responses to Child Sexual Abuse (2017) *Final Report: Historical Residential Institutions*, Volume 11, Commonwealth of Australia, available at:www.childabuseroyalcommission.gov.au/sites/default/files/final_report_-_volume_11_historical_residential_institutions.pdf (accessed 11 December, 2018), p. 79.
28 Keenan, M. (2012) *Child Sexual Abuse and the Catholic Church: Gender, Power and Organisational Culture*, Oxford: Oxford University Press, p. 104.
29 Kinsey (1953), cited in Gathorne-Hardy, J. (1977) *The Public School Phenomenon, 597–1977*, London: Hodder & Stoughton, p. 261.
30 Gathorne-Hardy (1977), op. cit., p. 206.
31 Unal, F. (2000) "Predisposing factors in childhood masturbation in Turkey", *European Journal of Pediatrics* 159 (5), pp. 338–342, doi:10.1007/s004310051283, p. 340.
32 Mallants, C. & Casteels, K. (2008) "Practical approach to childhood masturbation—a review", *European Journal of Pediatrics* 157 (10), pp. 1111–1117, doi:10.1007/s00431-008-0766-2, pp. 113–114.
33 Schaverien, J. (2004) "Boarding school: The trauma of the 'privileged' child", *Journal of Analytical Psychology* 49 (5), p. 695.
34 Renton, A. (2017) *Stiff Upper Lip: Secrets, Crimes and the Schooling of a Ruling Class*, London: Weidenfeld & Nicolson, p. 229.
35 Ibid., p. 226. See also Duffell, N. (2000) *The Making of Them: The British Attitude to Children and the Boarding School System*, London: Lone Arrow Press, p. 160.
36 Ibid.; Duffell (2000), p. 173.

37 Berk, L. (2007) *Development Through the Lifespan*, Boston, MA: Allyn & Bacon, p. 188.
38 Keenan (2012), op. cit., p. xx.
39 De Symons Honey, J. R. (1977) *Tom Brown's Universe: The Development of the Public School in the Nineteenth Century*, London: Millington Books Ltd, p. 169.
40 Renton (2017), op. cit., p. 228.
41 De Symons Honey (1977), op. cit., p. 176.
42 Renton (2017), op. cit., p. 229.
43 De Symons Honey (1977), op. cit., p. 181.
44 Keenan (2012), op. cit., p. 149.
45 Ruether, Radford R. (1974) *Religion and Sexism: Images of Women in Jewish and Christian tradition*, New York: Simon & Schuster, p. 157.
46 Kennedy, S. (1985) *Faith and Feminism: Catholic Women's Struggle for Self-Expression*, Sydney, NSW: Studies in the Christian Movement, p, xiv.
47 Renton (2017), op. cit., p. 223.
48 Ibid., p. 218.
49 Ibid., p. 223.
50 Maxtone Graham (2017), op. cit., p. 246.
51 Renton (2017), op. cit., pp. 223–224.
52 Simpson (2019), op. cit., p. 81.
53 Duffell, N. (2014) *Wounded Leaders: British Elitism and the Entitlement Illusion*, London: Lone Arrow Press, p. 143.
54 Duffell (2000), op. cit. p. 171.
55 Renton (2017), op. cit., p. 231.
56 Schaverien (2015), op. cit., p. 42.
57 Duffell (2014), op. cit., pp. 143–145.
58 Sexual Grounding Therapy (2015) "The body matters", available at: www.sexual grounding.com/index.html (accessed 19 December 2018).
59 Simpson (2019), op. cit., pp. 18, 81.
60 Robinson, K. H. (2013) *Innocence, Knowledge and the Construction of Childhood: The Contradictory Nature of Sexuality and Censorship in Children's Contemporary Lives*, Abingdon: Routledge, p. 271.
61 Ibid., p. 271.
62 Ibid., pp. 259–260.
63 Miller (2009), cited in Duffell & Basset (2016), op. cit., p. 131.
64 Barclay, J. (2011) "The trauma of boarding school", *Self and Society* 38 (3), p. 126.

Chapter 5

A strange new world

In spite of what happened, the dormitory remained a central place for me, probably because it contained *my* bed with *my* blankets, *my* pink mohair blanket and *my* eiderdown on it. My bed was the only place in the school that ostensibly belonged to me. When the primacy of a personal bedroom is denied the boarding school child, the bed then becomes the last bastion. Nikki Simpson remembers hiding under the duvet and praying "in desperation: for my parents to come and take me home".[1] Her memory positions the bed as a safe space where she could say and send off into the ether what needed to be voiced. Similarly, James X cried "hidden under the bedclothes, away from the gaze of the other boys".[2]

Some boarding school students had a favourite soft toy they could cuddle at night. We were not allowed to bring any toys or personal objects that might serve as a "transitional object": something that soothes a child, giving psychological comfort and connecting them back to the parent.[3] Functional items such as uniforms and linen were the important things on the lists of many boarding schools.[4] However, my soft pink mohair blanket was a treasured object on my bed and I would wrap myself in it in winter before getting between the freezing sheets. It was something I continued to do well into secondary school. I remember being sad as a young adult when the blanket deteriorated to such a degree that it had to be discarded. It is only now that I realise that it *was* an unintentional transitional object: something beautiful, soft and chosen by my mother, capturing her care in its woollen threads.

The only heating in the school was a small heater in the study room. The temperature ranged in winter from below 0°C to 12°C and sometimes it would snow. We were taught to knit and the first thing we produced was a "pixie": two coloured squares sewn together on two sides with a tie attached. We wore them outside to protect our frozen ears. We weren't given any toys, except when it rained and we had to stay inside for play. Then, there were some board games. The exceptions were that we were allowed to have a pair of roller skates, a set of jacks, a tennis ball and racquet and a camera. I was good at skating on the concrete near the study but still carry scars on my knees from the many falls I took when I was trying to do a complicated turn. I also spent a lot of time playing jacks with other students as did many boarding school girls in that period.[5]

It was a week or two into my time at the school when I was asked to do something in the dormitory that brought me into conscious awareness of what had happened to me. Every day we had to be meticulous in making our beds. Straightening the sheets and blankets, tucking them back into the mattress, pulling up the bedspread and finally folding the spare rug and eiderdown and placing them at the end of the bed. Pyjamas were carefully placed under the pillow. The whole bed had to be crease free. I coped quite well with the routine until one morning the nun told us to *strip our beds*. I had no idea what she was talking about, thinking to myself: *What is "stripping your bed"?* I looked about me to see what the other children were doing and saw that they were taking all the linen off the bed, putting it into a bag at the entrance, collecting a new set of sheets and remaking it. I had never been asked to make a bed from the start in my life and I thought to myself in amazement: *Oh, this is a very hard place to be.*

Researchers into boarding school trauma would refer to this experience as a "threshold memory": a discrete moment in which the student realises that they have crossed over into a new world from which they will never fully return.[6] The realisation can come to children in different ways; for me it was the simple event of remaking a bed. Now I knew that much would be asked of me and I had to learn to cope with it because there was no one to whom I could turn.

Christopher had a similar experience even before he went away to board. He began school at Miss Walter's day school where he sat next to Anne Dartington. The year before he went to preparatory school, he was sent to Gibbs School on 15 January 1929—the only date that as an adult "survived" from his "childhood unforgotten", revealing its significance. His hair, worn long until then, was cut somewhat shorter and he had on his "new bright red blazer" along with a "rather large and loose-fitting peaked cap". Olive took him there and brought him back. When he returned, he rushed into his father's library to tell him the most amazing story that at school they had to call the male principal "Sir". He expected his father to be equally astounded and irate because that was what those who worked for the family called them and not what "boys like him had to call anyone"! He was even further amazed that his father was not surprised, "gently" explaining to him that it was common practice in schools. It was an initiation into "the newness and strangeness" of the world in which he now found himself.[7] While he was at Gibbs, he was still living in the nursery with Olive who was still "very much at the centre" of his life. He was a shy introverted boy and at eight, with the onset of a stammer, she spoke for him.[8] A year later, she was gone and he was sent to Boxgrove boarding school, perhaps somewhat prepared by the Gibbs experience. Again, he described his new school as "a strange place amongst strange people", signalling his continued journey into a foreign world.[9]

In the much loved Winnie-the Pooh books, the fictional Christopher Robin is the adult, always resourceful and competent, a hero "brave and godlike to the toys", as well as being the comforting parent.[10] In sharp contrast, Christopher in his first memoir describes his young self as underweight, small for his age, with unusually long hair and dressed in girlish clothes (his parents had wanted a daughter), "shy and un-self-possessed", "not very bright", "good with his hands" and clever with mechanical things.[11] In his second memoir, he wrote that at boarding school he experienced the world as a "shy and self-conscious" child who found it difficult to mix socially and was "embarrassed" by his name and appearance.[12] He remembered that he wanted to be called John or Peter so that he could be like everyone else, because at "school one lives the life of a herd, and in the herd there is no place for the individual who is different".[13]

It seems that he lived his school life surrounded by others but still alone. He remembered loving a book by Richard Jefferies, *Bevis: The Story of a Boy* (1882). The book is fictional but based on Jefferies' boyhood on a Wiltshire farm. Bevis and his friend Mark play at being "savages, soldiers and explorers" living free in the countryside—all the things Christopher was, did or wanted to do. He described this book as being "really the autobiography of a solitary, lonely boy and so makes its appeal to other solitaries"—someone with whom he could identify.[14] He also felt different because he was a city rather than a country child. At school, he was ashamed of the fact that he came from the city and was envious of the boys who were "born as well as bred in the country". While he spent a good deal of time at their country home, he had been born and lived much of his life in London, yet he never really felt himself to be a "Londoner". In spite of the time he spent in the country during the holidays, at school he couldn't claim full country status and this made him feel less acceptable.[15] It is a sign of the strength of the pressure to fit in.

The country girls who attended boarding school with me expected that they would be sent away. The fact that older siblings or friends from the local district were already at the school when the young child arrived might have lessened the impact for some students, although not for all. Dianne was one of the nine ex-students I interviewed from my preparatory boarding school. She was the youngest of five and, as their country property was too far away from either primary or secondary schools, they were all sent to boarding school. Her brothers went at five but for some reason she was allowed to stay at home until she was seven. When she arrived at the school her older sister was already there, but it didn't stop the pain she experienced. She cried out her grief in public and soon got the message that her behaviour was unacceptable. She never saw her parents during the term and once she had to stay over during the Easter holidays as there was not sufficient time to go home. She remembered also how cold the school was, as there was no central heating.

Her way of coping with this, with the strictness of the school routine and with the pain of separation, was "to steel herself".[16]

Her words bring to my mind the idea of an "iron curtain" that is impenetrable. They also resonate with Schaverien's notion of "an encapsulation of the self" that takes place for some students as they form a shell, cutting themselves off from their emotions, abandoning the need for love and adopting an "I can cope alone" mentality.[17] Dianne went on to join the religious order in adulthood and was sent back to the same school. There she identified with the "homesick children" but she was not allowed to reach out to them as she wanted to do. Again, she was on her own because she wasn't a successful teacher and there was a lack of helpful support. This time she interpreted her suffering as a test of her love for God.[18]

Those who have suffered from abuse in childhood are, according to Judith Herman who draws on the work of John Bowlby, "at great risk of repeated victimization in adulthood".[19] Unless that trauma is brought out into the open and addressed in a therapeutic way, it can leave a trail of destruction in subsequent life. Men are more likely to act it out as aggression, while women "are more likely to be victimized by others or to injure themselves".[20] While Dianne did not suffer from specific instances of abuse, it is a central argument of researchers into the impact of sending young children away to boarding school that it is a form of abandonment that causes similar trauma.[21] It is also, writes Schaverien, "a form of imprisonment".[22] I believe that Dianne recreated her childhood suffering in her adulthood, allowing herself to be made "captive" again, as she had been in childhood. It is, as I will discuss in a later chapter, what I also did in my early 30s.

While the woman who established the preparatory school I went to might have hoped for a homely environment there for the young children, it was not the case. The nuns were not allowed to talk to us except by way of duty and were not allowed to form or express any emotional attachment to us, such as cuddling evokes. They had given their lives to God and that was officially interpreted to mean no "particular friendships" (as they were called) with each other and certainly not with the students. Emotions of all kinds were suppressed. There were so many places where we had to be silent and being "boisterous" was simply not allowed. The physical environment was also difficult.

The lack of central heating meant that in my first winter I developed itchy chilblains on my fingers and toes. I scratched them until they became open sores. My parents must have been told because they sent me a pair of fingerless mittens, which had been hand-knitted by my grandmother, and also a pair of fur-lined boots. I wore both these articles of clothing every winter's day and clearly recall the brown suede covering of the ankle boots, with a zipper in the middle, and the thick fawn-coloured woollen mittens.

My memory of these items has been strong across the years and when I first came to write about them I became "stuck" and could go no further. Then a university colleague, Linda Devereux, with whom I later wrote a paper on this topic, alerted me to Vamik Volkan's research into the notion of "linking objects".[23] In his work with traumatised people, Volkan realised that there were significant objects which they had either preserved or created in relationship to the trauma. The usually inanimate object provides a symbolic "meeting ground" between "what has been lost and the mourner's corresponding self-illustrating image".[24] Uncomfortable feelings connected with the trauma are displaced onto the objects.[25] This allows the person to postpone the complicated grieving process and the objects continue to be associated with "hot feelings" until the work of mourning the loss is finally achieved.[26]

After reading Volkan, I began to explore the boots and mittens as "hot objects" containing powerful emotions that had not been processed. I knew the boots and mittens were symbols of love and care sent to me from home. They made a significant difference to my life, keeping me warm and stopping the pain of the chilblains; yet the comfort they offered was paradoxical. On one hand, they showed that I had not been forgotten and was loved; but they also evoked grief because I had lost my home, my parents, my pet cat who slept with me, my bedroom, my toys and my freedom. I was in a place where I was often in trouble and there was no one to comfort me. I was lonely, frightened and struggling to survive.[27]

There was no one to turn to and so I had to cope on my own. The term "homesickness" is often used in relationship to the boarding school child's distress at being sent away. Schaverien takes it more seriously, defining it as "the complex symptoms of unprocessed grief" because the child is "emotionally wounded (traumatised), exiled (homeless) and bereaved (grieving)".[28] This description well reflects my experience. When I was in my 20s and revisiting the trauma of my childhood experience, I remembered the green walls of the toilet cubicle where I escaped when it was all too much for me. I remember crying there, but that is all. It wasn't until I began to explore the boots and mittens as linking objects that the memories of what I said in the toilet cubicle came back to me.

When I could bear my grief no longer, I escaped to this place where I sobbed out the words: *Mummy, Daddy, Mummy, Daddy.* When I had cried myself out, I dried my tears and went out as though nothing had happened. Another of my coping strategies when I got into trouble or fought with my friends was to escape to the same space, saying to myself: *This time will pass.* It was now clear to me that for my younger self "boarding school was a place without consolation beyond what I could provide for myself".[29]

My boots and mittens showed love and thoughtfulness sent from home, but that meaning was paradoxical because the reality was that I was alone and abandoned. My three sisters remained at home and never went to boarding school. I was the "*sent away*" one. This dilemma is almost universal amongst boarders: believing that their parents love them, yet confused about being sent somewhere they hate, which suggests that perhaps they are either not loved or are bad.[30] Yet even when I recognised the confusion the objects evoked, I knew there was another meaning. It took me months to be able to see it.

The items of clothing were signs of care, but I had to deny my need for care because there was no one to meet it. Indeed, boarding school life was one of toughness where letting anyone else see your vulnerability was simply not done and I developed a personality organised to defeat all attack.[31] I learnt never to show my vulnerable side, never to let on that I cared about anything, never to aspire to be thought of as "good" by the nuns because I never achieved it and I didn't want them to know I wanted their affirmation.[32] My loss of memory about what I said in the toilet cubicle reveals that I had repressed my deep need for my parents. Again, it took me even more time to realise that, as a child, I had made a connection between love and abandonment. I did believe my parents loved me, but they had sent me away and I could not tolerate this paradoxical relationship. It led me to close down on feeling love owing to the fear of abandonment that came with it. That disconnect would plague me in adult life.

The teachers/nuns who cared for us at my preparatory school were forbidden to offer any affection. Yet we know that "children have a biological instinct to attach" and if their "caregivers are loving and caring or distant, insensitive, rejecting, or abusive" they will develop a "coping style" to try and get their needs met.[33] My way of dealing with the lack of love was to develop an imaginative world based on the ballet. My parents offered me a cultural education by taking me regularly to see classical ballets in which the central story-line was one of a prince who is deeply in love with the main female character. So I invented a world in which I was the princess who is loved and protected by the prince. I could endure the difficult times, being badly treated and the loneliness, because I had a magical door into a fantasy world where I was safe and loved.[34] There is a long history in psychoanalytic literature that recognises the role of unconscious fantasy in the psyche of the troubled child.[35] For me, it was a conscious place of refuge that was easily accessed, providing me with what was lacking in my immediate setting—love and safety.

We were required to write weekly letters home to our parents, ones that were read and corrected by the nuns, but I never included any problematic experiences. I doubt that any other students did either. They were circumstances that had to be dealt with alone. Neither did I talk to my parents about it when I saw them and I have no memory of them ever asking me how I liked the school. So begins the process of silencing traumatic events, as John Bowlby puts it: "What cannot be spoken to the [m]other cannot be told to the self".[36] Parents believed they were doing the best for their children; some would have made significant financial sacrifices to pay the exorbitant fees; while others would be continuing a family tradition, perhaps even sending their children to the same school they attended, contributing to "family identity". Most children would have been aware of what their parents thought they were offering them and so there was a recognition by boarding school children that it was their duty "to reassure" their parents "that they were having a lovely time, even if they weren't".[37]

The splitting off of painful emotions is essential for the survival of the boarding school child, with the result that they can "appear to be coping even though that is far from the emotional reality".[38] That was true for me and also for many students who were at British boarding schools as children. One of the British women Maxtone Graham interviewed remembered "longing" for her "mother physically—just longing for her to bend towards me in her rustling evening dress and kiss me goodnight".[39] Sometimes homesickness broke out in dormitories "and soon the whole wing of a school could sound like a field of bleating lambs in search of their mothers".[40] Another student remembers it as "a bewildering and lonely experience".[41] Canadian Indigenous children soon learnt that crying would do them no good, realising they needed to "shut down".[42]

While many students, including myself, suffered grief at the loss of our families and home, the impact on me went further. Not long after I arrived, I had what in retrospect is identifiable as a psychotic episode. One day, while in the dormitory, I started to hear and see church bells that weren't there and I told the supervising nun what was happening to me. The nuns, so my mother told me later, told my parents and they all decided it was because I was reading too much and so they put a stop to it for a period, although I have no clear memory of that happening. I didn't have another episode until I was 28 and began to face the trauma of my boarding school years.

It was friendships that helped me to survive the loneliness, as it was for many other students.[43] Trauma research reveals that the capacity for friendship remains even under the most difficult circumstances, so that forming close relationships is an important factor in psychological survival.[44] I don't remember how I made friends but I did and this was central to my survival. We clung together, although we didn't share our feelings. When I fought with my friends I found it incredibly painful and I called the fights "World Wars". British ex-boarder Marianne Simpson recounts that at boarding school the "making of and maintaining friendships" were "the key to survival" but that there was "plenty of practice in making and breaking up".[45]

Judith, my best friend, was fearless and I basked in her glow. She took on a rebellious position from the start and maintained it across the years. She was untidy, late in getting ready for Mass in the morning, argued with the nuns and was continually punished. Once she was made to wear her pyjamas all day for being slow in getting dressed. Other punishments included being stopped from reading novels, from going out on a Sunday at the invitation of her friends' parents (including mine) and being excluded from taking part in special school events such as puppet shows and plays. She endured her punishments by taking the view that the nuns were wrong and she was right. Like the Christian martyrs, whose lives we had to read on Sunday mornings, she would suffer for her beliefs.[46]

Probably the most difficult event for Judith was when her older sister was killed in a car accident. Her parents decided they didn't want her to attend the funeral, so they came later to tell her what had happened. They took her out of the school for the night and the students were told that her older sister had died. I remember looking at her empty bed that night and wondering what it would be like to be told that your sister was dead. Judith came back the next morning and we just went on as we had before as if nothing had happened. She couldn't understand it all so she used to "lie in bed at night and think she is in America".[47] The event illustrates that, when a child is taken from the family and doesn't participate in its significant events, they are cast adrift and removed from the shared emotions and interpretations that bond it together. Judith had to make meaning of her sister's death alone and she was not allowed to share in the grieving. This also happened to me.

When I was about eight, Poppy, my grandfather, died. He often came over to our house to look after me before I went away. I would sit on his lap and take the chocolate he always brought for me out of his pocket. I liked him but, when he died, it was left to the nuns to tell me. My parents didn't visit during that period and I didn't attend the funeral. That night when we knelt to say our group evening prayers in the study room, the nun leading it mentioned that my grandfather had died and asked the group to pray for him. I knew that I should be upset but I felt nothing, so I pretended to cry, while at the same time feeling ashamed of my deceit. Even now, I can still feel the shame of not being able to connect with any emotion associated with his death.

When I was writing about this experience I continued to be perplexed, just as I have been for most of my life, asking myself: *Why couldn't I feel any grief around the death of my grandfather?* Pondering this question has led me to realise that the crying I did in the toilet for my parents stopped after a few months. Many might say: *Oh, she got over her "homesickness".* Researchers into boarding school trauma would say: *No.* My grandfather died when I had been at the school for almost two years and at a time when I no longer cried for my parents. I had shut down, removing myself from emotions that could not be expressed now, even to myself. This is the core of Schaverien's notion of "Boarding School Syndrome" in which the child learns that her real self is unacceptable and must be kept hidden, including her grief. So I had shut off my feelings and that included any emotions around connection to my family, including my grandfather. I have kept a picture of him in my childhood prayer book all my life. It is the only picture I have of him and I still feel as though I didn't say goodbye to him.

My friends and I spent many hours of our recreation playing imaginary games. Some were taken from Enid Blyton books and I remember one which involved rowing to an island to escape pirates—we were always rowing but never seemed to arrive. When we went down to the back field for afternoon recreation, we built homes rather like Aboriginal gunyahs out of bark taken from the tall eucalyptus trees. Our constructions consisted of large sheets of bark propped up against a tree trunk. The nuns left our constructions there for some time but then one day we would come down to find they had been taken away. We never complained or were surprised; it was just what happened and we accepted it. We didn't have a discourse for unfairness that we gathered around in our conversation. We were at their mercy and never thought to complain.

What looms largest in my memory are the many weeks we spent making secret plans of running away. We especially planned what we would do when we got out the front gate, heading for the railway station and a train to take us home. We did have pocket money that was kept by the nuns and given out to us on odd occasions when there was something to buy, for example at the annual fete held to raise funds for the overseas Catholic missionaries. Perhaps we thought of holding some of this money back to fund our escape. There was an orchard in the school grounds, so we raided it once and hid some of the fruit for our journey. A nun discovered our cache and walked into the classroom with the fruit displayed on a tray, announcing: *The cat's out of the bag! The cat's out of the bag!* I suppose we owned up and got into trouble yet again.

It is interesting from the perspective of child-centred play therapy to think about the meaning of our games. Our play about home and escape evidences that we considered that we did see ourselves as "captives" in the school.[48] While I entered into the escape plans we made, I knew I would never go through with them. The foreignness of what lay beyond the walls of the school seemed too hard for me to navigate. Judith was one of a small number of individual students who did run away. I don't remember her making the decision to go; she just did it one day. Perhaps it was a spur-of-the-moment decision, as it was for Nikki Simpson's mother.[49] Judith walked the mile or so into the local town where she bought some lollies, only to be captured and brought back by the police. Her parents were notified and her father drove all the way from their remote country home to see her. She expected him to congratulate her on what she considered her daring and was stunned when he admonished her and went straight home again. In adulthood, when she told me about her father's response, I was amazed that she thought for a moment that her father might support her![50] Years later in secondary school, I too turned to my father for rescue and he too took the side of the nuns. Renton notes that "adults seldom reacted with much sympathy either to the self-harming or to the runaways".[51] It was a clear message that we had been handed over and that we were totally subject to the rules of the school. It was a very powerless place in which to reside.

Yet "captive" people find ways to escape their confinement sometimes through an "overdeveloped ... solitary inner life".[52] Christopher coped at preparatory school by withdrawing into the "private world" of his imagination which he "visited at night before going to sleep".[53] Elizabeth Routledge reported: "My imagination saved me".[54] It was a strategy I also used and I tried to stay awake as long as possible so that I could enjoy my "ballet" fantasy. I also escaped to it during lessons, taking myself to another place, and this probably earned me the tag the nuns gave me of "having an attitude" of disrespect, something I did because I could see no value in what they taught us.

The desire and capacity of the child to escape confinement through imagination is well reflected in literature. In her book *The Golden Age*, Australian author Joan London draws on the trope of children and young people seeking inner freedom when physically confined. Her novel is set in a small hospital for polio sufferers who must remain there for a significant period. Elsa, one of the young patients, spends time in an isolation ward where there is a single window that becomes her "backyard, her freedom, her picture show". She watches as "the sky slowed itself to a silent, endless semaphore of shapes and colours, as if it were signalling a message".[55] London's inspiration for understanding what happens to young people when they are physically confined came partly from reading *The Diary of Anne Frank*.[56] The young Anne, hiding from the Nazis in an attic along with her Jewish family during the Second World War, finds a friend in her diary and lets her imagination soar out of the one window available to her. It is another book I read a number of times when I was boarding in secondary school. The desire to escape through the imagination is a sign of the child's unconscious awareness of the captivity and the inner drive for freedom.

References

1   Simpson, N. (ed.) (2019) *Finding Our Way Home: Women's Accounts of Being Sent to Boarding School*, Abingdon: Routledge, p. 31.
2   Schaverien, J. (2002) *The Dying Patient in Psychoanalysis: Desire, Dreams and Individuation*, New York: Palgrave Macmillan, p. 24.
3   Triebenbacher, S. L. (1997) "Children's use of transitional objects: Parental attitudes and perceptions", *Child Psychiatry and Human Development* 27 (4), p. 222.
4   Maxtone Graham, Y. (2017) *Life in Girls' Boarding Schools 1939–1979: Terms and Conditions*, London: Abacus, p. 116.
5   Ibid., p. 209.
6   Schaverien, J. (2015) *Boarding School Syndrome: The Psychological Trauma of the "Privileged" Child*, Abingdon: Routledge, p. 58; Duffell, N. & Basset, T. (2016) *Trauma, Abandonment and Privilege: A Guide to Therapeutic Work with Boarding School Survivors*, Abingdon: Routledge, p. 33.
7   Milne, C. (1974) *The Enchanted Places: A Childhood Memoir*, London: Pan Books, p. 80.
8   Ibid., p. 81.
9   Ibid., p. 86.
10 Thwaite, A. (2017) *Goodbye Christopher Robin: A. A. Milne and the Making of Winnie-the-Pooh*, London: Pan Books, pp. 156–157.
11 Milne (1974), op. cit., pp. 32–35.
12 Milne, C. (1979) *The Path through the Trees*, London: Eyre Methuen, p. 218.
13 Ibid., p. 218.
14 Milne (1974), op. cit. pp. 132–133.

15 Milne, C. (1982) *The Hollow on the Hill: The Search for a Personal Philosophy*, London: Eyre Methuen, p. 141.
16 Trimingham Jack, C. (2003) *Growing Good Catholic Girls: Education and Convent Life in Australia*, Melbourne, Vic: Melbourne University Press, p. 94.
17 Schaverien (2015), op. cit., p. 141.
18 Trimingham Jack, C. (1997) "School history: Reconstructing the lived experience", *History of Education Review* 26 (1), pp. 239–241.
19 Herman, J. L. (1992, 2001) *Trauma and Recovery: From Domestic Abuse to Political Terror*, London: Pandora, p. 111.
20 Carmen, E. H., Ricker, P. P., & Mills, T. (1984), cited in Herman (1992), op. cit., p. 113.
21 Schaverien (2015), op. cit., p. 7; Duffell & Basset (2016), op. cit., pp. 4–5.
22 Schaverien (2015), op. cit., p. 137.
23 Trimingham Jack, C. & Devereux, L. (2019) "Memory objects and boarding school trauma", *History of Education Review* 48 (2), pp. 214–226.
24 Volkan, V. (2006) *Killing in the Name of Identity: A Study of Bloody Conflicts*, Charlottesville, VA: Pitchstone Publishing, p. 53.
25 Ibid., p. 255.
26 Ibid., pp. 53–54.
27 Trimingham Jack & Devereux (2019), op. cit., p. 222.
28 Schaverien (2015), op. cit., p. 164.
29 Trimingham Jack & Devereux (2019), op. cit., p. 223.
30 Duffell & Basset (2016), op. cit., p. 140.
31 Ibid., p. 154.
32 Trimingham Jack & Devereux (2019), op. cit., p. 223.
33 Van der Kolk, B. (2014) *The Body Keeps the Score: Mind, Brain and Body in the Transformation of Trauma*, London: Penguin Random House, p. 115.
34 Trimingham Jack & Devereux (2019), op. cit., p. 223.
35 Levin, K. (1996) "Unconscious fantasy in psychotherapy", *American Journal of Psychotherapy*, Spring 1996; 50 (2), pp. 137–153.
36 Bowlby, J., cited in Van der Kolk (2014), op. cit., p. 232.
37 Maxtone Graham (2017), op. cit., p. 86.
38 Schaverien (2015), op. cit., p. 131.
39 Maxtone Graham (2017), op. cit., p. 77.
40 Ibid., p. 78.
41 Ibid., p. 80.
42 Rose, H. A. (2018) "'I didn't get to say goodbye … Didn't get to pet my dogs or nothing': Bioecological theory and the Indian Residential School experience in Canada", *Journal of Family Theory and Review* 10, p. 356.
43 Maxtone Graham (2017), op. cit., p. 79.
44 Herman (1992), op. cit., p. 91.
45 Simpson (2019), op. cit., pp. 40–41.
46 Trimingham Jack, C. (1997) "Kerever Park: A history of the experience of teachers and children in a Catholic girls' preparatory boarding school 1944–1965". Thesis submitted in fulfilment of the requirements of Doctor of Philosophy, University of Sydney, School of Social and Policy Studies in Education, pp. 296–300.
47 Ibid., p. 297.
48 Schaverien (2015), op. cit., p. 137.
49 Simpson (2019), op. cit., p. 41.
50 Trimingham Jack (2003), op. cit., p. 56.

51 Renton, A. (2017) *Stiff Upper Lip: Secrets, Crimes and the Schooling of a Ruling Class*, London: Weidenfeld & Nicolson, p. 89.
52 Herman (1992), op. cit., p. 87.
53 Milne (1979), op. cit., p. 407.
54 Routledge, E. in N. Simpson (ed.) (2019), op. cit., p. 123.
55 London, J. (2014) *The Golden Age*, Sydney, NSW: Random House, p. 10.
56 Sullivan, J. (2014) "Interview: Joan London", *The Sydney Morning Herald*, 8 August, available at: www.smh.com.au/entertainment/books/interview-joan-london-20140804-zza13.html (accessed 12 September 2019).

Chapter 6

Hidden longing

The nuns who taught us were prepared for teaching in closed novitiates where they were taught by older members and certified externally by a registered inspector. The teaching approach they were taught was that "knowledge was to pass from the mind of the Mistress to that of the child".[1] Indeed, the key teaching practices of most schools in this period were based on teachers engaging in "exposition"—description and explanation of an idea—which students then had to memorise and demonstrate understanding of, usually through written work. There was no notion of students constructing their own knowledge—that would come later with Progressive Education. I remember well the production of "perfect work" undertaken by copying out poems and memorising them. We wrote compositions that were corrected, mistakes removed, then copied into "feast books" that were presented to the reverend mother on the day of her namesake saint. We did mathematics, learnt English history, grammar and a lot of parsing (analysing the structure of sentences).[2] The emphasis on grammar certainly gave me a sound understanding of constructing correct and readable text.

The nuns also placed value on nature study as a means of awakening the young child to see God through the beauty of nature.[3] I remember learning about plant structure which included some walks through the garden for observation. It was a beautiful garden and I loved it. My parents also took me to the occasional open garden in the area in spring when they visited and my appreciation of gardening has lasted into my adulthood. Sometimes we were taken down to the river, where we collected tadpoles and put them in fish tanks in a garden shed, hoping (vainly) to see them emerge into frogs. I enjoyed this contact with something that was real and had the potential for discovery.

Alice Miller has found that children who grow up in settings in which their emotions are not acknowledged often turn to nature as a place in which they can be "attentive, lively, and sensitive". It becomes a safe place in which they are "free of conflict", which can arise when they express emotions that are not acceptable to their parents.[4] Both Christopher and I grew up in a historical period when the inner life of the child was not acknowledged. He began his love of nature when he was a child and it lasted all his life. It was perhaps his way of dealing with his ambivalence around the fictional Christopher Robin. His writing about his experiences of country rambles have a vivacity to them that support Miller's argument. He recorded that as an adult he loved to see the primroses turning the Devon hills yellow in the spring, bringing back to him the childhood thrill he had first felt as a child at their country home at Cotchford.[5]

There is research on what is termed "place-identity" as being significant in the formation of self-identity.[6] That is, not only do children learn about who they are in relationship to the significant people in their lives but they also form constructs of who they are by "the objects and things, and the very spaces and places" in which they live. When we form autobiographical narratives about our lives, we include "the environmental past" consisting "of places, spaces and their properties which have served instrumentally in the satisfaction of the person's biological, psychological, social and cultural needs". In summary, people become attached to "geographically locatable places" that provide them with "a sense of belonging and purpose which gives meaning to his or her life".[7] This was true for both Christopher and myself.

When Christopher went to secondary boarding school at Stowe, he coped by going for long solitary walks in the countryside.[8] It was a place of refuge, where he could go when troubled and turn to for consolation: "All my life I have found reassurance in the countryside; have found sorrows and anxieties benefitting from a walk through the meadows".[9] He found a trip out into nature was curative, "restoring as a cool drink on a hot day". It demanded nothing of him, simply let him bathe in its pleasure and in escaping from his worries. His admission reminds me of a lonely boarding school child who, having no parent to throw oneself on in time of need, must find solace where it can be found.

English boarder Patricia Morris also turned to nature for imaginative freedom. She remembered that she would creep to the dormitory window to look out over "the park at night, watching the trees, and listening to the owls". She relished the fact that "no one knew I was there. I was free, it was my only escape". It led her to "appreciate the beauty of the countryside".[10] Joy Schaverien has also found that in the absence of the significant relationships boarding school children experience at home, the young child may substitute places rather than people.[11]

Nature was also a place of freedom for the young nuns who taught at my preparatory school. Suzanne was unusual because she was an outsider—one who hadn't attended a school run by the religious congregation. When she came to the school she was full of ideas about teaching the children through discovery learning, based on the child-centred Progressive Education approach. She saw her students as "curious, active learners", but discovered that the required teaching based on memorisation left little time for creative teaching.[12] She conformed to what was expected of her but found it frustrating. She believed the children should have been free to run in the garden and play their own games rather than being subject to all the strict discipline. She knew that not all of the children were suited to living under such a regime and that some were very unhappy. Her way of dealing with the repressive strict discipline was by being "conscious of the great sense of beauty there, so that the whole ambience of the place was one to lift up the soul".[13]

Mary, another young nun, also tried to respond to the children by establishing relationships with them, praising them so as to build up their self-esteem. However, she found herself to be powerless to change the practices based on conformity and to make the students conform to what was expected in the school regime. She remembered, after she left the preparatory school and had moved on to the senior school, seeing a young child "go to her mother as if she were a stranger".[14] She advised the parent to take her child home and send her to a local school. She, too, turned to the garden at the junior school as a place of refuge, experiencing the love of God through nature: "I just felt His closeness in all that beauty".[15]

Patricia was one of the lay sisters who did the domestic work and who were not allowed to interact at all with the children. They were given no further education, even being restricted to reading the children's library. Many years later, she questioned the waste of the potential of these women. The lay sister system ended in the 1960s and it needed to end, as it kept these women in uneducated servitude.[16] When Patricia visited the convent after the school had closed, the garden remained important to her:

> It's very precious, very precious to me because I've seen the garden change, develop and grow with the trees … I always walk around the garden and say hello to the trees and I remember when different ones were planted and what they're like now; what we've lost, what has died and I see improvements there too.[17]

Her reflections reveal that the garden was a source of place-identity for her in which she found belonging. It was also essential in the narrative of her life as a nun, incorporating significant changes in how that life was lived, providing an "*environmental past*" with its physical continuities and discontinuities.[18]

Patricia's need to return to the garden resonates so well with my experience. The beauty of the Southern Highlands, with its four distinct seasons, has remained significant for me across my life. I returned to live there when I retired. Our weatherboard cottage was built the year I was sent to boarding school in 1957 and it seems fitting that a home I would love so much was being prepared for me in those traumatic years. The house is perched high on a hill and surrounded by a cold-climate garden, including large Japanese maples that turn brilliant red in autumn. My favourite sitting place is in the lounge room looking out across the raggedy old fir trees to a wide sky with its changing light. The school closed in 1965, becoming a retreat house run by the same religious congregation. A few years after I came back to live here in 2008 it was sold, returning it to private ownership. The grand country house and gardens remain, with the school finding its place only in historical memory. It is an outcome that pleases me.

Nature became, for these boarders and nuns, essential in constructing themselves as a "free person". Yet the *leaving* contains the possibility of moving *towards* something. When I think back over three of my key memories from those early boarding years, I believe that there was something germinating within me, as it did in Christopher, that was to come to fruition many years later. First, there was my escape to the toilet cubicle when things were difficult, telling myself: *This time will pass.* My second memory is of standing in the small attic at the top of the old converted stables, where we sometimes did craft work, and looking down over the large school property, taking in the buildings and the surrounding gardens. It was the sense of distance that mesmerised me—being able to look down on the whole property and see the entire vista of it. It was such a new way of seeing it. At the time I could not have told you why it mesmerised me, but it did, and I have retained it as a clear memory across the years. The third significant memory involves an event that took place at the back of the school where we played every afternoon. I was lying on my back in the grass watching the clouds pass by overhead. I stayed there for some time, caught up in the movement in the sky, just watching, until suddenly I thought to myself: *I wonder what my life will be about?* When I think about these events, which have been clear but discrete events in my memory, it seems to me that what was occurring was the beginning of my historical imagination: a growing consciousness of time as encapsulated and in which, with distance in place, past events can be interrogated.

The young nuns who cared for and taught us at this school were also trying to make a life for themselves. Their decision to join the congregation meant, at that time, turning their back on all close relationships, including those with their families whom they now rarely saw. Like the children they taught, I am sure they too had to suppress their grief, making it difficult to be available to the emotional needs of the children under their care. Additionally, the social order of the school, which didn't allow for attachments to each other or to the children, meant they could not respond to the children's needs, even if they recognised them. One nun acknowledged that they were not given any information about the children's families which may, in her opinion, have given her some understanding of "difficult behaviours". She also admitted that she "discounted the physical needs of the children when they were sick".[19]

I have no doubt that the nuns at the school I attended as a child regarded each child as one of individual value and I certainly felt that the reverend mother (the principal) of the school valued me, but she was distant. The nuns were subject to a regime of living which thwarted expression of individuality and this was passed on to us. The 1922 curriculum plan for the school included a statement referring to "strong studies" that are about "sustained effort" on the part of the teachers, based on

> Seriousness, which develops the mind: sure and deep principles to direct the will and keep the heart for God—these are the things we need for the education of our children, who are all too prone to take prettiness for beauty, and the interesting for the true.[20]

Education was directed towards the traditional role of upper-class women as wives and mothers. There was an emphasis on perfection, expressed through "self-control and self-deprecation", self-monitoring, absolute obedience, modesty, suppression of individuality in service of the school "family" and curbing of children's behaviour so that they were not "disruptive of the group". One ex-student referred to it as a "moulding haven" (a metaphor bringing together pressure and safety), designed to turn out "the gracious, disciplined, educated lady".[21]

In that period, girls were trained "to keep themselves hidden", to feel ashamed of their bodies, leading to "a false modesty, a false femininity". The goal was for them to adopt a position of "subservience" through "service" to their men.[22] In the male elite British Establishment this behaviour was ultimately seen to be for the country, while in convent schools it was for God. When boys began boarding school at seven or eight, they learnt to distance themselves from any "sissy" behaviour, acquiring a "veneer of masculinity, a kind of bravado to disguise the vulnerable child self". As with the girls, so the boys develop a "false" understanding of masculinity acquired in preparatory school, becoming "useful" in adulthood as one who has "endured and survived" this "lengthy initiation process". The endurance provides membership of an elite "brotherhood", fostering social advancement as part of the British Establishment.[23] Yet suppression of vulnerable emotions means they do not go away and they find expression in adulthood in "unpredictable behaviours or emotional outbursts, often in reaction to simple triggers".[24]

Alice Miller argues that the child requires positive parenting involving "respect, echoing, understanding, sympathy, and mirroring" the needs of the child. The young child's feelings, including "jealousy, envy, anger, loneliness, impotence, anxiety", must also be accepted, enabling the child to separate from the parent and move towards "individuation and autonomy". When this is not available, it leads to the "true self" being "deeply and thoroughly hidden": "But how can you love something you do not know, something that has never been loved?"[25] Christopher remembered that as a child he never lost his temper, being, in his opinion, spared "the most distressing of all childhood emotions".[26] I could not find any further information about why he thought this, which leaves me to hypothesise that at times he got so angry and upset that he found it hard to bring himself under control. Children do need assistance in learning to experience intense emotions and then bringing themselves back from them—the process of emotional self-regulation. It may have been that he had little support in doing this and so, when his anger did erupt, it was overwhelming for him. This may also explain why he was also given to "burst[ing] into tears on too many occasions for too little reasons". He remembered that he could be "jealous and resentful and unbearably shy". He was also afraid of the dark, of witches and at school of "boys who liked hitting other boys". He became ashamed of expressing his emotions, although in adulthood he recognised it as a gendered practice: "We [men] are (rightly) proud of our ability to reason, to think logically. We are (excusably) a little ashamed if inadvertently we display our emotions rather too publicly" and those "childhood memories still haunt us".[27] His reflection reveals buried shame about such behaviour.

My father, an only child, was adopted (although not formally) and was only told this fact when he was sent to boarding school aged seven. This led to two significant disruptions to his world. In the same year he developed a stammer and indeed I started to lisp when I was sent away at seven. Christopher's "stammer" (the same as stuttering) began when he was eight, before he went to boarding school. No doubt being different by having a major speech defect must have been at least problematic at boarding school for my father and Christopher, probably triggering shame. Feelings of shame about my lisp were there for me but not strongly. I was given private elocution lessons (as they were called) from an outside speech teacher (female) to try and cure me of the problem. I do remember a nun chiding me for the way I spoke, but none of the students did so. What I find interesting for me now is that, when I talk about being at boarding school as a child, I often slip back into the lisp and the associated bodily sensations, feeling teary, weak and full of grief.

Contemporary explanations for the causes of stuttering are that it is genetic-ally based rather than trauma-induced, although researchers agree that they have not yet arrived at a full explanation of the causes.[28] Paul Brocklehurst, a researcher associated with the British Stammering Association, argues that a proportion of sufferers attribute its onset to some kind of trauma. He notes that people who stammer frequently relate its beginning to having to speak in front of a class. Brocklehurst does not deny genetic influences, but argues that it is only the "predisposition that is inherited" and that the persistence or onset "almost certainly depends on environmental factors".[29]

Virginia Axline also believed that "snarls and tangles in the child's feelings, quite often show up in a language difficulty".[30] Her words echo Christopher's description of his voice getting "knotted up".[31] He explains the source of his problem as a hereditary link to his grandfather who also suffered from shyness. However, his discussion of the problem is embedded in discussion about Olive, to whom he was so emotionally connected when he was sent to board-ing school. It may be that Brocklehurst is right and the predisposition to speech problems shows up under stress. My sisters did not go to boarding school and none of them suffered from speech problems. Interestingly, Virginia

Axline found that speech problems such as "stammering, stuttering, baby talk, repetitive language, garbled language" are corrected in play therapy. This supports her linking of them to psychological difficulties.[32] If a traumatic event is part of the cause, then being sent away to board would account for the onset of speech problems for my father and myself. It is less clear in the case of Christopher, although it may be that his shyness in the face of the relentless publicity he endured was a factor.

As I have worked through key memories from my years at boarding school, I can see that they were associated with suppressed emotions. There is a memory from my time at the preparatory school and it has haunted me across the years, although I have never explored why it was so important. Each year we spent many months preparing for a concert to be given to our parents on a special visiting weekend. On that weekend, even country parents who never visited during the term came to attend the concert. The reverend mother who ran the school was a fine pianist and very keen on Gilbert and Sullivan operettas. She directed us in performances of *Mikado* and *The Pirates of Penzance*, accompanying us on the piano. A stage was put up at the back of the study room and a curtain ran in front of it. I was always in the chorus and never had a part, much to my chagrin.

On one occasion, before the performance started, I was hiding behind the curtain with a couple of other girls, peeking through a slit to watch our parents taking up their places on the rows of seats. When we looked out, I saw that my mother and father were already seated in the front row, so that we had a full view of them. My mother was very beautiful and that night she was wearing a pale green dress with very soft pink flowers washed into the filmy material. It had a scoop neck stretching out across her shoulders and a cocktail-length finely pleated skirt caught at her narrow waist by a green belt with a marcasite clasp. She sat upright, legs crossed at the ankles, hands in her lap, eyes looking down. She made a stunning picture. As soon as she was sighted by the girls one of them gasped: *Who is that!* There was no need to inquire as to the source of her attention and I responded immediately with great pride: *That's my mother!*

Many years later, when I was writing my doctoral thesis on the school, I did an analysis of the school iconography that included an image of Mary, the mother of Jesus, as a young woman. It is a mural painted on the walls of a convent in Rome owned by the religious order. Mary is painted surrounded by symbols of womanhood: a spinning distaff, sewing basket and a lily representing purity. She is wearing a soft flowing pink dress and is seated with *her eyes cast down*. Behind her is an open window through which you can see the distant town. While I was writing about the image, some of the words of the poem "The Lady of Shallot" (1832) by Lord Alfred Tennyson kept wandering through the back of my mind: "She left the web, she left the loom. She made three paces thro' the room ... She look'd down to Camelot".[33] The analysis I was undertaking, at the time, involved deconstructing sacred symbols, something that was challenging for me as a person brought up in the Catholic tradition. It took courage to proceed. Still, I went ahead because of a belief that it was important because some sacred symbols convey powerful unconscious messages to students about the traditional subservient role of women in society—not ones to which I subscribed.[34]

At the time, when I reflected on the words of the poem drifting through the back of my consciousness, I realised that I wanted the figure of Mary to *look up*. It was the work of American academic bell hooks, who has written so powerfully on the intersection of class, gender and race, that gave me the words to theorise my desire. She considers the "gaze" to be political, especially for "colonised black people" in that by looking we declare our resistance: "Not only will I stare. I want my look to change reality".[35] I interpreted my desire for Mary to look up as wanting her to challenge the way in which women were depicted in a subservient position. I published a paper on my analysis. It was very well received and I didn't think more about it until now.[36]

At that time I was only at the beginning of using reflexivity in my writing—becoming aware of my thinking as a researcher and trusting that what may seem to be, at first, irrelevant thoughts may have something important to tell me about the project. Now, 25 years later as I returned to those events, I asked myself: *What was it that led you to turn to the poem in the first place? What made you want Mary to look up?* When I finally asked myself that question, I was immediately thrust back to the memory of peering out from behind the curtain and seeing my mother in the front row. The answer came quickly: *I wanted my mother to look up, I wanted her to see me. I wanted her to come and get me and take me home.* My associated feelings are ones of longing and grief as I look out from behind the curtain at the parents I cried for in the toilets, but with whom I could not share my grief. Many years later, a therapist asked me why I didn't tell my parents that I wanted to come home. My response was immediate: *It never occurred to me that I could!*

References

1 Trimingham Jack, C. (2003) *Growing Good Catholic Girls: Education and Convent Life in Australia*, Melbourne, Vic: Melbourne University Press, p. 28.
2 Trimingham Jack (2003), op. cit., pp. 20–35.
3 Ibid.
4 Miller, A. (1981) *Prisoners of Childhood: The Drama of the Gifted Child and the Search for the True Self* (R. Ward, Trans.), New York: Basic Books, p. 10.
5 Milne, C. (1982) *The Hollow on the Hill: The Search for a Personal Philosophy*, London: Eyre Methuen, pp. 70–71.
6 Proshansky, H. M., Fabian, A. K., & Kaminoff, R. T. (1983) "Place-identity: Physical world socialization of the self", *Journal of Environmental Psychology* 3, pp. 57–60.
7 Ibid.
8 Milne, C. (1979) *The Path through the Trees*, London: Eyre Methuen, p. 407.
9 Ibid., p. 97.
10 Morris, P. in Simpson, N. (ed.) (2019) *Finding Our Way Home: Women's Accounts of Being Sent to Boarding School*, Abingdon: Routledge, p. 106.

11 Schaverien, J. (2015) *Boarding School Syndrome: The Psychological Trauma of the "Privileged" Child*, Abingdon: Routledge, pp. 10, 41.
12 Trimingham Jack (2003), op. cit., p. 84.
13 Ibid., p. 88.
14 Ibid., p. 90.
15 Ibid., p. 92.
16 Trimingham Jack, C. (2001) "What's in a veil? Discourses informing a study of lay sisters", *Change: Transformations in Education* 4 (1), pp. 76–90.
17 Trimingham Jack (2003), op. cit., p. 109.
18 Proshansky, Fabian & Kaminoff (1983), op. cit., p. 66.
19 Trimingham Jack (2003), op. cit., pp. 106–107.
20 Ibid., p. 22.
21 Ibid., p. 34.
22 Schaverien, J. (2015), op. cit., p. 43.
23 Ibid., pp. 41–43.
24 Ibid., p. 50.
25 Miller (1981), op. cit., p. ix.
26 Milne (1982), op. cit., p. 67.
27 Ibid., pp. 67–68.
28 Buchel, C. & Sommer, M. (2004) "What causes stuttering?" *PLoS Biology* 2 (2), pp. 1059–1063; Packman, A. (2012) "Theory and therapy in stuttering: A complex relationship", *Journal of Fluency Disorders* 37 (4), pp. 225–233.
29 Brocklehurst, P. (2016) "Stammering and post-traumatic stress – some food for thought", The British Stammering Association, available at: www.stammering.org/speaking-out/article/stammering-and-post-traumatic-stress-some-food-thought (accessed 31 October 2018).
30 Axline, V. M. (1989) *Play Therapy*, Edinburgh: Churchill Livingstone, p. 59.
31 Milne, C. (1974) *The Enchanted Places: A Childhood Memoir*, London: Pan Books, p. 125.
32 Axline (1989), op. cit., p. 59.
33 Tennyson, A. (1832) "The Lady of Shallot", available at: www.poetryfoundation.org/poems/45359/the-lady-of-shalott-1832 (accessed 6 November, 2019).
34 Trimingham Jack (2003), op. cit., p. 114.
35 hooks, b. (1995) "The oppositional gaze: Black female spectators", in P. Z. Brand & C. Korsmeyer (eds) *Feminism and Tradition in Aesthetics*, University Park Pennsylvania: Pennsylvania State University, pp. 143–144.
36 Trimingham Jack, C. (1998) "Sacred symbols, school ideology and the construction of subjectivity", *Paedagogica Historica: International Journal of the History of Education* 34 (3), pp. 771–794.

Chapter 7

Resistance and acceptance

Virginia Axline writes that: "A child whose emotional life is in conflict and turmoil is not a satisfactory pupil".[1] Recent research has shown that when children are subject to stressful situations for a lengthy period of time their memory and learning are undermined due to "the release of toxic amounts of corticosteroids from the stress response circuit".[2] It also explains why it can be difficult to remember highly traumatic events. This may offer some explanation as to why I had become a difficult student. My reports always included statements like: "Has been respectful, but not yet obedient"; "Lacking in docility and respect"; "If Christine would put her mind to her work, her progress in general would be more satisfactory"; "Desire for notice makes her disrespectful and self-willed". I was indeed desirous of attention and I found ways of misbehaving that bonded me with my friends. My misbehaviour involved breaking low-level rules, such as talking when silence was required, finding ways to hide from the nuns during recreation, being silly and inattentive in class. The teachers' approach at the time was to punish children for such behaviour and I was often excluded from special activities, such as having a leading part in a play or sharing in fun craft activities. It didn't work because my negative behaviour was reinforced by the attention I got from other students and especially from the feeling of belonging that came from being a member of a naughty group. This attention far outweighed the punishments I was given. My way of behaving is well explained by the work of Rudolf Dreikurs, an Austrian psychiatrist and educator.

Dreikurs developed a method of understanding children's problematic behaviour based on the work of Alfred Adler whom he met at the University of Vienna. In the 1990s Dreikurs moved to Chicago where he played a significant role in developing teaching strategies based on positive approaches to managing children rather than the traditional punitive model. He believed that the primary goal of all humans, including children, is to belong and that the capacity for social connection is the basis of successful development in life. His approach is based on the positive encouragement of appropriate behaviours and logical consequences that have been well explained to children when their behaviour is inappropriate. He argues that, if children grow up in an authoritarian punishing environment in which they are not encouraged to engage with adults in a democratic way by having some say about their lives, they become discouraged. In their search to fit in, they adopt one or more of four "mistaken goals": (a) seeking attention; (b) engaging in power struggles, especially with significant adults; (c) seeking revenge towards those who have hurt them; (d) giving up and adopting a position of hopelessness and inadequacy. These four "mistaken goals" are on a continuum and, by the time a person gets into revenge or inadequacy, it takes significant effort to realign them with positive goals.[3] Attention seeking and power struggles were certainly my two mistaken goals, especially at preparatory school.

Fitting in at boarding school is critical and I had chosen not to conform to what the nuns wanted of me, but instead to seek affirmation by getting noticed by other students. It is hard to say how this came about but I think I enjoyed the excitement of being naughty. American psychologist Frank Walton (1996) extended Dreikurs' four categories by including one that he considered emerged in adolescence: "excitement", which included being good at "being bad" rather than failing at trying to be good.[4] I know I enjoyed the exhilaration of being with my friends and doing what we were not supposed to do at preparatory school. This became stronger when I moved on to secondary education.

Investigation into the impact of childhood trauma is ongoing, although it does seem clear that those who experience childhood trauma involving lack of parental support exhibit poor attachment behaviour.[5] They become "distant from" or engage in "oppositional behaviour towards parents, caregivers, and authorities".[6] I do have one memory of expressing my unhappiness at being sent away to boarding school as a seven-year-old child. It occurred when my parents visited me at school and took me out for a picnic. During the afternoon my father wanted to photograph me and asked me to smile but I refused. An emotional struggle ensued between the two of us. I knew that he wanted a happy photograph, perhaps unconsciously to assure him that I liked the school and was glad to see my family, but I would not give him what he wanted, so he took it anyway (see cover). The photograph is one of very few I have from my boarding-school years. It reveals an anxious and unhappy child. Roland Barthes, who has made a study of signs and symbols, states that: "The photographic message is a continuous" one.[7] Across the years, that photograph has been a physical memory repository of my unhappiness. At the time my refusal to smile was spontaneous, springing, I suspect, from an unconscious desire to let them know how I felt. I continued similar resistant behaviour when I was home, refusing to participate in family outings and, if I was forced to go, resisting enjoyment. At school all that mattered was my friends and during the holidays I didn't see them because they lived too far away.

My parents must have been concerned about my academic results because they decided to take me out of the preparatory school when I was eleven, a year before it finished. However, instead of being taken home and being sent to the same day school as my sisters, I was sent to a weekly boarding school in Sydney run by the same order of nuns who ran my previous school. It is hard to fathom their thinking. Perhaps they thought that continuing with the same religious order would provide some continuity for me. They may have thought the academic quality of what was offered in a city school was better than that offered in a country school. Perhaps they even thought I liked boarding school! After all, I had never said that I didn't. I don't remember any discussion about the move. It just happened and I accepted their decision. Reflecting back, I wonder, if I had been asked, what I would have said? I was used to it and my friends were there. Also, I hadn't liked the day school I had attended for the first two years of my education (aged five and six). I was sometimes caned, which I never mentioned to my parents, but perhaps they knew and it contributed to their decision to send me away to board.

The students I had befriended accepted that boarding school was how we lived. We might have hatched a plan of escaping but we never discussed making our parents realise that we didn't like it. There was no discourse around talking to our parents about our distress. Indeed, I had become cut off from those emotions after some months of being at the preparatory school. The words of novelist L. P. Hartley (who wrote, amongst other books, *The Go-Between*) about his time at boarding school resonate with me: "He had repressed his feelings so often he had none left to repress".[8] After all, we knew our parents had chosen to send us there, so there was an embedded reason for it—it was our lot and we needed to just get on with it.

The twentieth century saw a growing interest in child development.[9] It has been argued that "the British elite abandoned emotions around 1850" only to rediscover them in the 1970s when "child development theory penetrated middle-class homes".[10] Theories around child development led to a reduction in an emphasis on obedience.[11] This change had not reached my home or school in the 1950s and 1960s. Catholics were still embedded in a culture of "unquestioning docility of mind".[12] It was only with the advent of Vatican Two in 1962 that Catholics were encouraged to rely more on our consciences than on slavish reliance on rules. Parents of my generation didn't enter into discussions with their children about how they felt. They had aspirations for them to be socially successful and, if they were girls, to make a good marriage. My parents wanted their four daughters to be educated so we could earn a living if we ever needed to, but they aspired to us marrying someone who could support us without us having to work.

So I obediently left the preparatory school for yet another new world. My new school, an hour's drive across the city from where we lived, was both a weekly boarding and a day school in Sydney. I went there as a weekly boarder. My mother shared the driving with another doctor's wife whose daughter (much older than me) also attended the school. Each Monday morning I was driven across the city to board again until Friday when I came home. The move required considerable adjustment.

My preparatory school had been made up of many country girls and I felt out of place there because I was a city girl. Now I felt out of place in my new school because these girls, aged from 11 to 18, were city girls, They were far more sophisticated than I was, having spent my previous years with country girls. At the preparatory school, horses and country life were what passed for social cachet. At my new school, being sophisticated and knowing about current popular music and other social mores was the new social currency. I simply did not have sufficient "funds" to keep up. I remember one evening at the dinner table, which was presided over by two older stylish girls, making a significant social blunder. Exactly what it was totally eludes me, but I remember the amazed look on their faces and the derision from one of these girls who corrected my error. It was humiliating. Still I managed to adapt, made new friends and again fitted in.

There is one key memory from my time there. One day we were in a class being taught by a woman who was not a nun. In the middle of the class I told her I was feeling sick and asked her if I could go up to the dormitory and lie down. I wasn't at all ill. I just wanted some space to myself and thought that she would fall for my claim of being sick (the nuns were far less likely to respond). She gave me permission and I went upstairs to the dormitory and lay on my bed doing nothing, just gazing into space. I remember the pleasure of being in the dormitory on my own.

At home I had been brought up virtually as an only child. My next sister was almost five years younger, with the other two coming in quick succession after her. They formed a group so, when I was home, I spent a lot of my time playing on my own. I also spent time alone in the holidays because my boarding school friends lived far away and I had no local friends. My isolation was compounded by the fact that we lived on a busy main street, so there was no street play with other children. I learnt to occupy myself, not looking for the company of others. When I was eight, my report noted that I preferred to "isolate myself" and did not "blend in readily with others". The comments could be read as a criticism of something lacking in me, but investigation into my background would have provided at least a partial explanation. At home I was used to being on my own and was not required to "blend in".

After some time lying on my bed in the dormitory, a student came up to find me, telling me that the teacher was listening to them reading aloud in front of the class. She had been told to tell me that I needed to come down and do my reading because I was likely to get the reading prize for the year. Public reading was an important part of the process in ascertaining who would get the award. Over my boarding school years I became an avid reader. Books were what I loved to explore because they took me into another world that was so much better than the one in which I lived. At my new school I quickly read my way through the junior library, so I was given permission to move on to the senior library. It seems the teachers were aware of my interest in and capacity for literature and giving me the prize would have made sense. Still

I was surprised that I was being considered for it. I was also stubborn. I listened to what the student told me, weighed up my options and decided that coming down would be a loss of face. I wasn't going to admit, by returning to class, that I really wasn't sick. Indeed, I realised that the teacher's invitation was a sign that she was aware that I was not ill. Even the lure of the prize did not entice me, so I told the student to tell the teacher that I was too sick. By so doing, I entered into Dreikurs' mistaken goal of a power play which, of course, did me far more damage than it did anyone else.

My resistance was also partly because I didn't see myself as one of the "players" when it came to trying to excel at school work and for many years I had considered that what they offered was not worth investing in. It bored me. I also had no idea that I was at all clever, even though each year I usually won a prize associated with English. I hardly registered that accomplishment and it did not convince me of my capacity or encourage me to be more engaged in classes.

I lasted a year at that school. Many years later my mother told me they moved me because they considered that one of my friends was undermining my confidence. She was right. The girl was very sophisticated, with an older sister who had left school and moved with a group of very smart people. The sister's antics were reported with relish by her younger sibling—parties and outrageous behaviour—and I found them amazing. I tagged along behind her, as did the rest of our group, courtiers in her court. I didn't question my parents' decision. There may have been part of me that was pleased because I was going to the secondary boarding school where all my friends from the preparatory school would join me. Ironically, I discovered the next year that the girl my parents moved me to avoid had also transferred to my next school.

Yet again my parents decided not to take me home and send me to day school with my three younger sisters. I can think of no explanation for their decision except that I was now a difficult child. They may have thought that having me at home was too much for them, especially for my mother. She had enough difficulties. One of my sisters was very sick with asthma. The next one had almost died just after her birth and that was also a worry for them in terms of what the outcome would be for her. My youngest sister had allergies which meant she was often covered with rashes that were painful for her to bear and for my parents to treat. Research into children who have suffered separation indicates that many become difficult, leading to abandonment by subsequent caregivers which creates a new trauma.[13] My parents moving me from one boarding school to another may have been their attempt to rectify what they saw as a growing problem. However, it just made life more difficult for me in having to adjust again.

The secondary school which I began in 1962 at age 12 was another boarding school run by the same congregation of nuns. However, many of my new fellow students had attended a day school attached to the senior school until they were 12. Then they had no option but to board or move to another school. Some lived within walking distance of the school. There were many elite private girls schools in Sydney, including some Catholic schools, so they could have attended day school. Their parents had also decided, for whatever reason, that boarding was preferable. Apart from a continued belief in the primacy of elite schools, another possible explanation is that it meant no contact with boys. Most Catholic parents had ingested the Church's fear of sexuality and a great worry in those days was that their daughters would fall pregnant and be forced into marriage—a source of shame for them. Indeed, it happened to many girls I knew when I left school, before the advent of the pill. We secretly felt ashamed of having sex, so not using some form of contraception was a form of denial of our behaviour. We were also ignorant about it. This may have contributed to the parents' motivation, but I am hypothesising. Certainly and probably more importantly, there were family traditions of sending my fellow students to the school because mothers had gone to school there. One of my friends from secondary school, who lived just up the road from the school, told me recently how every Sunday when she went home for the day, she screamed and cried, begging to be allowed to go to day school. It didn't work and she was there as a boarder for six years. Her way of coping was to be a good girl, becoming a school prefect. She didn't do well academically.

The period after the war, between 1951 and 1975, was one of optimism in Australia following two decades of "austerity" due to the depression and then war. There was peace and the economy began to grow and so the national government was finally able to turn its attention to schooling. Completing all the five years of secondary education had been the preserve of the elite, many of whom went on to university. Now there was a growing expectation that all students would have access to some years of secondary school. The numbers of students enrolled in primary and secondary school rose from 975,000 in 1947 to 2,839,000 in 1972.[14] Australian middle-class parents embraced secondary education as a path to white collar work and the professions. If they could afford it, they tended to choose either government selective schools or non-government schools for their children.[15] The United Kingdom followed a similar pattern of extending schooling into secondary education for all students and government schools were opened to accommodate them. However, a growing number of middle-class parents aspired to send their children to elite secondary schools which had previously been the domain of the upper classes.[16] In response to the demand, new private schools were opened and Christopher was sent to one of them.

Christopher's father had completed his secondary schooling at the famous Westminster School (established in the twelfth century or earlier). Before he went there, he attended the private school his father ran which also took in boarders. He was assisted in adapting to Westminster because his older brother Ken, having started there before him, coached him in its ways. However, later in life, he would say that in his orientation Ken concentrated on "this meaningless, artificial life … in which all morality was convention", only right because it had been done for 300 years.[17] Still, he recalled when he went to the school that he went through a "conformist phase", explaining that "public schoolboys often adopt a protective colouring".[18]

Duffell and Basset, as a result of the many years they had spent working with ex-boarders, identified three typologies of Strategic Survival Personalities that students adopt to cope. They can become "Compliers or Conformers" by identifying "with the values of the school"; "Rebels" who take an "anti-authority stance"; or "Casualties or the Crushed" who cannot develop "a competent survival personality" and are often subjected to "bullying and scapegoating" from teachers and students.[19] Milne realised that he became a conformer and his words about developing a "protective colouring" reveal insight into the adaptation students must go through in these settings. Yet he maintained an affection for Westminster, leaving the school a large share of his estate when he died. Ann Thwaite believes he valued it not so much for the education it offered him but because "he had shared so much of it with Ken", his beloved brother.[20] This may be true but John Bowlby provides a better explanation: "A school or college, a work group, a religious group or a political group can come to constitute for many people a subordinate attachment 'figure', and some people a principal attachment".[21] Still, Milne did question his schooling enough to send his son to a different one, although not enough to avoid sending him to boarding school altogether.

Christopher won a scholarship to Harrow for secondary school but his father turned it down as he wanted him to go to the newly opened Stowe, a selective independent school in Buckinghamshire.[22] The school was established in 1923 and John Fergusson Roxburgh, a Scottish school master, was founding Headmaster. His brief was to develop a modern public school that focussed on the individual, giving them self-confidence through a liberal education and values based on Christianity. Milne chose the school because it had rules that were based on "reasons not custom".[23] However, Roxburgh "was notorious in his pursuit of titled families to furnish pupils who would attract the middle classes". He wanted to abolish corporal punishment and fagging (the use of younger boys as personal servants by older students) but shied away from the decision for fear of being "too untraditional".[24] He was also worried about sexuality and had the seats in the choir designed so the boys couldn't face each other and exchange "ravenous glances".[25]

Christopher recalled that, when he left for boarding school, his goodbye to his father was only "partial" because "part of him would be remaining with me, hovering over me, lovingly and anxiously watching me through the term".[26] It was his father who advocated to have some of the physical conditions at the school changed, such as the over-crowded changing room. He was the one, rather than his mother, who came to see him on visiting days and who could chat easily both with the masters and other students.[27] Milne's decision to send his son to a different school, not continuing the tradition of Westminster, may be explained in two ways. First, when Milne was 12, a teacher at the school had, unfairly, given him a "crushing report" which he claimed turned him into someone who questioned "the establishment".[28] Yet he required the patronage of members of the establishment to buy his books and support production of the many plays he wrote. This dual position of insider and outsider may account for his continuance of the tradition of sending his son away to board, while picking a school that he thought was less traditional. It is hard for parents to break away from tradition, especially where children are concerned, with the imagined danger of somehow thwarting their children's lives if they break with it. The known path seems safer.

A second explanation for his school choice may have been his awareness that Christopher was different to the majority of boys in their echelon. Early in his son's life, Milne revealed his awareness that Christopher was perhaps not going to become the imagined and hoped-for son. In 1925, when Christopher was five, his father wrote to Ken that he doubted that Billy could be as clever as the older Milne men and suspected him "of striking out on an entirely new line of his own". But he said he was prepared not to mind "as long as I love him as I do now".[29] Christopher loved music, especially classical music, while his parents preferred musical comedies like Gilbert and Sullivan. At Cotchford, their country home, he had his own carpenter's shop full of tools he had bought with his pocket money, each "labelled" in his "mind with the date and occasion" on which he had purchased them. He made a burglar alarm and at one stage turned a gun that fired blanks into a gun that fired real bullets (his father allowed it for two years). He enjoyed sewing, knitting, making tapestry pictures and using a Meccano set. He also pulled things apart, including dissecting a dead mouse "to see how it worked", and he was designated the family's "Chief Mender". None of these interests was known to the public.[30] In contrast, his father told a journalist that Christopher's interests were cricket and mathematics, taking after the things he was good at as a boy—no doubt also because they were acceptable interests for boys at elite schools.

However, it was the fictional Christopher Robin that was to cause the greatest problem for Christopher at school, especially secondary school. He described life at boarding school as involving a splitting of oneself "down the middle" to "become a schoolboy at school, reverting to homeboy during the holidays".[31] In describing this process, he said that for himself the "split was particularly deep" because of the "love-hate relationship" with his "fictional namesake". At home he liked being able to "bask in some of his glory", while at school his dislike of being associated with Christopher Robin grew.[32] So he formed two identities. At home he was Moon (as he was called) *and* Christopher Robin. At school he wanted to be one of the group of students, Christopher Milne, with no other associations. No doubt there were painful emotions attached to this dilemma, but at this stage he didn't express them.

After Olive left, he developed a very close relationship with his father. Just as he had clung to her for nearly ten years, now he turned to his father for that intense relationship: "For nearly ten more years I was to cling to him, adoring him as I had adored Nanny, so that he too became almost a part of me, at first, no doubt to his delight, later perhaps to his anxiety".[33] When he was young, Olive had spoken for him when he was too shy to speak. Now his father took that role because his "knotted up" voice, which had begun when he was eight, was by adolescence "sadly jammed". He adored and admired his father, accepting his ideas, yet he thought it must have been hard for his father. Christopher remembered that he was an "immensely sensitive" child who was "easily wounded, quick to take offence", resulting in tears.[34] No doubt he was in his turn unconsciously careful what he said to his father, to others and to himself, around his increasing difficulty in being enmeshed with Christopher Robin.

Christopher had begun to have difficulties with speech when he was eight but by 12 when he went to Stowe his trembling and stammer were significant.[35] They dominated his school life where he struggled to get his words. Even as he wrote his memoir when he was in his 60s, he found it difficult to recall the pain and suffering it caused him. Reading aloud, using the telephone, making small talk with adults, all of these things were difficult. He particularly remembered one Greek class when it took what seemed like half an hour to negotiate the "comparative" and "superlative" forms of the word *"fronimos"* (meaning wise).[36] By this stage it was also becoming obvious to him that he could not achieve what his father hoped for him, especially becoming an outstanding cricketer.[37]

Milne did little to shield his young son from the publicity he attracted, yet he must have had some doubts. In a letter to Ken, he said that a boy who was a "nursery celebrity" might have had difficulty at school in the past, but that "those days are gone, thank goodness!" This letter is included in Ann Thwaite's 1990 biography of Milne and her response to his claim is: "How could he have felt so sure?"[38] It is a keen question, challenging Milne's certainty (perhaps hiding his doubt), because of course those days had *not* gone. The Winnie-the-Pooh books and Milne's books of children's verse in which the fictional Christopher Robin starred were famous. It would have been a rare child who had not heard of them, including Christopher's fellow students. More than likely they had been given one as a present, had them read as bedtime stories and perhaps learnt to read using them. Christopher may have managed to avoid full confrontation at Boxgrove, his preparatory boarding school, but at Stowe it was not the case. By then being associated with Christopher Robin had, in his words, become "a sore place that looked as if it would never heal up".[39] The stammer would have made him an easy target for his fellow students at Stowe. Adolescents have a low tolerance for difference. Milne's friendship with the masters may have been a strategy aimed in some way to protect Christopher from being beaten by the masters and bullied by his peers. It may have worked with the masters, but it failed with the students. Similarly, my parents may have thought that moving me to a school run by the same nuns as those who had educated me in primary school would somehow be a productive move. My parents and Christopher's father were wrong.

References

1 Axline, V. M. (1989) *Play Therapy*, Edinburgh: Churchill Livingstone, p. 139.
2 Sarto-Jackson, I. (2018) "Wired for social interaction: What an interdisciplinary approach from neurobiology, evolutionary biology, and social education can teach us about psychological trauma", *International Journal of Child, Youth and Family Studies* 9 (1), p. 22.
3 Ballou, R. A. (2002) "Adlerian-based responses for the mental health counselor to the challenging behaviors of teens", *Journal of Mental Health Counseling* 24 (2), pp. 155–156.
4 Ibid., p. 158.
5 Erozkan, A. (2016) "The link between types of attachment and childhood trauma", *Universal Journal of Educational Research* 4 (5), p. 1076.
6 Ibid., p. 1071.
7 Barthes, R. (1961) "The photographic message", in S. Sontag (ed.) (1982, 2018) *A Barthes Reader*, New York: Penguin, p. 196.
8 Hartley, L. P., cited in Renton, A. (2017) *Stiff Upper Lip: Secrets, Crimes and the Schooling of a Ruling Class*, London: Weidenfeld & Nicolson, p. 175.
9 Schaub, M. (2010) "Parenting for cognitive development from 1950 to 2000: The institutionalization of mass education and the social construction of parenting in the United States", *Sociology of Education* 83 (1), pp. 46–66.
10 Renton (2017), op. cit., p. 178.
11 Schaub (2010), op. cit.
12 Campion, E. (1982) *Rockchoppers: Growing Up Catholic in Australia*, Melbourne, Vic: Penguin, p. 70.
13 Benz, U. & Axelrod, T. (2004) "Traumatization through separation: Loss of family and home in childhood catastrophes", *Shofar* 23 (1), pp. 85–99.
14 Campbell, C. & Proctor, H. (2018) *A History of Australian Schooling*, Sydney: Allen & Unwin, pp. 178–179.
15 Campbell, C. (2007) "The middle class and the government high school: Private interests and public institutions in Australian education in the late twentieth century, with reference to the case of Sydney", *History of Education Review* 36 (2), p. 4.
16 Renton (2017), op. cit., p. 166.
17 Thwaite, A. (1990) *A. A. Milne: His Life*, London: Bello Pan Macmillan, p. 56.
18 Ibid., p. 37.
19 Duffell, N. & Basset, T. (2016) *Trauma, Abandonment and Privilege: A Guide to Therapeutic Work with Boarding School Survivors*, Abingdon: Routledge, pp. 53–56.
20 Thwaite (1990), op. cit., p. 87.
21 Bowlby, J. (1971), cited in Partridge, S. (2011) "British upper-class complex trauma syndrome: The case of Charles Rycroft, psychoanalyst and psychotherapist", *Attachment: New Directions in Psychotherapy and Relational Psychoanalysis* 5, p. 158.
22 Thwaite, A. (2017) *Goodbye Christopher Robin: A. A. Milne and the Making of Winnie-the-Pooh*, London: Pan Books, pp. 247–248.
23 Thwaite (1990), op. cit., p. 56.
24 Renton (2017), op. cit., p. 166.
25 Ibid., p. 219.
26 Milne, C. (1974) *The Enchanted Places: A Childhood Memoir*, London: Pan Books, p. 87.
27 Ibid.
28 Thwaite (1990), op. cit., p. 66, 86.
29 Ibid., p. 277.

30 Milne (1974), op. cit., pp. 34–35.
31 Ibid., p. 86.
32 Ibid.
33 Ibid., p. 125.
34 Ibid.
35 Thwaite (1990), op. cit., p. 517.
36 Milne, C. (1979) *The Path through the Trees*, London: Eyre Methuen, p. 47.
37 Milne (1979), op. cit., p. 24.
38 Thwaite (1990), op. cit., p. 378.
39 Milne (1974), op. cit., p. 144.

Chapter 8

Abuse and torture

The most significant event of Christopher's time at boarding school involved an incident at Stowe that, in his explanation of it, caused him to shut down from his feelings both at home and school. It involved a recording his mother had encouraged him to make when he was seven. The record, made in the HMV studio, was of him singing four of his father's poems, including "Vespers". The poem is about a small golden-haired boy kneeling beside his bed, struggling to say his evening prayers. It was the first of Milne's children's poems to be published and was a great commercial success.

A group of Stowe boys had acquired a copy of the recording and they tortured him by playing what Christopher refers to as "the famous—and now cursed—gramophone record remorselessly over and over again" in the room next to his study, so that he couldn't fail to hear it. Eventually, when they tired of the "game", they handed him the record. He took it and "broke it into a hundred fragments, scattering them over a distant field".[1] He developed an answer to the problem of being taunted about Christopher Robin by practising "not bothering" about it and he did this at home and school. As a child, it never occurred to him that he "ought to be blaming somebody for it"[2]; it was his problem to solve alone. As Duffell puts it, the boarding school child reinvents himself as someone who does not require love and cannot be betrayed.[3] In deciding to position himself as a person who did not care about what happens to him, he adopted a survival personality of one who can't be touched. However, the bullying he experienced and his withdrawal into himself, wandering alone in the countryside around the school, suggest that in Duffell and Basset's terms he became a "Casualty".[4] It took him well into his 20s to realise that he did need to bother and, when he did, it came out as anger and resentment towards his father.

The age of the boys has much to do with what the students did to Christopher. In a self-perpetuating cycle involving official teaching and student social norms, many forms of childish, effeminate or boastful behaviour were suppressed. This was reinforced during the transition into secondary school which involved cruel and humiliating initiation ceremonies.[5] By this stage, after their time in preparatory boarding schools, many boys had adopted "a veneer of masculinity, a kind of bravado to disguise the vulnerable self".[6] However, what remains in the unconscious becomes a projection. Christopher offered the boys who participated in the incident an opportunity to project on to him their own fears of being seen as sissy, weak, childish and vulnerable. What they wanted was for him to break down, to cry, to be a weak child. Breaking him would give them temporary evidence that they were strong and confirm that they were the opposite of him, thereby affirming their notion of what it is to be a man. Anything associated with childish ways of behaving (as represented by the "Vespers" poem) and what may be considered as an unmanly body (represented by Christopher who was by his own description a shy "girlish" boy easily given to tears) was to be rejected.[7] Such bullying has a long history in British public schools and the classic book *Tom Brown's Schooldays* (1857) includes reference to the bullying of boys who prayed besides their beds in the dormitory (the subject of the "Vespers" poem).[8]

Academic Philip Corrigan has written powerfully about his experience of not having the right body in the sort of school Christopher attended. Corrigan began life in a working-class English family, winning a scholarship to an "elite fee paying" secondary school. There he was "the skinny kid from South London" and was continually confronted by violence both from fellow students and the masters. It led him to live in "a state of terror, of fear, of bodily turmoil".[9] He was taunted for his "thin body" and his "physical, muscular inadequacies". Once he was publicly derided by being likened to the starving Holocaust survivors when a film about The Camps (Belsen, Auschwitz) was shown to the boys. "There's Corrigan", followed by "ribald laughter", echoed through the darkened room. His experiences led him in adulthood to see "the connection between male group violence *and* masculine ... sexuality". He argues that what is taught, and of course learnt, is "the *grammars* of dominance which leads to a denial of the bodily and emotional", which are co-opted "as much by the left as the right" side of politics in the name of "progress".[10] This way of being asserts and affirms that the student belongs to an "entitled elite", an "unspoken brotherhood". It is learned through a "long initiation ceremony", beginning in prep school and into secondary school, so that finally the "graduate" can join "men equipped to become part of the British establishment, to run companies and to enter government and, in the past, to run the Empire".[11] Corrigan believes that the beginning of the "unmaking of the boy" is signalled by engaging in "caring, involving as it does repairing, entails remembering, catching up the lost threads, the funny, awkward, difficult silly moments when we felt this, or sensed that".[12] It is his somewhat idiosyncratic way of trying to change the boarding school resistance to caring for self and others.

Christopher's coping strategy of "not bothering" resonates with my behaviour at secondary school. I had formed no connection with any of my teachers, I was bored by the work and I had a rich fantasy world which was far more enticing. Lessons interrupted my life, which was either having fun with my friends or living in my imaginary world. I have only one memory of being academically encouraged at the school and it came as a shock. We were sometimes required to write compositions. Mostly the topic set didn't interest me but this time it was a test, so there was silence as we did our work without interruption. The topic was "late afternoon" and we were totally free to approach it as we saw fit. It worked for me and I sank down into that clear space that I can still sometimes fall into when writing, drawing on some deep well of unconscious creativity. I remember the pleasure of imagining dusk in the countryside and concentrating on writing about the fading light and its impact on the landscape and animals as they find their way home. I wonder if it came out of a deep longing in myself to go home? I finished the few pages and handed it in. I had relished the process but gave it no further thought.

In class a few days later, the same elderly nun told the class she wanted to read us something. She offered no explanation. A moment or two after she began, I realised it was my composition. I was shocked but said nothing. It was obvious in her reading that she considered it to be good writing. The silence of the class, and my sensitivity to effective writing honed from all the reading I had done, affirmed her evaluation. When she had finished she asked the class who they thought might have written it. No one knew, so she finally gave the name: *Christine Jack*. That was it. No further discussion, either with the class or with me, then or later. Just my name. The message I took from the event was her surprise that I was capable of doing such a good piece of work. Her performance, the reading of the piece with no name attached, leaving the students to guess, extended the message to the class. This message may not have been what she intended. Her performance may have been her way of telling me and the class that I was an able student. Yet leaving it at that with no further discussion with me did nothing to move me towards engaging in lessons.

Judith, whom I had met in preparatory school, continued to be a close friend when I met up again with her at the secondary school. She was a clever girl, but remained resistant to the nuns and continued to be punished for it. She spent most nights of the four or so years she lasted at the school sleeping in a cupboard in the corridor behind a partition. She was untidy and their response was to move her bed out into a relatively public place to humiliate her. It made no difference. Whenever possible, she and I escaped from required activities and hid somewhere, relishing our rebellion. If I couldn't escape, especially during lessons, I took myself into another world. When the nuns spoke to me, I responded with little interest and certainly conveyed a message that I was not interested in pleasing them. It led to them dubbing me as "insolent": rude and arrogant. It was a reasonable assessment.

The nuns tried to get me to participate in school activities, but they used negative reinforcement rather than rewards. Their major strategy in managing our behaviour was a system of Weekly Notes—a highly organised ritual that took place each week. Students and teachers would gather in the large hall, with the nuns sitting in a semicircle and students in rows in front of them. Moving from the lower to the higher classes, each child's name would be called with their rating for the week: Very Good, Good, Fair and Unsatisfactory. The student would have to come up and receive the small piece of cardboard which had their rating printed on it.

A student would be rated as "Very Good" if they behaved themselves in every setting. "Good" was assigned when they "failed in punctuality, order or some point of fidelity". "Fair" involved "negligence" arising from being "disobedient", disrespectful or failing to obey a rule. "Unsatisfactory" was for "serious or persistent breaches" including "rudeness and disobedience".[13] It was a practice that gave the nuns the power, in the words of Michele Foucault, to "qualify, to classify, and to punish".[14] Most of the time I got a "Good" Weekly Note but occasionally I was given a "Fair". The system of Weekly Notes did little to change entrenched student behaviour, especially in the case of difficult students such as Judith and me.

When I was at secondary school, the nuns had a new impetus to try and get us to be conscientious with our school work. The state of New South Wales where my school was located had brought in significant changes to secondary education. Our class was the first year to be part of the Wyndham Scheme, a new system introduced in 1962 that had the goal of all students having at least four years of secondary education. The curriculum consisted of some core subjects (English, History, Mathematics and Science), with electives offered to "cater to a range of interests and aptitudes".[15] Students could leave school at 16, having completed the School Certificate, with those wanting to go on to tertiary education completing two more years and the final Higher School Certificate exams. Generally, this new system, apart from adding an extra year, had little impact on the elite non-government schools, which had a much higher retention rate (85%) than either government schools (28%) or systemic Catholic schools (35%) that served the majority of that population.[16]

The students at my school came from high socio-economic families, which are usually associated with good educational outcomes. So they should have sailed through the six years of high school, doing well in the Higher School Certificate and going on to university or perhaps a teachers' college. Yet it wasn't the case. In 1998, when I went to a 30-year reunion of the school, I was confronted by the anger that the ex-students felt towards the school because they believed the nuns had not offered them an adequate education. Virtually none of them had gone on to higher education. This outcome needs further exploration.

Australian educational historian Craig Campbell argues that while secondary education was valued by the rising middle classes, "the children of farmers … had needed little prolonged schooling in the securing of their futures".[17] The vast majority of the brothers of the country girls I went to school with attended elite private Catholic boarding schools. It was a rare country boy who stayed on and completed high school, most returning home after three years of secondary education (before the Wyndham Scheme) to work on the family property. The same was expected for the country girls, in that they would leave school early, undertake some sort of training, such as a year at secretarial school, and come home to work in the local town before they married. Some of the city girls came from very wealthy families and their parents also antici-pated a suitable marriage for their daughters to men that would support them. Still, I know the nuns were worried about our failure to perform academically. So in the last year before the formal external examination called the School Certificate, they purposely failed the recalcitrant students (my friendship group all fell into this category) in as many subjects as possible in order to give us, and perhaps our parents, a wake-up call.

Part of the problem, I suspect, was that we were clever girls who were not at all motivated by their teaching approach based on "exposition" and the notion that all knowledge moved in one direction from the mind of the teacher into the mind of the student. The job of the learner was to memorise and reproduce what had been conveyed.[18] It was not a good use of our inquiring minds, so we put them to use in thinking of ways to thwart or avoid the les-sons. However, it wasn't just the teaching that was problematic for me. Being away from home for so many years was taking an emotional toll.

When I was 13, my older cousin who had attended the school and whose mother had suggested I also go there, got engaged. It was a common practice at convent boarding schools for ex-students to bring their fiancées back to the school to meet the reverend mother. My cousin was engaged to a doctor and one afternoon she brought him to the school. After she had seen the nuns, I was sent for and brought into the formal parlour to see them. The three of us were left alone and I don't remember what was discussed. I do remember feel-ing rather removed from the whole situation although, no doubt, I responded politely. Many years later my cousin told me that, when they left, her husband was quite distressed, repeating to her a number of times: *She shouldn't be there!* His conclusion was based on patients he had seen from other boarding schools who were suffering emotionally from the experience. He was right and I was expressing it by becoming increasingly desperate to see my parents. At secondary school we were allowed the occasional phone call and I would seek permission to ring home. However, I was not in touch enough with my feel-ings to say what was going on for me, so the conversations with my parents were superficial. My school experience was also becoming more difficult for me to manage because I was increasingly being punished by what can only be defined as a form of torture: solitary confinement.

The principal of the school, again a nun as were most of the teachers, was determined that the spirit of resistant students such as myself was to be broken. Her solution was a process of isolating us from any contact with other students. I was subjected to it a number of times. It was my attitude towards the nuns that was problematic to them—resistant. I fell into Duffell and Bas-set's category of boarders who develop a Strategic Survival Personality by being a "rebel". These researchers have identified that one characteristic of this group is that they "reject their own potential".[19] This characterised me to some degree, except that I didn't know I had any potential. There is, however, a need to explore the intention behind the rebellious position.

Dreikurs argues that misdirected attempts to belong can include a desire for power which comes to the child and teenager when their desire for attention is not fulfilled. They reject the "community standards", seeking the power to find their own place in the setting when it is not granted by those in authority.[20] A way of dealing with students who engage in power plays is for the adult to withdraw from the struggle, acting kindly and respectfully, "let routines and policies be the boss", set achievable demands and "redirect" the struggle for control into some positive aspect of power.[21] These kinds of strategies, based on positive approaches rather than punishment, became a key part of teacher education in the last quarter of the twentieth century. However, my education, in common with approaches used in most schools of that period, was based on punitive practices. They left us diminished and defeated, as well as reinforcing our negative behaviour. At boarding school these approaches dominated our lives, so there was no escape.

Solitary confinement, as it was called at the school, involved total removal from the student body: no classes, recreation or dining with other students. You were also required to get up and go to bed at separate times, with no going out on Sundays. The strategy is in keeping with what Alice Miller refers to as "*poisonous pedagogy*" with the deliberate intention of "breaking the child's will in order to socialise".[22] It was punishment sometimes handed out to students when they received an "Unsatisfactory" Weekly Note. I know I was not the only student subjected to this practice.

My place of isolation during the day, when other students were at classes, varied. Once I was sent down to the end of the property to the junior school and placed in a small room at the top of the two-storey building. Secondary students never went down to the junior school, so it was a very unfamiliar place and I felt even more isolated. I would be left with some school books, although no actual work was set, until a nun came to collect me. Another time, a small desk was set up for me in the office of the Mistress of Discipline (rather like the Deputy Principal) where I sat all day. I didn't mind being there so much, because I think she had some sympathy for my plight, although she never overtly criticised what was happening to me. At meal times I would be put in the large scullery where the lay sisters served out the food and washed up. They too never spoke to me. They were long, lonely days. I would manage the process quite well for the first few days and, usually after three days, would stand again outside the principal's office and offer my apology. She would listen quietly, accept it, but say that she didn't think I was ready to join the other students yet. The following days would be more problematic and the description I have given it over the years is "crawling up the walls".

One Sunday, some students and I absented ourselves from morning Mass. Somehow the nuns found out who the offenders were and at about 10 a.m. our names were called and we were told to go and stand outside the principal's office to await our punishment. I hadn't chosen a good day to miss Mass because it was the day we were allowed to have outings and for me it was the day I went home. Each Sunday, my father faithfully drove the hour or so across the city to pick me up and take me home for a few hours. These days were a great relief, although I didn't spend much time with my parents because we had a tennis court and every Sunday there was a regular tennis party. It was made up of a large group of local doctors, their wives and the occasional older child, so my parents were preoccupied with playing tennis, socialising and serving afternoon tea. Sometimes I would be sent to the shops to buy an extra cake when it seemed that there was not sufficient food and I quite enjoyed being given that freedom—at school we never left the grounds. I spent most of Sundays by myself because my younger sisters had their own games that were well established in my absence and I was really too old to enter into them. Still, I liked being home and sometimes I would play tennis with some of the adults, regretting when the time came for my father to drive me back to school.

On that Sunday, when the names of the disobedient students were called and we stood in a silent line outside the office, I realised that my father would be waiting in the car outside to take me home. The image of him being so close led something in me to break and, without another thought, I bolted and ran outside the school doors and jumped into my father's car when I finally found it. I blurted out to him that I was in trouble and it was likely I wouldn't be allowed to come home that day. He listened quietly, with his face expressing some consternation. I suspect he was turning over his options, pivoting between a desire to respond to me and the unspoken contract most parents, especially at that time, have when they put their children into an elite school: to let the teachers do what they consider to be in the best interests of the student. Then, quietly, he told me I had better go back inside.

The energy I had when I ran out dissipated and I hunkered down into myself. Without another word, I got out of the car and went back to stand outside the office again. Of course, the nuns knew what I had done and I alone, out of the group of students, wasn't allowed to go home that day. Even now as I write these lines, I can feel the distress it caused me when my father sent me back inside. My desire was for him to save me, now that finally I had reached out to him. Instead, he capitulated to the system, as Judith's father had when she ran away from preparatory school. In my mind, he chose them over me but, of course, it is not that simple.

John Raymond de Symons Honey argues that the development of British public schools included the "general transfer of function from the parent to the school" and that this shift "is perhaps unique in modern history".[23] While headmasters often reinforced in their speeches that the values of home and school were totally in accordance and were to be "cherished", in reality it was anything but an equal partnership.[24] It was the same in girls' boarding schools. In my time there were no parent/teacher interviews and many parents would have no contact with the school except via the term reports. When parents handed over their children, they relied on the school to shape them for future life, including entry into the status of the elite. This was true in the nineteenth century and it was still true in the 1950s and 1960s, although in my setting it included induction into Catholicism.

Church and school were powerful institutions when I grew up. Parents were deferential to both, especially when they had paid significant money for their children to be educated in an expensive school. My father's decision is an excellent example of how Foucault's notion of "discourse" works. Discourse, using the definition I included in the introduction, is a "preconceptual, anonymous, socially sanctioned body of rules that govern one's manner of perceiving, judging, imagining, and acting".[25] I could see, as I sat in the car, that my father was struggling to decide what to do, no doubt tossing around ideas of concern that I had been driven to turn to him in this way, but in the end he suppressed them. He chose the discourse of power and authority and followed the rule of deferring to power of the school. It was not an unusual way for parents to act at the time but, of course, it had serious implications for me.

My action was done on the spur of the moment and did not involve any thought about consequences. It was an expression of my "unconscious and unmet needs" to come home to my family.[26] I had been captive in various schools for almost eight years, being subjected to what Erving Goffman calls "total institutions". The characteristics of these institutions are that "all aspects of life are conducted in the same place and under the same single authority", with requirements to "do the same things together". Daily activities are "tightly scheduled" and controlled by "explicit formal rules" which are based on "a single rational plan, purportedly designed to fulfil the official aims of the institution".[27] Conformity in actions is what is required of the "inmate", keeping hidden any questioning.[28] Schaverien believes that children in boarding school go through a process similar to that of people who are subjected to total institutions: "they apparently adapt to the system whilst keeping a part of the self hidden and so protected".[29] That was the case for me. I had kept the part of myself that was unhappy suppressed until that moment. Yet I didn't tell my father anything beyond that I was in trouble, with an unstated hope that he would help me. I didn't have the language, the words, to convey my distress. I couldn't tell him what I was unable to tell myself. It was the same when I phoned home from the school—I wanted to connect but I didn't know what to say. My feelings of desperation to contact my parents indicate that emotions I had suppressed for so long were bubbling to the surface, but I couldn't attach thoughts to them. The lack of access to one's emotional life makes authentic relationships, those based on revealing one's inner life, impossible.[30]

When my father sent me back into the school, I didn't feel any anger towards him. Rather than thinking of what I had done as an act of self-preservation and an expression of my need for my family, I blamed myself for my impulsiveness: *If I hadn't bolted, I could have still gone home. It is all my fault.* When there is no way that anger can be expressed in such situations, the person turns it into self-blame.[31] This may explain my thoughts but Goffman writes that the aim of total institutions that are religious is not just for "compliance", as in work situations or prisons, but for the person to internalise full acceptance of the rightness of institutional aims.[32] My self-blame seems to arise from this position—a belief that I had not followed the rules properly and, hence, I only had myself to blame. The other students were allowed to go out and I had learned a powerful lesson—that the school had ultimate authority over my life, not my parents. Many years later, I too aligned myself with teachers in the case of my youngest child in his first year at school. I failed to stand up to the principal when he told me that he had put soap on my son's teeth because he had sworn. My cowardice came from a fear that they would expel him, something which they did anyway at the end of the year. Later, we would realise that his difficulties at school were due to profound disability: autism and schizophrenia.

Even though the school principal rejected and tortured me, I still tried to make a connection with her, so desperate was I for some attention. Identification with the aggressor, rather than rejection, is often referred to as the Stockholm Syndrome: entering into "a psychological alliance" with the captor "as a survival strategy during captivity".[33] It is a "reaction formation" in which the person takes up "the opposite feeling, impulse or behaviour".[34] The captive person tries to "find the humanity in her captor" where the "attachment between hostage and captor is the rule rather than the exception".[35] It is also a form of "psychological infantilism" which "compels the victim to cling to the very person who is endangering their life".[36] This is what happened to me. I should have been angry and rejecting of the principal. I was certainly extremely frightened of her but I still wanted her approval, so thirsty was I for real attention, to be noticed just for myself, for someone to see me for who I was, to connect. So I sought it from her. She had a practice of having private talks with students on the open patio looking over the harbour in the evenings after dinner. There was a roster sheet for the talks outside her office and you could put your name down to have a 15-minute private walk and talk with her. I did it a number of times, rattling on to her about nothing in particular. She just listened to me and I have no recollection of any meaningful discussion. We didn't connect and she went on punishing me.

My final experience of being out into solitary confinement was in a room near the infirmary. The school employed a nurse, an older woman, probably in her 70s. It is likely she took the job because it came with live-in accommodation and allowed her to earn a living without being excessively demanding for a woman of her age. I was in Year 9 (aged 14) and, after a few days of solitary confinement in the room, I developed a severe headache in the right corner of my head. It was the beginning of persistent migraine headaches which I suffered from for many years afterwards. I went to the nurse to ask for some pain relief. She gave it to me and also spent some time talking to me about what it was like to be in solitary confinement. I don't think I said much, just that it was hard. In retrospect, I refused to be broken, but it was at a significant cost. The last bastion of control over my life was my refusal to capitulate—all that was left after my failed attempt to connect with the principal.[37]

The following day, the nurse came to the room in the infirmary where I was confined and asked me to come with her. I followed her down the main stairs. That walk is still clear in my mind, as is my bewilderment at seeing the principal standing at the bottom, awaiting us. The nurse must have set up the meeting but not told the principal what it was about. When we arrived at the bottom of the stairs, the three of us stood in a small circle. Then the nurse turned to me and said: *Christine, I want you to remember that we have had this conversation.* Then she turned to the principal and in a clear and firm tone said: *I will no longer be responsible for this girl's mental health.*[38]

It was a brave action on the part of the nurse who, no doubt, needed the job and was putting it in jeopardy. Yet she refused to be a silent bystander watching the abuse of a student. Although a Catholic, she was to some degree an outsider because she was not a nun. She was able to think and speak for herself, unlike the members of the congregation who were totally subjected to the authority of their superior, the principal of the school, who "was the voice of God", requiring "respect and deference". What she commanded was to "be executed promptly, humbly, cheerfully and definitely without consultation". A "good" nun was one who obeyed at all times, suspending their "good judgement, common sense and rationality".[39] Some of the nuns, including the Mistress of Discipline in whose office I was confined, may have had sympathy and perhaps even allowed the thought to emerge that this was not good practice. However, they had been trained to suppress any questioning of those in authority, a practice described as "radical obedience".[40]

But what of the principal who instigated the practice? Before she entered the order, she was a medical doctor. My thinking was that perhaps it was this background, which at times requires detachment from the suffering of others, that facilitated her actions. No doubt she thought her actions were necessary or she would not have engaged in the practice, not only with me but with other students. In her mind, my rebellious behaviour needed to be curbed in order to save me from my wilfulness. Foucault has written extensively about the rise of the prison system and the practice of placing prisoners in solitary confinement as a way to discipline the body in service of the soul.[41] A key goal for schools run by the religious congregation to which she belonged was to develop what they considered to be "women's gifts", including "the excellence of self-restraint and the loveliness of perfect service".[42] Indeed, training girls to have "a sense of service" (contrasting with the male sense of entitlement) was a common goal of private girls' boarding schools at the time.[43] No doubt the principal believed that she was failing in cultivating these behaviours in me and saw it as her duty to try and curb my behaviour. So she turned to extreme measures and there was no one to challenge her. In her mind, it may have been like a medical procedure in which suffering must be inflicted in order to save the patient, although in this case it was to save the student from herself. It was certainly true that my behaviour was problematic, not only to the teachers but also to me. However, she distanced herself from my suffering, supressing any recognition of the cause of my behaviour or the impact of the "treatment".

Acting "out of character" is not unknown for people working within authoritarian regimes where there is a duty of obedience to its values and the edicts of its leaders. The school principal was first and foremost an "insider" to the religious congregation, with her medical background being left behind when she became a nun. In contrast, the nurse was an "outsider" who, although a Catholic, had her first allegiance to her nursing profession, with its imperative of care for the whole person. This positioning gave her a wider perspective and she had the independence to question the actions of those in authority. The discourse paramount in her mind was commitment to her patients, allowing her to explore, through discussion with me, the impact of the practice and finally to act on my behalf. The principal's thinking illustrates that authoritarian regimes can also exist in the mind of the individual—suppressing unaligned thoughts and doubts. Her commitment to the discourse of obedience resulted in elimination of any qualms she may have had about solitary confinement.

Over the writing journey, I have had some helpful people who have given me initial feedback which I have usually taken up and included in subsequent drafts. However, feedback about my use of the word "torture" regarding solitary confinement has been problematic. One reader told me that they believe the word to be "over stated", the other that it is a "strong word", needing further explanation if I wanted to use it. Both statements suggest the word is perhaps not appropriate. There is a part of me that agrees with them, but changing the word has not been something I could readily do. The obvious alternative is "abuse". So I turned to published definitions to try and give me some insight. The verb "abuse" is defined as: "to use or treat so as to injure or damage", and the noun as: "a corrupt practice or custom", "improper or excessive use or treatment", "physical maltreatment" including reference to child and sexual abuse.[44] "Torture" is defined as: "the infliction of intense pain (as from burning, crushing, or wounding)", "to punish, coerce, or afford sadistic pleasure".[45] I have gone in search of other synonyms but none seems appropriate. Certainly "abuse" does cover what happened to me and is common in public discourse in relationship to those who have suffered at the hands of institutions. Yet when I think of "abuse" in relationship to solitary confinement, it feels like a blanket has been thrown over me and I am powerless under it. In contrast, when I think of "torture", I can picture having something done to me in order to extract something from me. This gives me some agency.

It seems to me that the word "torture" is applicable to what happened to Christopher, to Phillip Corrigan and to myself. In regards to the two boys, they are being tortured because they do not have the appropriate bodies. When I use it, I feel more in control, because the woman who inflicted solitary confinement on me was in search of something she wanted from me. The practice was inflicted on me in order to "coerce" me into submission, because there was a sense that there was a part of me that I was holding back. It is true, I was holding back, but I didn't know what it was they wanted. I simply would not give of myself, my true self, because I didn't feel safe and because my "self" was not consciously known to me. It had been suppressed at an early age and would take me most of my adulthood to slowly emerge. So I have left the word there because, for me, it is more descriptive of how I experienced, and now understand, what happened to me.

I have no memory of what happened after the nurse intervened on my behalf. All I can remember is that, by the end of the year, my parents had taken me out of the school and sent me to the local Catholic day school which my three younger sisters attended. Many years later, my mother told me that the principal had advised them to take me home because they were academically ambitious for me and I wasn't doing well at the school. That was true, but I believe it was the intervention of the nurse that made the principal realise that she had gone too far.

References

1 Milne, C. (1974) *The Enchanted Places: A Childhood Memoir*, London: Pan Books, p. 145.
2 Ibid.
3 Duffell, N. (2014) *Wounded Leaders: British Elitism and the Entitlement Illusion*, London: Lone Arrow Press, p. 108.
4 Ibid., p. 56.
5 De Symons Honey, J. R. (1977) *Tom Brown's Universe: The Development of the Public School in the Nineteenth Century*, London: Millington Books Ltd, p. 216.
6 Schaverien, J. (2015) *Boarding School Syndrome: The Psychological Trauma of the "Privileged" Child*, Abingdon: Routledge, p. 41.
7 Milne (1974), op. cit., p. 33.
8 De Symons Honey (1977), op. cit., p. 24.
9 Corrigan, P. D. R. (1988) "The making of a boy: Meditations on what grammar school did to, and for, my body", *Journal of Education* 170 (3), pp. 142–161.
10 Ibid.
11 Schaverien (2015), op. cit., p. 43.
12 Corrigan (1988), op. cit., p. 158.
13 Trimingham Jack, C. (2003) *Growing Good Catholic Girls: Education and Convent Life in Australia*, Melbourne, Vic: Melbourne University Press, p. 26.

14 Foucault, M. (1975, 1977) *Discipline and Punish: The Birth of the Prison*, translated by A. Sheridan, New York: Pantheon Books, p. 197.
15 Campbell, C. & Proctor, H. (2018) *A History of Australian Schooling*, Sydney, NSW: Allen & Unwin, p. 190.
16 Ibid., p. 191.
17 Campbell, C. (2007) "The middle class and the government high school: Private interests and public institutions in Australian education in the late twentieth century, with reference to the case of Sydney", *History of Education Review* 36 (2), p. 1.
18 Trimingham Jack (2003), op. cit., p. 28.
19 Duffell, N. & Basset, T. (2016) *Trauma, Abandonment and Privilege: A Guide to Therapeutic Work with Boarding School Survivors*, Abingdon: Routledge, p. 55.
20 Ballou, R. A. (2002) "Adlerian-based responses for the mental health counselor to the challenging behaviors of teens", *Journal of Mental Health Counseling* 24 (2), p. 160.
21 Ibid., p. 157.
22 Miller, A. (1983), cited in Duffell & Basset (2016), op.cit., p. 154.
23 De Symons Honey (1977), op. cit., p. 147.
24 Ibid., p. 149.
25 Flynn, T. (1994) "Foucault's mapping of history", in G. Gutting (ed.), *The Cambridge Companion to Foucault*, Cambridge: Cambridge University Press, p. 29.
26 Duffell & Basset (2016), op. cit., p. 170.
27 Goffman, E. (1961) *Asylums: Essays on the Social Situation of Mental Patients and Other Inmates*, New York: Anchor Books, p. 6.
28 Ibid., p. 118.
29 Schaverien (2015), op. cit., p. 149.
30 Duffell & Basset (2016), op. cit., p. 168.
31 Schaverien (2015), op. cit., p, 149.
32 Goffman (1961), op. cit., pp. 118–119.
33 Wikipedia (2019) "Stockholm Syndrome", available at: https://en.wikipedia.org/wiki/Stockholm_syndrome (accessed 20 January 2019).
34 Duffell & Basset (2016), op. cit., p. 169.
35 Herman, J. L. (1992, 2001) *Trauma and Recovery: From Domestic Abuse to Political Terror*, London: Pandora, pp. 81–82.
36 Dutton, D. G. & Painter, S. (1981), cited in Herman (1992), op. cit., p. 92.
37 Trimingham Jack, C. (2018) "Lucky or privileged: Working with memory and reflexivity", *History of Education Review* 47 (2), p. 213.
38 Ibid.
39 Rosemarie, J. (2017) "That was then, this is now: The understanding of authority and obedience by a selected group of women religious in Australia", *Australasian Catholic Record* 94 (3), pp. 309–310.
40 Trimingham Jack (2003), op. cit., p. 104.
41 Foucault (1975, 1977), op. cit., p. 237.
42 Plan of Studies, cited in Trimingham Jack (2003), op. cit., p. 31.
43 Schaverien (2015), op. cit., p. 43.
44 Merriam-Webster (2019) "abuse", available at: www.merriam-webster.com/dictionary/abuse#synonyms (accessed 7 March 2019).
45 Merriam-Webster (2019) "torture", available at: www.merriam-webster.com/dictionary/torture (accessed 7 March 2019).

Chapter 9

Shame

I finished the previous chapter by saying that I had no memory of what happened after the intervention by the nurse. So I proceeded to write the next chapter about moving to the new day school and my long journey of recognising what had happened to me. For many years I believed that I was the resilient survivor of my solitary confinement and that the principal had not crushed me. Yet, as I went on with the writing, I began feeling disengaged from the narrative, bored and distant. When I thought about the text I was now writing, it looked like it was greyed out, as it is when you can't undertake an action on computer text. When I thought about what I had written previously, it was black and accessible. Then I suddenly became resolute that I needed to read some of Carl Jung's writings again. I found a copy of *Man and His Symbols* (1964)[1] and read the book well into the night, stopping at a section in which he writes about the crucial and anticipatory dreams presented by two of his patients.

One dream came from a male client who was involved in what Jung describes as "shady affairs" (no further information) and who was compensating for his behaviour with a "morbid passion" for extreme mountain climbing. Jung immediately saw the danger and warned him to "restrain himself" in these climbs, but to no avail. The man continued and one day "he stepped off into space", carrying himself and a fellow climber to their deaths. The second dream was from a woman who considered herself to be "high and mighty in her daily life" but had "shocking dreams" that reminded her of "all sorts of unsavoury things". When Jung tried to get her to take the dreams seriously, she refused. Then the dreams became "menacing, and full of references to walks she used to take by herself in the woods". Jung saw the danger that lay for her in the walks which were fulfilling "a secret longing for adventure". She didn't heed him. Eventually, she was set upon by a sexual pervert and would have been killed if her screams had not been heard.[2] Jung was clear that such dreams come from the unconscious which is already informed about what our consciousness "does not yet know".[3] The two dreams were the unconscious struggling to warn the person's conscious mind.

I put the book aside and went to sleep. That night I dreamt that I was being pursued and I sought safety by climbing into the basket of a hot air balloon which was a few metres off the ground. The woman who was pursuing me (a version of my younger self) threatened me with a spade that almost reached up into the balloon basket. I became frightened, thinking that she would cut through the rope tethering the basket to the ground. So when she left, I climbed down to inspect it and found that the basket was connected to the ground by a thickly knotted ancient trunk with roots sunk deep into the earth. I realised there was no way she could cut through the connection with a spade, so I felt safe and climbed back up into the basket. When I started to move out of the dream into consciousness, I asked myself: *What danger would Jung see I was being warned about in my dream?* His answer came quickly and emphatically: *You are in danger of floating away!* I immediately realised that I had not been honest when I had left the previous chapter at the point of not remembering what happened between the intervention of the nurse and, months later, leaving the school. I had unconsciously decided to leave out an incident that was embarrassing and shameful by "floating away" into the next chapter. My younger self had "cut off" the memory from my conscious mind. It explained why I later felt disconnected from the writing.

I spoke publicly about solitary confinement for the first time in a conference paper I gave in 2017. It was also my first foray into the field of boarding school trauma, although when I started writing the paper I had no idea of where I was headed. Even though I was retired and had not been engaged in any academic writing for some years, the convenor of the annual Australian and New Zealand History of Education conference contacted me and asked me to give a paper at a forthcoming event. After some initial resistance, I agreed to write about going into teacher education in 1975, which was a time of significant change in Australian education. The resultant paper led me to revisit my experience of solitary confinement and how it had influenced my later decision to leave a teaching job after I saw what the principal, a nun, did to a female staff member.

The conference where I gave the paper was made up of educational historians, most of whom I had known for over 20 years. They were a very supportive group of people, so there was a degree of safety for me, but when I addressed the group my voice became hoarse and I was filled with shame in talking about something so personal and awful. Afterwards, I felt suicidal. Leigh Gilmore and Elizabeth Marshall, in their 2019 book *Witnessing Girlhood: Towards an Intersectional Tradition of Life Writing*, describe my experience so well: "Suicide becomes a form of thinking about the relationship between unbearable situations and unbearable feelings".[4] My suicidal thinking was driven by the meeting place between the situation of speaking publicly about something so personal but important to me as an educational historian who wanted to give testimony to her experience *and* the shame that came with exposing my vulnerable and inadequate "girl" self. However, my experience is not unusual. Research has found that "suicidal ideation" is "statistically associated" with trauma.[5] Still, I was determined to speak out and put the paper in for peer review. It was well received and published the next year. It explores the power of slippage between memories, showing that "shadow stories may lay hidden, revealing narratives that have the power to significantly change our understandings of educational experiences".[6] At that stage, I still had a belief that I was someone who had been tested and survived the ordeal and I would have gone on with that belief if the message from my unconsciousness via the dream had not intervened. If I hadn't turned back, remembered and included in the pages of this book what happened to me after the intervention of the nurse, I would indeed have "floated away" into a grand narrative of the resilient person who was not crushed by the experience. Now I can see that my suicidal thoughts after giving the paper were indicators of how deeply I had been affected by being put into solitary confinement.

What I finally remembered was that the day I left the school for the last time I left it from the infirmary. That memory held the key. A "normal" leaving of the school would have been when all students finished the year and left together with their parents. I left alone. There was a period of time, perhaps a couple of weeks, perhaps a month, perhaps less, between the intervention of the nurse on my behalf and my leaving. I now remembered that the nurse told me to come to see her whenever I felt ill. I took up her offer, finally finding someone who saw that I was suffering, although I could not acknowledge that to myself. That led to the infirmary becoming a place of refuge, a sanctuary. I spent my final day at the school there, perhaps even sleeping in the room the night before.

This is what I remember from my last day: *The infirmary room is large with a wooden floor, high ceiling, a picture rail around the walls which are painted a soft pastel. There are two beds, both covered with pretty floral bedspreads. It is morning and I am dressed in my uniform and waiting because the nurse has told me she has rung my parents and told them to come and get me. The room is bright because the sunlight is coming in from the large windows that face outwards onto the concrete area where cars pull up when they come in through the large stone gates. It is where my father was parked when earlier in the year I ran out to seek his help when I was in trouble and he sent me back inside. In my memory, the room seems almost luminous.*

Next door I can hear muffled noises coming from the nurse in the dispensary, attending to the needs of other students who have come to see her. Then I need to go to the toilet, which involves walking out of the room and crossing over in front of the dispensary into the bathroom. I do so and return back to the infirmary room, closing the door behind me. I don't know how long I wait there but eventually I need to go to the toilet again, but I am too ashamed to be seen having to fulfil this bodily function so quickly after the last time. It is too shameful to have such a need and I simply cannot leave the room, but I do need to urinate. So I find a metal waste paper basket and quickly wee into it.

There isn't much fluid but I know the nurse will find it after I am gone and have to deal with it, so I am sorry to do it to her. Yet there is a part of me that believes she will understand and not think too badly of me.

This memory is such a source of shame. No wonder I didn't want to include it in a public narrative and had cut it off from my conscious memory. A 14-year-old girl who wees in a waste paper bin! However, its inclusion is essential. It is a sign that I did not leave the school intact and unbroken, as I had believed all those years. I *had* been broken. I was what Duffell and Basset refer to as a "casualty"— one who "puts on a brave face, just enough to avoid annihilation".[7] I had done this when I was in solitary confinement because I could not, would not, acknowledge my distress either to myself or to anyone else. I had learnt early in my life at boarding school to endure. This was just one more time when I had to draw on my strength to do so. I had learnt that reaching out for help, as I had to my father in an unstated hope that he would take me home, was futile. So I turned it inwards, "crawling the walls", meaning that my inner turmoil was so great that I felt like a wild animal that had been caged and I was deteriorating from the inside. I had joined the group of boarding school students who had been "crushed"—those who were "abused at boarding school ... and were unable to make a cry for help" or, if they did cry out for help, it "was glossed over or ignored". Those who fall into this category exhibit "signs of distress".[8] My inability to leave the room and fulfil a bodily need is a sign of my torment and anguish, causing me deep shame.

Marie Louis von Franz who worked closely with Jung sees the tree (so significant in my dream) as symbolising the process of individuation: that "slow, imperceptible process of psychic growth" that if given attention by the person leads to "a constant extension and maturing of the personality".[9] However, in her retelling of a story by a Chinese sage, Chuang-Tzu, about a "gigantic old oak" tree which is "useless", she adds another element to the symbol: it gives "a lesson to our short sighted ego" because individuation requires us to "surrender consciously to the power of the unconscious".[10] This surrender may lead to the "swallowing of all sorts of bitter truths".[11] My ego had led me to believe that I had come through the solitary confinement experience unbroken, which was not the case. Remembering just how broken I was and my actions in the infirmary is indeed a "bitter truth". Writing about it is even more painful.

Judith Herman writes that "traumatic events violate the autonomy of the person at the level of basic bodily integrity ... control over bodily functions is often lost".[12] I see my behaviour as a form of regression to an earlier stage of life. I felt safe in the infirmary room but unsafe outside it (James X also found "respite" in the infirmary at his boarding school).[13] It is a reverse of what happened to me in solitary confinement when I saw life with the other students outside the room of confinement as a place of safety. I had become a little child again, with no internal parent to guide my behaviour. I succumbed to my fear of what lay outside the place of safety and could not look after myself properly, leaving the adolescent girl with a legacy of shame.

The nature of shame has a long history. Unlike guilt, which is about *actions* (what one did), shame is about what one *is*, thereby impacting on the whole self. In the fourth century BC, Aristotle undertook a phenomenological analysis which Swiss psychiatrist Léon Würmser builds upon, outlining three forms. First, one can experience anxiety and "fear of disgrace" in *anticipation* of the shame associated with being exposed because of something one has done, leading to a sense of the "dishonoured" self.[14] The second form relates to the feelings that arise from being *exposed* for failing to live up to the expectations of others or oneself. These expectations may be social expectations which one can break by, for example, cheating, stealing or lying. However, unrealistic personal expectations may also lead to shame, such as being seen as being weak and vulnerable. Feelings related to this form are about being inadequate, unworthy, dishonoured or having contempt for oneself. Würmser argues that this may lead to a desire not to be seen: "You should disappear for being the person you have shown yourself to be—failing, weak, flawed, and dirty, out of control over your emotional, physical or social self".[15] Disappearance is the ultimate punishment for the failure. It is what I wanted to do after giving the paper in 2017—to annihilate myself so I wouldn't be seen for being as weak and flawed. I was also afraid of stigmatisation, arising from what sociologist and social psychologist Erving Goffman (1961) calls "the spoiled self".[16]

In the third form, Würmser draws on Aristotle's discussion about "the protective attitude of shame".[17] He calls this a "character trait", whereby one both inhibits oneself from "self-exposure or disgraceful acts of behaviours" that may lead to shame and also acts in direct contradiction to their desires. Psychologically this is referred to as a "reaction formation".[18] It is a defence mechanism employed when a person is in danger of expressing feelings or acting in a way that may be perceived by others to be "disturbing" or "socially unacceptable". In order to protect the self, the person behaves or expresses feelings that are *directly the opposite* of what they secretly think, overcompensating for "the embarrassment, guilt or repulsion the person feels regarding his private thoughts". This behaviour may be "extremely exaggerated, compulsive and inflexible".[19] For example: "A young man who fears he might be gay joins a conservative church and becomes very involved with anti-homosexuality activism".[20] Würmser argues that this form of shame may also arise from respect for others and oneself, invoking "reverence, discretion, tact", as well as sexual modesty—a guard against "the privacy and intimacy of the self".[21]

In summary, Würmser's three forms of shame are, first, fear of being disgraced leading to anxiety about the humiliation that comes from exposure; second, feelings of contempt expressed towards oneself when one has been exposed for failing to live up to one's own expectations or those of others; and third, the suppression of feelings and actions in service of social acceptability (perhaps triggering a reaction formation) or as protection of "the privacy and intimacy" of oneself and others.[22]

I believe I suffered from all these forms of shame as a result of the many years of being at boarding school. I was afraid of being exposed as someone who was inadequate (the first form). At my preparatory school, I believed that I had nothing to offer. I was not a country girl and I was not a "good girl". I remember as a child spending a term sitting next to a girl in the study room who was both a "good girl" and well-liked by the nuns and the other children. She had a beautiful colouring-in book based on French art works and I was so envious of it. Her ownership of something so beautiful was, to me, a symbol of her value and my lack of such an object was a sign of my inadequacy. When I was caught masturbating, I was exposed by being seen then moved into the open dormitory so I could be supervised (the second form). The third form applied to me because I developed expectations of myself that I would not reveal any aspect of myself that showed need and vulnerability. It explains my reaction after giving the conference paper on what had happened to me. Nick Duffell writes that: "The classic boarding pattern for school survivors remains one of achieving a pseudo-independence at the expense of belonging needs".[23] I was ashamed that I had broken the privacy of myself and that I had somehow breached the "personal" boundaries of the listeners. It also explains my struggle in the present to include in this book what I did in the infirmary. It is another reason why I needed the psychological companionship of Christopher Milne in writing this book—to deflect the imagined gaze of the reader *away* from me.

I suspect that Christopher also carried feelings of shame. In adolescence, being aligned with the fictional Christopher Robin stopped working for him. The fictional character is one associated with childhood—an identification to be left behind in adolescence. The taunting by Christopher's peers based on the character was an attack on his personhood, including his body, leading him to reject all aspects of Christopher Robin and to be disparaging about himself. While he does, in his first memoir, re-claim the story of the real child rather than the fictional Christopher Robin, he still describes himself in a binary, disparaging fashion: "Girlish" [vs manly]; "very shy and un-self-possessed" and "not very bright" [vs the all-powerful, un-contestable knower embedded in Corrigan's description of the public school boy]; "good with his hands" [vs the upper-class man who does not engage in manual work].[24]

In my early boarding school years there was no recognition of the suffering I experienced in being removed from my home and family in such a sudden and traumatic way. When I withdrew into myself as a result of this, refusing to participate, I was punished and made to feel ashamed. There was a vast discrepancy between the loved, valued and beautiful person I was in my imaginative world and the unattractive, unlovable child in the real world. As I grew older, I also felt shame about continuing to engage in a fantasy world. Additionally, I did not experience being "seen" as a child, with any innate capacity that was recognised, developed and enhanced in my education. When I was noticed, it was for doing the wrong thing, including the dreadful, shameful sin of masturbation. As an adolescent, my needs and will, and my very self, were treated as a thing to be tortured into acquiescence. Later, as an adult, when I did allow myself to be "seen", especially by sharing my vulnerability when I gave the first paper about my boarding school experience, I felt that I had broken a social norm and embarrassed myself (Würmser's third form of shame).

Both Christopher and I employed a reaction formation in response to instances of being abused. Instead of feeling deep anger and resentment towards the woman who put me into solitary confinement, I did the opposite—I wanted her approval and tried to connect with her. That desire for approval continued well into adulthood. Christopher decided "not to bother" about the impact of the fictional Christopher Robin on him but, of course, the opposite was true. He was, in fact, deeply bothered by it, only allowing his true feelings to surface in his mid-20s.

Shame emerges about the age of 3½ but it is at its peak in adolescence, especially due to enhanced capacity for thinking (cognition) through brain growth. The young person now has the capacity for reflecting on and evaluating his/her self, especially in comparison with others. Adolescents are highly self-conscious and subject themselves to personal "scrutiny" in comparison with others, often amplifying their own importance and believing they are constantly being looked at, the object of the attention of others.[25] My fear of leaving the infirmary to urinate the second time was firmly located in the adolescent view that I was being watched by "the world", my trips to the toilet noted and shameful in such an infantile, physical need. There is a deep association between being seen and shame, recognised by Aristotle so many centuries ago. He stressed the role of the eyes and the importance of being seen: "The eyes are the abode of shame—*to en ophthalmois einai aido*".[26]

Being brave enough to include my shameful infirmary event was also helpful in leading me to understand another event that happened to me almost ten years ago. I started seeing a therapist at the beginning of 2011 after my father died in December 2010, aged 93. He lived in a nursing home for the last 18 months as he was in a wheelchair. The weekend before his death I had spent with my mother, supporting her in making the decision not to make any heroic attempts to save him. My thinking, which I shared with her, was that, if we saved him from the illness he was experiencing, he would only have to go through it all again, so it was best to let him go. He was also suffering from dementia, with what had been his fine intellect diminishing rapidly. So we made the decision to let him go. My sisters stayed with him over the night before he died while I went home with my mother. When they rang in the morning to say he was gone, I experienced a sense of psychological deterioration and great fear that I would come apart. When we returned to the nursing home to view his body, I went into the room alone and was filled with such a rage that I almost tore the room apart, picking up pillows and slamming them down, saying over and over: *I cannot go through this again!* Although,

at the time, I was not really sure what it was I could *not go through again.*
My balance was finally restored when a nurse came in and listened to me
recount the losses I had experienced over my life.

When my father died, I immediately put myself into therapy and for the
following year whenever I went into the therapy room I started to shiver,
experiencing a deep physical coldness. It is interesting that, in contrast, James
X experienced the therapy room as "warm", reflecting the "emotional warmth
within the therapeutic relationship". His response was due to the acknowledgement by the therapist of the suffering he experienced when he was sent
away.[27] My experience was the opposite but not because of a lack of a warm
relationship between myself and the therapist. The cold was an expression of
the loss of my father and I believe it went back to the abandonment
I experienced when, aged 14, I had to leave the safety of his car and return to
the school. It was a form of flashback which Schaverien describes as being
like a form of "time travel", reliving "in the present the trauma of the past".[28]
She draws upon the work of Judith Herman to explain that "psychological
trauma is an affliction of the powerless".[29] My father's decision left me powerless with nowhere to turn and was the beginning of a spiral into despair, finally
expressed by not being able to come out of the infirmary to go to the toilet.

At the time, neither the therapist nor myself was aware of the UK research
on boarding school trauma and so I didn't explore that as a key experience in
my life and had no idea of the connection. Indeed, even as I write in 2019,
unlike in the UK, there continues to be no public discussion in Australia about
psychological difficulties children might experience in being sent away to
board. Gilmore and Marshall refer to Judith Herman's contention that "psychological trauma becomes visible only when there is a transformation in cultural
politics such that people who suffer it have value".[30] A possible explanation
for the absence of public discussion about boarding school trauma in Australia
is that our country's violent and shameful history of forcibly removing Aboriginal children from their families makes the suffering of "privileged" children
seemingly irrelevant. Indeed, some Aboriginal children are still attending
boarding schools, often thousands of kilometres from their families. Although
there continue to be concerns about sending them to boarding schools, a recent
government report did not problematise the notion of "homesickness" and the
discussion was not informed by the UK research into boarding school
trauma.[31] Another explanation for the absence of discussion in Australia about
boarding school trauma, driven by a discourse of egalitarianism, may be
a belief that our experience of boarding has no links to the experience of those
"privileged" children sent to board in the UK. A simpler explanation may arise
from the feelings of discomfort around disclosure of vulnerability that come
with speaking about trauma. An outcome of the absence of discussion is that it
contributes to a self-perpetuating cycle in which the lack of discourse around
boarding school trauma means, as in my experience, that those who have suffered it have no language to bear witness to it.

I suspect that in 2011, if the therapist and I had known about the boarding school trauma research and read it, as I did six years later, it would have led to an understanding of what was happening for me. Perhaps I would have connected the experience of my father turning me out of the car and my physical manifestation of coldness. At one stage of the therapy, the psychologist encouraged me to remember myself as a young child and my mind immediately went to myself as a boarding school child. I saw her as a smelly unlovable child—not one I would want to know or be. However, after a period I was able to accept and acting lovingly towards her.

At the end of the year I decided to stop therapy, although my therapist reiterated that I had been traumatised as a child and that I needed at least two more years of therapy. While I knew intellectually that he was right, and I had known it for many years as this was not the first time I had been in therapy, I could not see my way forward because I did not understand exactly what it was that had traumatised me. It was only six years later when I came across the UK boarding school research that I was finally able to fully understand what had happened to me. When Joy Schaverien named the deep grief James X felt when he was sent away, he stated: "This is what I have been looking for all my life but I did not know what it was".[32] Finally, someone acknowledged "the state of perpetual loneliness that had haunted him since that time".[33] I had the same experience when I came across the UK research on boarding school trauma. I ordered all the books, underlining sentence after sentence because it described *my* experience. Finally, someone was witnessing what had happened to me, explaining how it had led to childhood trauma and its impact on my adult life. It reveals the freeing power of theorising experience, especially through psychological lenses which assist people to find a framework in which to locate their experiences. I believe it also needs to be part of the work of educational historians.

When the memory of what happened in the infirmary first came, I could hardly bear the thought of writing about it and having others read it. I lost interest and belief in the value of writing the book. For a time, I thought perhaps all of it had been leading me to this point and, now that I could recognise what had happened to me, I could leave it all behind. There was no need to go on writing. It was a dream that helped me realise that I could return to the project.

I dreamt that I was walking in an old part of the city. It had once been an industrial area, so the walls of the stone and brick buildings were dark with black soot. However, as often happens in derelict parts of a city, the value of its location had been recognised and it was now a boutique shopping area frequented by tourists. I wandered through the area until I came across some shoe shops. In one shop I put on a lovely red suede boot, then I left and went into another shop that had the same shoes in a dirty beige colour. I put one of these shoes on the other foot, then wandered out of the shop wearing the different coloured shoes, because I couldn't decide what colour I wanted. After a while, I realised I hadn't paid either shop for the shoes and that I needed to go back and sort it out. Now I wanted the red shoes but I couldn't find either shop, yet it seemed to me that the shop owners weren't worried about my having the boots. Finally, I asked someone I met what I needed to learn from all I had seen. The person's response was that children need to be told how to turn a television on and off. Then I came across a shop full of beautiful pieces of pottery that were discounted. A former senior colleague owned the shop (he was someone who had valued my writing when I was a young woman working at a teachers' college). He showed me through it and the discounting didn't seem to diminish the beauty of the objects. They were colourful and densely filled the space. As I walked through it, I moved past a decorated pottery snake that was made up of connected pieces; it moved as I passed it—seemingly alive.

The interpretation I gave to the dream, at the time when it occurred, was that the old derelict area is the scene of my childhood, which I was now exploring and restoring to myself. In writing the memoir, I was engaging in a form of therapy in which "the person riffles through the treasures and terrors that have lain hidden away for years".[34] My consciousness and sense of self still bore the signs of my childhood history (the blackened walls), but it was being reimagined as a place of value. The shop that was full of beautiful discounted items represented my thoughts that perhaps writing about my childhood is not worth the effort. In contrast, I also believe that writing honestly about what happened to me not only provides me with insight into the trauma but it has also thrust me into the creative process of writing—a capacity that has slowly emerged across my life.

In my first interpretation of the dream, the odd shoes symbolised the lack of control I often felt in the writing process. I was either full of fire and feeling rather grandiose about it (the red shoes) or believing that what I produce would not be of interest to others and that it is an egocentric and shameful thing to do (the dirty beige shoes). What I wanted was not to be either driven (red) or despondent and shamed (beige) about the project, but at the time I concluded that those feelings were a normal part of the writing process. I decided I wanted to bring into the mix a pair of green boots that manage both aspects (being able to turn on and off the television), giving me permission to go forward with the project, but with caution. I started writing again and completed the book.

The full meanings of dreams take time to appear and rarely "emerge immediately".[35] Many months after I had the dream and wrote my initial interpretation of it, I returned to it after re-reading parts of Bessel van der Kolk's book, *The Body Keeps the Score: Mind, Brain and Body in the Transformation of Trauma*. The particular section I found helpful was his discussion about the "self-system" of the traumatised person breaking down when "parts of the self become polarised and go to war with one another".[36] The person then swings from "self-loathing" to "grandiosity", from "loving care" for the self to "hatred".[37] His words well describe my experience of writing when I had the dream, swinging from seeing what I was doing as highly valuable to seeing it as useless and unworthy.

Van der Kolk, drawing on the work of Richard Schwartz, explains that: "Beneath the surface of the protective parts of trauma survivors there exists an undamaged essence, a Self that is confident, curious and calm".[38] This Self remains undamaged and will "spontaneously emerge" when it feels safe to assist in reorganising "the inner system" and integrating those cast off parts.[39] Mindfulness, being in touch with bodily sensations and exploring the different parts of oneself, is important in this process.[40] The finding reinforces how important I find it to meditate twice daily, noticing what is happening in my body and allowing myself to acknowledge without judgement aspects of myself that emerge. Trauma specialist Janina Fisher has worked closely with Bessel van der Kolk. Her book, *Healing The Fragmented Selves of Trauma Survivors: Overcoming Internal Self-Alienation*, has also been extremely helpful in navigating my way to understanding the journey and the value of mindfulness. She outlines a mindfulness process a person can go through in order to "unblend", separating out from "the intense reactions of parts" of ourselves that have been previously discarded, bringing them respectively into the present.[41]

Reading about the undamaged Self provided me with a new interpretation of the dream. I was indeed engaging in a war between the parts of myself and I was aware of the parts, naming them as either "grandiose" and "driven" or "despondent" (the words being very close to those used by van der Kolk). Now it seemed to me that in wanting to bring into the mix "green boots that manage both aspects", I was calling on a part of myself, the undamaged part of myself, the integrating self that has remained patiently hidden, waiting for a safe space to emerge. It is the curious and calm part of myself that enjoys the process of writing and research.

References

1 Jung, C. (1964) "Approaching the unconscious", in C. Jung (ed.), *Man and His Symbols*, New York: Dell Books.
2 Ibid., pp. 34–35.
3 Ibid., p. 66.
4 Gilmore, L. & Marshall, E. (2019) *Witnessing Girlhood: Towards an Intersectional Tradition of Life Writing*, New York: Fordham University Press, p. 42.
5 Fisher, J. (2017) *Healing The Fragmented Selves of Trauma Survivors: Overcoming Internal Self-Alienation*, New York: Routledge, p. 127. In this reference she is writing about Post Traumatic Stress Disorder arising from trauma.
6 Trimingham Jack, C. (2018) "Lucky or privileged: Working with memory and reflexivity", *History of Education Review* 47 (2), pp. 208–216.
7 Duffell, N. & Basset, T. (2016) *Trauma, Abandonment and Privilege: A Guide to Therapeutic Work with Boarding School Survivors*, Abingdon: Routledge, p. 56.
8 Ibid., pp. 55–56.
9 Von Franz, M. L. (1964) "The process of individuation", in C. Jung (ed.), op. cit., p. 161.
10 Ibid., pp. 164–165.
11 Ibid., p. 171.

12 Herman, J. L. (1992, 2001) *Trauma and Recovery: From Domestic Abuse to Political Terror*, London: Pandora, p. 53.
13 Schaverien, J. (2002) *The Dying Patient in Psychotherapy: Desire, Dreams and Individuation*, New York: Palgrave Macmillan, p. 151.
14 Würmser, L. (2015) "Primary shame, mortal wound and tragic circularity: Some new reflections on shame and shame conflicts", *International Journal of Psychoanalysis* 96 (6), p. 1618.
15 Ibid., p. 1618.
16 Goffman, E. (1961), cited in Lewis, M. (1998) "Shame and stigma", in P. Gilbert & B. Andrews (eds) *Shame: Interpersonal Behaviour, Psychopathology and Culture*, New York: Oxford University Press, p. 130.
17 Würmser (2015), op. cit., p. 1618.
18 Ibid.
19 Ibid.
20 Pedersen, T. (2018) "Reaction formation", *Psych Central*, available at: https://psychcentral.com/encyclopedia/reaction-formation/ (retrieved 23 February 2019).
21 Würmser (2015), op. cit., p. 1618.
22 Ibid.
23 Duffell, N. (2000) *The Making of Them: The British Attitude to Children and the Boarding School System*, London: Lone Arrow Press, p. 247.
24 Milne, C. (1974) *The Enchanted Places: A Childhood Memoir*, London: Pan Books, p. 33. Corrigan, P. D. R. (1988) "The making of a boy: Meditations on what grammar school did to, and for, my body", *Journal of Education* 170 (3), p. 144.
25 De France, K., Lanteigne, D., Glozman, J., & Hollenstein, T. (2017) "A new measure of the expression of shame: The shame code", *Journal of Child and Family Studies* 26 (3), p. 770.
26 Aristotle, fourth century BC, cited in Würmser (2015), op. cit., p. 1617.
27 Schaverien (2002), op. cit. p. 26.
28 Schaverien, J. (2015) *Boarding School Syndrome: The Psychological Trauma of the "Privileged" Child*, Abingdon: Routledge, p. 57.
29 Herman, J. (1992/1997), cited in Schaverien, ibid., p. 57.
30 Gilmore & Marshall (2019), op. cit., p. 42.
31 House of Representatives Standing Committee on Indigenous Affairs (2017), *The Power of Education: From Surviving to Thriving Educational Opportunities for Aboriginal and Torres Strait Islander Students*, Canberra: The Commonwealth of Australia, available at: file:///Users/christinejack/Downloads/Committee%20Report%20-%20Final.pdf (accessed 30 September 2019), p. 102.
32 Schaverien (2002), op. cit., p. 24.
33 Ibid.
34 Ibid., p. 34.
35 Ibid., p. 100.
36 Van der Kolk, B. (2014) *The Body Keeps the Score: Mind, Brain and Body in the Transformation of Trauma*, London: Penguin Random House, p. 281.
37 Ibid.
38 Ibid, p. 283.
39 Ibid., pp. 283–284.
40 Ibid., p. 283.
41 Fisher (2017), op. cit., p. 263.

Chapter 10

A normal life?

When I left boarding school for the last time, it was from the infirmary. I had spent nine years in three convents run by the same religious congregation. Some of the nuns had known me both in childhood and adolescence, but none of them said goodbye to me. I remember in the months before I left the school the hierarchy had decided to give a special award to students who had been at their schools for ten years. I was disappointed that I would miss out by two years. I had spent five years of my childhood and three years of my adolescence in their care. I spent more time in their schools than at home, yet they simply let me go with no acknowledgement of my life there. I suspect I represented failure for them, so in their minds perhaps it was best to just let me slip away and pay attention to their successes. My best friend, Judith, was expelled the next year. In adulthood she opened a small alternative school for children struggling in mainstream systems.

The moving pottery snake I passed in the shop in my dream is symbolic of the changes that started to occur in me after I left boarding school—small pieces of insight about myself and my childhood. Colleague of Jung, Joseph Henderson, refers to the "universal quality" of animals as symbols of "transcendence".[1] The Jungian notion of "the transcendent function of the psyche" refers to the task of the adult to achieve a "union of the conscious with the unconscious contents of the mind", leading to achievement of the highest goal—"full realisation of the potential of the individual Self".[2] It is a movement of maturity away from any "confining pattern of existence".[3] My turning in on myself was certainly a confining way of living but the unfolding process took time to occur and when it did it was overwhelming.

Symbols provide a means of the unconscious entering the conscious mind. Attention to the power of symbols in this process, writes Henderson, drawing on Joseph Campbell's comparative studies of mythology and religion, can be traced back to the Lascaux caves in France, the object of my childhood fascination.[4] The snake is the most common dream symbol of transcendence. It is a "therapeutic symbol", originating with Aesculapius, the Roman god of medicine, and is still in use today—the non-poisonous snake coiled around the staff of the healing god.[5] My journey of healing and integration began when

I left boarding school, but insight came in pieces and has taken time to fashion into a connected whole (the segmented snake). Education was critical in that process.

Books were my companions when I was at boarding school. Books would eventually lead me into understanding what had happened to me during those nine years. For now, I decided to take textbooks seriously although, looking back, I can see that it was also a way of keeping my chaotic inner life together while splitting off the traumatised part of myself. Janina Fisher has found that traumatised people are often skilled at suppressing that part of themselves—the "trauma-related parts"—while they practise "going on with the normal life part" of their personality.[6] She explains that they are able to do this because the right part of the brain has the capacity to remain almost totally separate from the left side if required. The traumatic experiences are kept in the right part of the brain, which "does not 'forget' the nonverbal aspect of experiences and does not interpret it" because it is the left part of the brain that is able to describe the associated emotions.[7] This capacity provides an explanation for loss of memory around traumatic experiences—the memories are still there but compartmentalised. Fisher argues that it is "safer" for the traumatised person to "adapt using a system of selves rather than becoming a full integrated 'self'".[8] This was true for me when I left boarding school. I had been traumatised but I had managed to split off the painful parts while going on with a "normal" life and it was how I survived over the next ten or so years.

My new school, which I started when I was 15, was a convent boarding and day school which my three sisters attended as day students. My parents had intended to send my sisters away to board but my father put a stop to it, so my mother told me many years later, because: *He saw what a mess it made of me.* Acceptance into the new school required an interview and my mother took me to meet the reverend mother. The nun, a middle-aged woman, spoke to me briefly, looked me up and down, then turned to my mother and said: *She seems an intelligent girl. I think she will be fine here.* I wonder what she made of it all? She knew my mother quite well as they had worked together on a parents committee. She would have known that my three younger sisters had attended the school since kindergarten—they were all in primary school when I came, a separate school across the main road. Perhaps she thought that I was the child of a different relationship which was why I had been sent away? I also wonder what my parents knew about what had happened to me. I know the nurse told me she had rung for my parents to come and collect me from the infirmary—she must have told them something about what had happened. Perhaps that is why the nun who interviewed me at the new day school told my mother *I would be fine there*—she had some background that I had not been fine where I had been previously.

The nun was right. I *was* fine there. Now that I was home and interacting with my parents on a day-to-day basis, I stopped being resistant to the teachers, although I continued to be an attention seeker. My parents and

I didn't have a close relationship, as in sharing our inner thoughts and feelings, but I especially enjoyed being an older sister to my siblings. I took them clothes shopping and sometimes made dresses for them. At my new day school, when I became bothersome the teacher simply told me to go and study in the library. There were no punishments and I don't think moving me out of the class was meant as such, just a way to deal with a problem. I was old enough to know and accept that I had indeed brought it on myself, so I didn't feel bad about it at all. They seemed to be exasperated with me rather than rejecting, although at times I walked a fine line, almost being sent to the principal. When I was sent to the library I just got on with my school work, which usually resulted in doing well in the examinations.

When I look back at that 15-year-old girl, I can see what she *did* but there seemed to be no inner self. She was like a ghost, a thin flat sheet of paper that hardly existed. When I got to this point in the writing, I found it hard to move forward, to understand why there was no self and so I took the problem to my therapist who came back with a clear answer: *You had been institutionalised for eight years. Your "self" had been suppressed because there was no place for individuality and so by the time you left it was gone.* This was hard to hear but also helpful. Judith Herman supports this view, writing that people who have been subjected to prolonged trauma may lose a sense of self and may feel that a part of themselves has died.[9] So I went back to the writing and began to look for signs of life in myself in the last three years of school. They were there but only surfaced fleetingly.

At first, I still tended to spend much of the classes reading the textbooks to myself, tuning in and out of the lessons, but gradually I became more engaged. The nuns were good teachers. Many had been to university and knew their subjects well. What they offered was generally interesting and intellectually challenging. My parents were keen for me to go to university and my new peers took their work seriously, so I settled down to studying. I fitted into a friendship group some of whom I could have known when I was a child attending the same school in Kindergarten and Year One, although I didn't remember them. They were a fun crowd and many of them were very beautiful girls (one was modelling already), so we were popular with the other students and with the local boys. A number of our parents, including mine, were part of the same social group, mostly made up of husbands who were doctors and pharmacists. I liked the sense of belonging that the close community created.

The year I started, 1965, was the initial year of the Year 10 public examination: the School Certificate, part of the new Wyndham System. The associated textbooks were well written, especially the science textbook which was an enormous blue tome and interesting to explore. We had thought-provoking novels to study such as Thomas Hardy's *The Mayor of Casterbridge* (1886)[10] and I enjoyed the analysis that took place in class. The nuns put me in all the top classes except science. I didn't receive any serious science education before I went there, so I was lacking in the area. However, in reality I was a humanities person and did well in all those subjects.

There was one event I remember well that revealed an aspect of myself that was surprising to my classmates, the teacher and me. It was a history class and the nun running it was a few minutes late. Before she arrived, I was standing at my desk, which was close to the door, and another student asked me something about homework that was to be done in preparation for the class that day. I realised I hadn't done it and engaged in a short conversation with the other student about my unintended omission. A minute or two later the nun walked into the classroom, sat us down and then set about asking various students to come to the front and read out what they had prepared the night before. The topic was something to do with the Second World War. She was a strict and unapproachable teacher but knew a lot about history and imparted it well. I valued her classes. After asking two students to read out what they had written for their homework, she called out my name. I was not deterred. I immediately picked up my folder, opened it at some pages I had written about something else and went out to stand on the platform. I found and sank down into that place of intuitive knowing out of which I later learnt to write. I spoke for some minutes on the topic, synthesising the material we had been talking about in class over previous days. It required no conscious effort on my part, the words seeming to come from another place within me. I know that what I said made sense and I can still see the slight expression of surprise on the teacher's face.

Then she asked to see what I had written so I walked to the desk where she was seated and put the open folder in front of her, moving my hand across the page saying: *Here it is.* She scanned it for a second or two, appearing to be perplexed, then told me to go and sit down. Nothing more was said by her but I suspect she had overheard the conversation I had with the student before she came into the class. Later, the student who knew that I hadn't done the work said: *I can't believe you could do what you did!* It wasn't planned on my behalf, I simply rose when she called me and did it. No premeditation—just a spontaneous action. I was as surprised as the student who knew what I had done. Yet I was also not surprised because there was a glimmer of recognition in me that it was something I could do. It was similar to the event when I had sunk down into my unconscious to write the piece of creative writing that the nun had liked when I was at my last boarding school. That event in the history class became an experience that stayed with me over the years, waiting for me to return to it again, waiting for interpretation that only came to me when I wrote the last chapter of this book.

I passed the year with a good result and moved on to Year 11. While I settled down to study, I was emotionally unstable. I had been taken out of boarding school, yet boarding school had not been taken out of me. I still led a secret inner life of fantasy and my emotions surfaced in ways that puzzled me. At times I would feel upset and wander away by myself to cry intensely.

There was no apparent trigger, grief just seemed to overwhelm me and I had no idea what caused it. My parents had a waterfront beach house with boats moored in front of it. Sometimes when I walked outside at night and heard the rigging clanging as the boats were moved by the wind, it brought out a deep grief and I often found myself crying. Nor did I ever talk to anyone about it. Indeed it never occurred to me that I had anything to talk about, so removed was I from the cause of these intense emotions. The intensity of that grief returned to me a few years ago when I went away with some of my friends from that day school. We had flown from Sydney up to the Gold Coast and had rented a unit together. One day, after we had returned from a day out together, we were having some time out and I was sitting on my bed reading. Suddenly, for no reason, I started crying. It was as though I was that 15-year-old girl again with all the feelings of shame and aloneness. A disowned part of myself needing acknowledgement and integration.[11]

In those three years at my new day school and in subsequent years, I was sometimes filled with ferocious anger, especially when I was crossed by my parents, and it would take me ages to calm down from my rages. I was also very greedy for love, so I turned to boys, craving the feeling of "being in love", wanting to be cuddled and held. If I had lived in another historical period, I would have been promiscuous but Catholic girls had trained themselves to make sure they didn't go "too far". It was the era that sociologist Anne Summers wrote about so eloquently concerning the Australian notion that women fell into one of two categories: "Damned whores" (women who were promiscuous) or "God's police" (the morality keepers of society).[12] The boys we knew were open in their disdain for girls who "slept around", although I suspect they might have enjoyed their company at times.

I worked hard in the last years of school, often making choices to study rather than go out. In retrospect, I can see that it gave me a sense of control about my life—keeping me together. When I was in my last year at school, aged 17, I met my future husband. Both of us had been unsuccessful in winning the attention of someone we wanted as our girl/boyfriend. So when we came together, we agreed that we would have a relationship based on "not being in love". For me, it was an unconscious avoidance of the complexity of love being associated with abandonment which I had formed in childhood. Long term, this was not a good decision but in the short term we each had a partner and were able to join a group made up mainly of the sons and daughters of our parents' social group. I liked and respected him. He was easy to be with and very supportive of me. I also enjoyed his large family and the associated feeling of belonging. He was in his first year of a law degree and it was another thing we had in common.

My intention was to study law and then to work in community law when I graduated. Community Legal Centres were established in Australia in the 1970s, growing out of a belief which gained momentum in the 1960s: that legal aid is a right of liberal citizenship.[13] I have no memory of where I heard about them or why I wanted to work in them but I know it was where I wanted to go. Perhaps my attraction to such a project was an unconscious desire to free my incarcerated self. I studied hard to get into Law School at Sydney University and I was accepted. Then when it came to actually going, I changed my mind and told my parents I wanted to do an Arts degree at University of New South Wales where all my friends were going. They were most unhappy with my decision.

I never told my parents, or indeed anyone at the time, why I reneged on my initial goal, but I am clear about what drove my decision. I firmly believed I couldn't compete with the men who dominated the law. All my boyfriend's university friends were male and I never met a female law student during that time, even though I often studied with him in the law school library. I had grown up in a family of women, with my father being the only male. I went to girls-only schools all my life, so I had never had any experience of competing with males. I didn't even play with boys, except for once and it taught me a lesson I never forgot.

One day, when I was about six, my parents asked a family from over the road to afternoon tea. They brought their two sons, who were a couple of years older than me. My parents ushered us three children outside to play in the backyard, while both sets of parents had afternoon tea inside the house. The boys chose a game I had never played before: cowboys. I had no idea of how the script worked and struggled to enter into the action. They also brought some lollies to share which were big black circles of strong liquorice. When they offered me one of the sweets, I accepted it, popped it into my mouth and sucked on it for a few minutes. It tasted disgusting but I didn't want to lose face in front of them by admitting my distaste. So I kept it in my mouth while they were looking and when I had a chance I went behind the garage and spat it out. It was my first encounter with boys and I decided then and there that I just wasn't in their league. I couldn't play cowboys and I hated their sweets. Boys and their activities were to be avoided if at all possible.

My home life reinforced my gendered view of the world. I saw my father as an "important" doctor and my mother didn't do paid work. In my view, men ran the world. Even at boarding school I realised the nuns were inferior to the priests. It was the priests who led the important church rituals, who had the power to say Mass, to christen and confirm people and to forgive sins. I had another experience at my preparatory school that reinforced the dichotomy between male and female. We were never allowed to leave the convent grounds except when accompanied by our parents. In contrast, there was a boys' boarding school within a few minutes' walking distance from our school and at weekends I would often hear the noise of the boys as they made their way through the bush to swim in the nearby river. We girls never went near the river and I envied the boys their freedom. I saw them as living in a very different and far more interesting world.

My decision not to do law may also be explained by the fact that I was still in what Mary Belenky and her colleagues refer to as the first stage in women's journey into engaging with knowledge: silence. In this stage "women see themselves as mindless and voiceless".[14] Indeed, I did not believe I could have any power in a male world, including engaging with their knowledge. Yet my decision needs to be considered in a wider context. Sara Delamont argues that the feminist pioneers of girls' education were "revolutionary" but had been successful by "manipulating" the classification of women/men while "not violating it".[15] They had purchased education by not publicly challenging the priority of women's domestic place in the family. This discourse was alive and well in 1968. In that year, the year I finished secondary school and was struggling with my decision of what to study, British anthropologist Edmund Leach gave a public lecture calling for women to undertake education that was "consistent with domestic feminine roles".[16] His concern was that higher education was likely to challenge the strict division of labour by sex, making women want to leave the domestic sphere.[17] Delamont states that the lecture was not widely known.[18] However, the fact that he felt he could utter such propositions in a public space means that discourses around women's priority place as being in the home still had currency. They certainly did in my world. My parents wanted me to be well educated but only as an insurance: if my husband became sick, leaving him unable to work, I had the capacity to earn a living.

When I was accepted into Law School at University of Sydney, I wanted to make a leap across the gender divide but I was lacking in any sense of identity or self-belief. All my friends were going to University of New South Wales to do an Arts degree. So I told my parents I was going to join them and do the same degree. It was my first attempt to make an important life decision for myself—a critical developmental aspect of the successful negotiation of late adolescence. It didn't go well. I fought with them for a couple of weeks, leaving home at one stage and staying with a friend. In the end, I acquiesced to their desire for me to go to University of Sydney (my father's *alma mater*) but they did accept my rejection of a Law degree and my decision to do Arts.

When I look through the lens of being a parent, I can see that they knew I had worked hard to get into Law and was one of only a small number accepted straight out of school into the faculty. They were disappointed for me that I was letting an opportunity go by. Like many others, they considered University of Sydney to be more prestigious than the University of New South Wales and so they must have thought that at least I could go there. I have no doubt that their intentions were about offering me the best chances in life, including going to the "best" university. What they missed was my need to make some decisions for myself. At that stage of life it would not have had serious consequences for my life because I would have still attained a degree. In my late 20s, when I did finally set out to make my own decisions, to drive my own life, the ramifications were serious, not just for me but for others I cared deeply about, especially my children.

References

1 Henderson, J. L. (1964) "Ancient myths and modern man", in C. Jung (ed.) *Man and His Symbols*, New York: Dell Books, p. 153.
2 Ibid., p. 146.
3 Ibid.
4 Ibid., pp. 146–151.
5 Ibid., pp. 153–154.
6 Fisher, J. (2017) *Healing the Fragmented Selves of Trauma Survivors: Overcoming Internal Self-Alienation*, Abingdon: Routledge, p. 25.
7 Ibid., p. 23.
8 Ibid., p. 25.
9 Herman, J. L. (1992, 2001) *Trauma and Recovery: From Domestic Abuse to Political Terror*, London: Pandora, pp. 49, 86.
10 Hardy, T. (1886, 2016) *The Mayor of Casterbridge*, New York: Vintage Classics.
11 Fisher (2015), op. cit., p. 21.
12 Summers, A. (1975) *Damned Whores and God's Police: The Colonisation of Women in Australia*, Melbourne, Vic: Penguin Books.
13 Noone, M. A. & Tomsen, S. (2006) *Lawyers in Conflict: Australian Lawyers and Legal Aid*, Sydney, NSW: The Federation Press.
14 Belenky, M. F., Clinchy, B. McV., Goldberger, N. R., & Tarule, J. M. (1986) *Women's Ways of Knowing: The Development of Self, Voice and Mind*, New York: Basic Books, p. 15.
15 Delamont, S. (1989) *Knowledgeable Women: Structuralism and the Reproduction of the Elites*, Abingdon: Routledge, p. 136.
16 Ibid., pp. 136–138.
17 Ibid.
18 Ibid., p. 137.

Chapter 11

An arduous journey

Long journeys can be gruelling. There is so much to take in. The traveller pushes the body, wanting to see everything, at times becoming overwhelmed by a plethora of stimulation. The daily regime becomes relentless and the crossing of time zones makes sleep elusive. Sometimes transport from one place to another is cancelled, re-scheduled or breaks down, so that the traveller gets stuck in one place, leading to frustration. Treacherous waters or borders may need to be crossed. Finally, exhaustion sets in, making one vulnerable to disease. That is what happened for me at this stage of the long journey of reconnecting with and writing about childhood trauma.

The process of writing resulted in nights when I couldn't sleep because my brain was flooded with ideas. Sometimes I was filled with emotions—joyful catharsis, grief, sadness, guilt, shame—that washed through my body, draining it of energy. At other times I became stuck and wondered how I would move forward in the writing—the dilemma producing a deep tiredness. The period after I remembered what had happened in the infirmary at the end of my time at boarding school was one of deep grief. I was unable to sleep properly, near tears much of the time and initially frightened I would fall apart. I had taken a deep dive into my unconscious and I was having trouble resurfacing.

What else made it hard for me was that I was moving from writing about my school and university years to writing about early adulthood. It was a shift from seeing myself as the powerless boarder into considering myself as an adult person who was now free to make decisions about my life, but then feeling guilty about many of my choices. One night I dreamt that a woman was on trial and the associated question was: *Is she a victim or a murderess?* On another night, I dreamt that I suggested to my mother that we pack up and find a different house—an expression of my desire to suppress and reject my life. In yet another dream, I am travelling with someone and we need to cross from one long thin body of water to another one. There is a small isthmus of land between, but we seem unable to negotiate the crossing.

Then I became sick. I developed shingles of the vagina that worked up my lower back. Who knew you could get such a thing! The first time I went to seek medical help, three doctors looked at me, puzzling about what was wrong, until one of them declared: *Now don't panic, but I have to tell you that it is herpes!* She was referring to the type that is sexually transmitted. I did panic, declaring that I had been with my partner for 24 years and that I had had only a couple of sexual partners previously. The doctors assured me that 80 per cent of people carry the virus in their bodies, but their attempts offered little comfort because I saw the hidden message behind their assurances that *it was indeed* something to feel mortified about. Shame set in. Three days later I went back to see one of the doctors, telling her that I had just about come to terms with what I had, when she pulled out a report, pushed it in front of me and said: *You don't have herpes, you have shingles!* She insisted I read the printed sheet from the pathologist so that I would be clear about the source of my illness. I am sure she felt guilty that they had pronounced on the illness before they were able to formally confirm it. For my part, I felt relieved, although I was somewhat perplexed as I had diligently had the shingles vaccination a year previously. When I expressed my annoyance that the injection had not prevented the illness, my doctor declared: *Vaccination is not always a guarantee!*

The drama of being first diagnosed with herpes and the valiant attempts of the doctors to stop me feeling bad about myself, including the last doctor insisting I read the report myself, with the coded message that herpes is a dishonourable virus, replicated the drama I was facing in my writing. The years of my young adulthood left me with deep guilt about many of my decisions, even though I tried to assure myself it wasn't my fault. When I was in my late 20s I confronted some of my childhood issues, but it didn't "vaccinate" me from further eruptions. There is significant evidence that traumatised children and adults suffer from somatic symptoms.[1] I knew writing my way forward would be an act of determination to remain truthful, while also viewing myself through a compassionate lens. However, first I had to deal with the memories that having this disease evoked in me.

Shingles is a virus (belonging to the herpes group) that attacks the nerves and the area around it. Painful blisters appear on the surface of the skin. Even when they heal, pain can linger for months. It is a reactivation of the chicken pox virus which lies dormant in the body, surfacing when your immune system is weak, often later in life. I contracted chicken pox when I was a child at boarding school and my mind immediately went back to that experience, an event which I hadn't included in the book because it didn't seem important. In many ways that is true. I remember being the only child in the school who had it at the time, but I think others had it before me, probably passing the virus on to me. I was placed in the infirmary, a room at the top of the stairs in the original Queen Anne building where I was cared for by a lay sister. My body was covered by large weeping blisters that were extremely itchy and painful. There was a big black and white old-fashioned bathroom off the infirmary and each day the sister filled the deep claw-footed bath, putting something in it that gave off menthol fumes and leaving me alone to soak in it for what seemed to be ages. Finally, she would return and I would get out, dry myself, dress and return to bed. I think she slept in one of the other beds in the room, but we didn't talk. Then I developed a painful ear ache and finally a doctor was called, who, after looking into the ear, announced that I had a chicken pox on my ear drum!

When I recalled this chicken pox time, I kept remembering getting measles when I was young, before I was sent away to board. I lay in my bedroom at home with a raging temperature, deliriously calling to Mummy and Daddy to get off the ceiling! At times, I could hear my parents walking up and down the hall outside my bedroom, often coming in to check on me. Their visits were reassuring and I felt safe. When I remember having measles, I feel warm. In contrast, I feel cold when I think of having chicken pox. The lay sister took good care of me, but there were no words of comfort, unlike being ill at home. Another memory came to the fore as I retrieved these memories. When I was a child and after I had been sent to boarding school, at home in the holidays I would sometimes experience lying in bed with the sheet over me, feeling as if I was covered with a stiff thin board. Many years later I told a therapist about this experience, asking what it meant. His response made sense to me: *It is a metaphor for how you experienced childhood.* I had externalised the pain of being sent away, my need for comfort and the lack of it in my life, turning it into a physical metaphor.

My experience of getting shingles, even though I had been vaccinated, is a physical expression of trauma. Like a virus, trauma can lie hidden and seemingly dormant in the body, only to suddenly resurface, doing considerable damage.[2] The eruption brings with it new memories that need to be addressed. An example is my reaction when my father died and I became overwhelmed with grief and fury. It also seems metaphorically fitting that shingles erupted in such an intimate, secret, unseen part of my body. Dealing with my trauma, writing about it, is a journey into the deepest recesses of a person's psyche. It is hard, taxing and laborious work that, while offering insight and hope, takes a toll and can be dangerous. Jung pointed out that the capacity of modern people to compartmentalise, with an erroneous belief in the unity of consciousness, makes us susceptible to an eruption of the unconscious causing fragmentation through the "onslaught of unchecked emotions".[3] I certainly felt vulnerable and at times even frightened that my descent into such difficult memories was not one from which I could return safely.

When I was ill, I fell into a yawning hole of depression. The feeling lasted for a few days and I lost any energy for writing. It seemed to me the loss was associated with the focus of moving from childhood into adulthood, which was closer to me as I am now and hence more challenging. Many people, including myself, view childhood as almost another world, while adulthood is about who we are now. I felt that I couldn't find a way forward. Then in the days around that depression, a number of significant things happened which for me fall into Jung's notion of synchronistic events: "a 'meaningful coincidence' of outer and inner events that are not themselves causally connected".[4] He believed that these meaningful occurrences "almost invariably accompany the crucial phases of the process of individuation".[5] He was right. They did lead me to take up writing again with a new vigour and resolve.

On the Saturday night, a week after the outbreak of shingles, I felt well enough to attend a local party. It is likely that the vaccination protected me from the full onslaught of the illness because I was not in great pain. While I was at the event, a friend told me about an exhibition of jewellery being held by the local art society and urged me to go and see it because the pieces were so unusual. Then another friend asked me to join a group who were going the next day to see a film from National Theatre Live of Alan Bennett's new play, *Allelujah!* The film and the exhibition were both coming to an end, so there was some urgency if I wanted to take in these events. I agreed to go but the next day I had to push myself to act on my agreement by convincing myself that the comedic aspect of the play would lift my spirits. The cinema and jewellery exhibition were in close proximity, so I asked my partner if we could look at the jewellery with a view that it might be a source of a seventieth birthday present for me, something that was approaching in some months. He agreed and we went.

The jewellery was stunning, made up of antique beads and artefacts including Roman coins. The designer sources her material from Afghanistan, North Africa, India (Nagaland), China, Japan, the Middle East and Nepal. The woman who made the jewellery grew up in South Africa and her pieces have a feeling of antiquity and close connection to symbolism. We wandered into the exhibition, moving through the first room and admiring the pieces. Then we progressed into a larger room where my eyes were immediately drawn to one piece. I loved it—just my colours—but, as it was expensive, I moved on, telling myself: *We haven't seen the rest yet.* In the last room, encouraged by the jeweller, I tried on a piece that was unusual for me, as the colours were different shades of green. I tried to tell myself to choose it because it was cheaper and different. Then I went back to the first piece that had drawn my eye. I asked my beloved what he thought and he quickly responded by pointing at the original one still on display, not the one around my neck: *That's the one!*

It is beautiful. The necklace begins at the back with a clasp of coral in a copper clasp which joins three ropes of small clear crystal beads. Next comes a small piece of worked copper, four red faceted glass beads, then another small copper piece followed by two long beads intricately painted in a blue, purple, yellow, deep pink and green design. The ropes continue with a long piece of copper holding in place the three descending strands of washed gold beads. The card that came with it says that it is made up of "Vaseline" trade beads (the washed gold ones) made in Bohemia in the 1800s. These have small pieces of vulcanite taken from broken 78 rpm records in between. The red beads are Millifiore Venetian trade beads and the long beads are African seed beads.

The piece seemed so appropriate for my stage of life and the process I was engaged in: putting old stories into a new narrative. The description of the exhibition includes the following statement referring to what will happen if you buy: "You will become a custodian of a rare and precious Wearable Treasure, complete with tales, fables and wild stories". Yes, it seemed fitting and I felt that owning it and seeing it as physical expression of my completed memoir would help me to keep writing. It would be a talisman—a keeper of mystical powers—drawing me on to completion.

The second event that helped me get back to writing happened immediately after buying the necklace. I attended the Alan Bennett play *Allelujah!* It was both enjoyable and confronting, being about elderly people in a UK hospital. At the end of the play, Bennett wraps up his views about the current state of the country, including a plea to be more inclusive towards displaced persons. It hit me that Bennett is a man in his 80s and he has reached an age which brings with it a freedom to say what he wants to say in his plays. I decided that I would be brave enough to do the same. I would continue to write, considering myself as the first and most important audience.

Another event that gave me courage to move forward happened the day after I bought the necklace. I meditate twice a day and find that it is calming but also helpful in the writing as ideas suddenly seem to bubble up. On this morning, as I sat still on the couch, eyes closed, hands resting on my lap with my first finger and thumb joined, a thought broke through the mantra I use. When I was deciding to buy the necklace, the artist told me about the beads and then left us alone to make our decision. Then she came back and told me she had forgotten to say that the pale golden Vaseline beads had between each one a small round piece made from broken 78 rpm records. As I meditated, it suddenly hit me that the necklace had a connection to the most significant story about Christopher's time at boarding school—being taunted by his peers who play a recording of him as a child singing the words of the "Vespers" poem. When they finished with it, they gave it to him and he broke it into pieces and buried it in a field. For me, the pieces of broken records in between the beads are symbolic of this memoir: a weaving together of our two stories. Again, I saw the purchase of the necklace as deeply meaningful.

The final synchronistic event occurred the next day. I had read a number of books on trauma as well as academic articles, many of which refer to Judith Herman's 1992 book *Trauma and Recovery: From Domestic Abuse to Political Terror.*[6] At first I thought I had read enough but well into the writing I decided I needed to order it. I had bought the necklace and seen the Alan Bennett play on the Sunday. The meditation that provided insight into the significance of the use of the pieces of old records happened on the Monday. Herman's book arrived on the Tuesday and I turned to it immediately, lying on my bed to rest (as instructed by my doctor), turning the pages and being struck by how different it was to read a book written by a woman as compared with those written by men (Bessel van der Kolk and Peter Levine). Her voice seemed closer, less clinical, more compassionate. I felt as though she had entered the room, put her hand on my shoulder and said: *I am here to help you with the rest of the journey.*

As I read, some pertinent sections caught my attention, giving me courage. She writes that the challenge for traumatised people is to "arrive at a fair and reasonable assessment of their conduct, finding a balance between unrealistic guilt and denial of all moral responsibility".[7] This was the challenge facing me in this part of the writing—trying to deal with my overwhelming feeling of guilt. My dream of crossing the thin isthmus of water was about the movement from childhood, where I had no choice, into adulthood where I had to take responsibility for my choices. Yet more of her words were helpful in understanding what had happened to me and the implications for my young adulthood. She argues that the experience of trauma in adolescence "compromises" the tasks of this stage of life: "the formation of identity, the gradual separation from the family of origin, and the exploration of a wider social world".[8] This was true for me and explains why I couldn't branch out on my own in late adolescence but, instead, accepted my parents' decisions and the cultural trajectory of early marriage.

These synchronistic events gave me the courage to try writing again but, when I tried to produce anything about my young adulthood, my heart started racing, my jaw became tight and constricted, and I felt exhausted. So I procrastinated and went back to some earlier chapters, tying up some thoughts and inserting some of Herman's work at pertinent points. Then I read the rest of her book, leading to a realisation that I had not fully processed my experience of solitary confinement. I had no feelings attached to it. When I first decided to put in the incident involving weeing in the waste paper basket, there was part of me that felt momentarily elated, thinking: *That was me acting to let them know what I thought of them! It is what they deserved!* But I knew it wasn't true. It was no act of resistance. I could not leave the safety of the infirmary and go into the dangerous outside world where I would be scrutinised.

Herman emphasises that in reconnecting with a traumatic event it is important to visually imagine the event, noticing bodily sensations and then, if possible, attached feelings. She argues that this stops the dissociation because recollection without emotional content is not sufficient.[9] With her words as a guide, I returned to thinking about solitary confinement and I was led straight into feeling as though I wanted to urinate. Then I felt exhausted and wanted to go to sleep—a sign of dissociation. Van der Kolk considers this reaction as being "the essence of trauma".[10] It happens because the "overwhelming experience is split off and fragments, so that the emotions, sounds, images, thoughts and physical sensations ... take on a life of their own".[11] When the person revisits the experience, they experience it through bodily sensations. Still I persisted.

When I recalled going down to the junior school it brought the experience into the present. It is a place which is so unfamiliar to me, I feel as though I had entered another world. I know there was a window there but I can't remember what I could see out of it. I know I must wait until I am released, until someone comes to get me. It is a place without time. Do people spontaneously urinate when they are really afraid? I think so. I am afraid. I am afraid again when I revisit being placed in the Mistress of Discipline's office. At least I have books and some work to do. She moves in and out of the room, so it is not as bad as the first place. Unlike in the attic in the junior school where it is silent, here I can hear the world around me. Now, as I return to the scene, I have contempt for the woman whose room I have been placed in: the passive bystander who observes "something that demands intervention on their part" but chooses "not to get involved".[12] It has been argued that living in authoritarian regimes, as convent life was in those days, "neutralised individual ethics".[13] This was so for this woman who put her allegiance to the community before the welfare of students. I am not alone in my anger towards this woman. Often the strongest emotion of those who have been held captive is towards those who stood by in silence.[14] I know I must have talked to another student about what was happening because I remember being told by her that, if I go and apologise, the nun who put me there will accept it but won't let me out, that she will want me to truly suffer. I knew that other students had been given similar treatment. I must have sought her out, another captive, needing to study the way the captor acts, to understand the process, to try to have some control over the situation. As I reflected on this, I wondered how I came to speak to the student about it, given that I was not allowed to have contact with other students? I remember there was some overlap with the student body when I was going to bed. I must have done it then.

Then I started to see the woman who had held me captive. She is small and in my imagination I demand she take off her wimple (a nun's traditional headdress) so that I can see her without that symbol of power. When the wimple is gone, I see her as a powerless person and I don't want to have anything to do with her. Up until this point I felt connected to her, continuing to want her approval, including visiting her in adulthood, which I will discuss later. Now I can feel anger. I suspect that making her take off her wimple also comes from a desire to humiliate her, as solitary confinement led me to feel humiliated by what I had done that last day in the infirmary. A hurdle has been negotiated and a line crossed.

As I began to write again, words emerged that described how I felt as that young girl: lost, alone, frightened, desperate, deserted and forgotten. It is the last two words that have the most power for me: my family have deserted and forgotten me. When I started to write again, constructing this chapter about what happened to me in the writing journey, I entered into the process that Peggy Penn describes so well in her analysis of writing about trauma. It allows one to reach "the needed words", to make "the unspoken spoken", to hear our own words, to say "things that have lived in the shadows" and to become our first audience.[15] We enter "deep time"—a place "where the past and future disappear and we feel totally present".[16] She argues that "when we write we are no longer being done to: *we are doing*".[17] And for me, in the *doing*, I entered into a process of mourning and terrible, terrible sadness about what happened to my young self, especially being lost to my family. I decided I did want to go forward with the writing, but I knew that the story of the impact of my boarding school years on my young adulthood was another painful place to visit.

References

1   Van der Kolk, B. (2014) *The Body Keeps the Score: Mind, Brain and Body in the Transformation of Trauma*, London: Penguin Random House, p. 98.
2   Fisher, J. (2017) *Healing the Fragmented Selves of Trauma Survivors: Overcoming Internal Self-Alienation*, Abingdon: Routledge, pp. 126–127.
3   Jung, C. (1964) "Approaching the unconscious", in C. Jung (ed.) *Man and His Symbols*, New York: Dell Books, p. 8.
4   Von Franz, M. L. (1964) "The process of individuation", in C. Jung (ed.) *Man and His Symbols*, New York: Dell Books, pp. 226–227.
5   Ibid.
6   Herman, J. L. (1992, 2001) *Trauma and Recovery: From Domestic Abuse to Political Terror*, London: Pandora.
7   Ibid., p. 68.
8   Ibid., p. 61.
9   Ibid., p. 155.
10   Van der Kolk (2014), op. cit., pp. 65–66.
11   Ibid.
12   Hoo, S. S. (2004) "We change the world by doing nothing", *Teacher Education Quarterly* 13 (1), p. 200.
13   Ibid., p. 201.
14   Herman (1992, 2001), op. cit., p. 92.
15   Penn, P. (2001) "Chronic illness: Trauma, language, and writing: Breaking the silence", *Family Processes* 40 (1), p. 49.
16   Gallagher, T. (1986), cited in Penn (2001), ibid., p. 49.
17   Penn (2001), op. cit., p. 50.

Chapter 12

Out of silence

Christopher spent four years longer at home than I did before going to boarding school. It allowed him to work through Erikson's middle childhood stage of industry versus inferiority in which the child develops "a sense of competence at useful skills and tasks", thereby enhancing their self-concept and pride.[1] At home, he was given freedom to develop his mechanical skills, becoming the family's "Chief Mender" and earning him a special place in the family.[2] Even though he later felt inferior at school, the positive sense of self he developed in middle childhood formed a basis for continuing to develop a sense of identity in adolescence. By contrast, the skill I developed in middle childhood was my capacity for reading, but my companions were also good at it so I didn't feel in any way special—it was just what everyone did. At that stage of life I fell firmly into what Erikson terms "the child's danger" in developing "a sense of inadequacy and inferiority".[3]

Adolescence involves transition from childhood to young adulthood and the challenge, as Erikson puts it, is to develop a sense of personal "identity" apart from parents: who I am as an individual in the world (versus role confusion). He argues that the formation of identity is built on what has been forming across the years of childhood, through the interplay between how one is seen by others and how one sees oneself.[4] The capacity of the adolescent to separate out from the parents, including their world view, is facilitated by the growth of the brain that fosters the ability to think abstractly: the capacity to think symbolically and philosophically. Being able to successfully negotiate the identity crisis has recently been found to be associated with a strong sense of self: knowing who you are, understanding your own personality and having your own opinion.[5]

James Marcia, who extended Erikson's theory on adolescent identity formation, found that some young people may superficially appear to have a committed set of beliefs and lifestyle.[6] However, their view of the world and career choice have been significantly influenced by their friends or parents and are not of their own choosing. They have "foreclosed" on a set of beliefs and not struggled to make them their own.[7] This characterises me at this stage of my life. I tried to push away from my parents and make my own decision about where I would attend university but failed in the process, thereby foreclosing on my parents' aspirations. I wanted to be a lawyer but could not achieve my goal because I believed I could not be successful and could not find my voice in such a male world.

Christopher's father wanted him to excel in mathematics and cricket but he, perhaps unwittingly, opened a door to a world that was far more interesting to his son. When Christopher arrived at his secondary boarding school, Stowe, he wrote home to his father that the school library appeared to be completely made up of the 55 volumes of the writings of Edmund Burke (1729–1797).[8] Burke was a prolific British author and philosopher. He was also a member of the British parliament from 1766 to 1794. His works were foundational amongst British conservatives and included his belief in the importance of religion and manners as forming the moral basis of society.[9]

Milne provided his son with some alternative, and more interesting, books. In particular, Christopher remembered reading books by H. G. Wells (who had been a teacher at his grandfather's school), Charles Dickens and Thomas Hardy, all of whom made a significant and "enduring impression" on him. What he particularly liked about those authors was that they wrote about the "dustmen rather than dukes".[10] He believed that it was at this stage that he began to identify himself with the Milne side of the family rather than his mother's aristocratic de Sélincourt side. The Milnes were proud of the fact that they came from a line of poor families. Christopher noticed that his father had the greatest sympathy for the "penniless" characters (such as Copperfield) or the ruined Michael Henchard in Hardy's *The Mayor of Casterbridge*.[11]

By encouraging him into such reading, Christopher's father created an environment that led him to explore an identity apart from the English Establishment whose sons were his school peers. Even more importantly, the country environment, which was so formative for Christopher at home at Cotchford, was reinforced when he went to Stowe. The school was set in a green valley and surrounded by highly landscaped gardens.[12] The founding headmaster of Stowe, John Roxburgh, hoped that a boy who went to the school would, through his interaction with the landscape, "know beauty when he sees it all the rest of his life".[13] Christopher turned 14 the year he started secondary school, an adolescent entering the period of identity formation. At that stage, birds became his obsession and the countryside both at Cotchford and at Stowe provided a setting to pursue his interest:

> Fields, woods, hedges, streams and lakes were all within an afternoon's ramble. No matter that I knew nothing of the birds that haunted the rocky coasts and river estuaries. I had enough here to keep me happy; and away I would go on my own with my binoculars over my shoulder.[14]

Yet there was purpose in these excursions. He methodically kept records of birds and nests he encountered, putting his observations into burgeoning folders. He imagined himself as an ornithologist.[15] Christopher's childhood love of nature continued to nourish him in adolescence, protecting him from becoming lost to himself and it also provided a potential career, not one he took up but it reveals an emerging identity separate from those around him.[16]

Christopher's memory of the Hardy book *The Mayor of Casterbridge* (1886) evoked my memory of also finding it enthralling when I read it in my last year at school. There were other books but this was the one I readily recall; it had captured my attention. My focus, in contrast to Christopher who was interested in the men in the book, was the plight of the woman. The plot involves 21-year-old hay trusser Henchard getting into a drunken rage and auctioning off his wife Susan and baby daughter to a passing sailor at a country fair near Casterbridge. The next day he tries to find his family but it is too late and Susan, who believes the auction to be legally binding, lives with the sailor as his wife for 18 years.[17] She well illustrates Belenky and her colleagues' notion of a woman in the stage of Silence who is "voiceless and subject to the whims of external authority".[18] Eventually, she sets out to find Henchard who, by now, is a successful grain merchant and the Mayor of Casterbridge. Her return is portentous for him because he had pretended that he was a widower. There were other female characters in the book but it was the plight of Susan I clearly remember. I think it was her powerlessness, something I had experienced for much of my life, especially at boarding school, that spoke to me, reflecting back my "female" experience. In retrospect, the power of the book for me was that it led me to begin to think about gender differences, but it was only a tiny step in beginning to be reflective about my life. Unlike Christopher, my boarding school experience, and especially what happened to me in the secondary school, had stifled any emerging sense of identity.

I left boarding school traumatised and somehow managed to complete school and a university degree, but I had no sense of who I was. So frightened was I of moving away from home that I refused to take up my parents' offer for me to go on a tour to Italy with the Fine Arts department at my university. I chose instead to study. Another part of my refusal to go on the Italian trip was that I had decided to marry the boy I had started dating when I was 17. My parents made it difficult for me when, two years earlier, I had broken off the relationship, realising that if I wasn't careful we were going to end up married. There was a part of me that had some ambition to see the world. However, after a few months I went back to him, partly because of the subtle pressure my parents put on me, but the reality is that I was complicit in what followed. I might have aspired to see the world but my desire to marry was stronger. I was seeking security and an identity—I would be safe with a husband and I would be a wife. So when I turned 21, just after I finished university, we married. We were both the same age and it was not uncommon to marry so young in 1971. Yet I am sure, deep down, both of us knew that we had reached for safety in our marriage rather than seeking and attaining a soulmate.

Hardin and Hardin have found that those who have been traumatised through the loss of their primary caregiver in childhood will often marry someone they define as "imminently losable or leavable".[19] There is "an element of consciousness" combined with an "unconscious ... intolerance of intimacy".[20] What these researchers are talking about is the capacity for emotional intimacy. It was lacking in my relationship with my new husband in that we did not talk about our inner life, making ourselves emotionally vulnerable by self-disclosure, which is the hallmark of true intimacy. It was also lacking in the relationship between Christopher's parents.

Ann Thwaite's research into the Milnes' marriage led her to conclude that Daphne went into the marriage "determined never to care deeply enough to weep".[21] It supports the hypothesis that Daphne had been traumatised as a child. Yet she was, in Thwaite's view, "devoted" to her husband.[22] I suspect that research into the impact of the loss of a primary caregiver on key adult relationships does not preclude the possibility of a deep, perhaps largely unconscious, emotional bond. While both of the Milnes were having relationships with other people by the time Christopher was in his early teens, they remained together for the rest of their lives.

Like Daphne, I considered my husband to be a person of real value (in contrast to being "losable") and the fact that I saw him that way contributed to my low self-esteem. In marrying, we were following a path that had been prescribed for us both by the culture of the time (marrying in our early 20s) and by my parents (in regards to my decision). What Hardin and Hardin don't write about is that the person who has lost her "self", who has no idea of who she is, cannot possibly self-disclose and therefore cannot find, or be, a soulmate. I am sure this would have been true for Daphne as well as for me. I had suppressed myself for so long at boarding school that I had little sense of my individuality or my inner life. Daphne lived in a period when women, especially those from wealthy families, were "trained" to be socially acceptable wives of successful men. She revealed these hallmarks, being "quick witted, lively and admiring" of her husband as well as "an amusing talker".[23] She had been to a French finishing school, which would have fine-tuned her capacity to be an engaging and attractive wife, but it seems she was not the "educated wife" imagined by the pioneers of women's education.[24]

However, while I valued my husband, I also held a belief that did fall into seeing him as "losable", illustrating that we often hold competing beliefs which we do not actively challenge. My low self-esteem led me to imagine that anyone who could love me was not worth having. If he loved me, which I believed he did, then he wasn't worth having, because he loved someone so unlovable. It is common for "adult survivors" of some form of childhood abuse to continue to view themselves with "contempt".[25] Still, like the Milnes, there was a deep connection there which has remained across the years.

Erikson's challenge in young adulthood is for a person to enter into a close, intimate relationship versus isolation, the latter involving "fear of ego-loss", leading to "a deep sense of isolation and consequent self-absorption".[26] I had not successfully negotiated the challenge of this stage. As I did all through my boarding school years, I held back my inner world. I kept up my inner world of fantasy, doing as I had as a child, imagining being loved by someone who was powerful, a leader, someone who had no vulnerability (someone not actually human!). Survivors of abuse in their childhood are, according to Herman, susceptible to seeking out "powerful authority figures who seem to offer the promise of a special, caretaking relationship".[27] My imaginings always involved being taken to live in a beautiful, grand house. I have known for some time that when I dream about a house it represents myself. It was only when I read Joy Schaverien's *The Dying Patient in Psychoanalysis: Desire, Dreams and Individuation* that I realised that those imaginings of a grand home are a metaphor for my sense of "psychological ... homelessness" generated by the loss of my parents when I was sent away.[28] However, over the next seven years, unconsciously I entered into a slow journey of initial self-discovery, eventually learning a language that would allow me to reflect on what had happened to me. The first key event was when I attended my graduation. The key note speaker gave a long talk which ended with the pronouncement: *You are just at the beginning of learning, not at the end.* I was shocked as I had no idea about life-long learning. In my mind, I had finished studying and was now on a familiar path of marriage and family. I took up a job teaching at the day school I had attended for the last three years, seeing it as a temporary job until we had children.

It is a tradition in convent boarding schools for girls to take their *fiancés* or husbands back to the school to introduce them to the nuns, as my cousin had done at secondary school. It never entered my head to visit the secondary boarding school and now I can see that unconsciously I knew it was to be avoided. However, I did want my husband to see where I had spent my earlier childhood. I knew that the reverend mother, the school principal of my preparatory school, still lived there in what had become a retreat house. So one day, when we were in the region, we drove up the gravel drive, parked the car and walked up the steps to the veranda and knocked at the front door, as my parents had done 15 years previously. We were asked to wait outside while the nun who answered the door found her. She walked out on to the veranda and almost the first words she spoke were: *Christine, can you ever forgive me for the things I did to you!* It was a statement, rather than a question, an admission of guilt. She then moved on to talking about a memory she had of tying my best friend to a chair for something she had done wrong. I was shocked and my mind immediately went to the dormitory incident of being caught masturbating. Then a thought came into my mind that was like a seismic shift: *Perhaps it wasn't me who was wrong. Perhaps it was them all along!*

It was a gift. As I look back now, I realise that I had felt cared for by her even though her ways, and the regime she followed, centred on strict, emotionally remote discipline that was not right for children. However, my admiration of her put me, as a child, in a bind. The fact that I saw her as intrinsically "good" led me to conclude that something was wrong with me. It was the same in relation to my parents. I had never thought to question being sent away and what happened to me in the process and so memories became sequestered.[29] This quarantining carried on into adulthood.

While I turned away from opening out my world, especially by going to Italy, Christopher expanded his world by joining the army. It was, of course, what many young men were doing, but he would have been allowed more time at university if he had so chosen. Instead, he felt confident enough to give up the mathematics degree and seek a new path. When he did this, two aspects of his identity came together: his interest in mechanical matters and his identification with ordinary people rather than the elite. In his third memoir, *The Hollow on the Hill* (1982), he writes that he had learnt as a young child that the "world was divided into a hierarchy with the British on top, other white men next and coloured people at the bottom".[30] He also knew that he had been born "upper class", leading him to feel "a twinge of guilt and moments of sadness for those who by misfortune were lower".[31]

When he joined the army he did so as an ordinary soldier in the Royal Engineers, a sapper—commonly known as someone who disengages mines and bombs but also lays them. They also undertake survey work, build camps, look after stores, drive trains and ferries, lay bricks, build roads, docks and bridges, and do carpentry work. When he did his recruit training it was with "miners, navvies and bricklayers".[32] He believed that in joining the army in this way he entered the world of the "Players" rather than the world of the "Gentlemen", referring to labels on the two entrance gates at the Lord's Cricket Ground. He describes the difference as being about class distinctions of the time. The Players "existed only to serve our needs"; that is the needs of the wealthier classes, the group to which he knew he belonged.[33] While in the army, he was known as "Robin" Milne, which gave him anonymity for the first time in his life and allowed him to mix freely and learn from the ordinary soldiers—an experience he relished.[34] By the time he sailed to the Middle East he had been made an officer, but he continued to be uncomfortable with the way ordinary soldiers were treated.[35] His decision was a statement about his identity. He may have been brought up in an elite world as part of The Establishment but his affinity was more with the working class.

He saw his decision to join the army as the ending of one world and the beginning of another. He believed "he had been on the leading rein quite long enough" and he wanted his freedom.[36] Now he was a young man "looking ahead to what might lie in the future, the other is looking back to what lay in the past. For the one a new world was just about to unfold. For the other a world is just ending".[37] He defines this decision as really about maturing into an adult by getting to know himself: "Who am I?" He knew that he wanted to do something heroic "but brave words were out of the question" due to his continuing stammer.[38]

When he returned to his own side, by becoming an officer, he was a platoon commander of 40 men. He asked to be allowed to accompany his men when they went to work rather than staying back at camp, which was what was normally expected from officers. He was denied permission. He stood firm in his request and was finally allowed to go. While he did enjoy the company of his fellow officers, he also felt a need to breach the barriers of rank and when he did so "it would be as if a sluice were opened and something gushed out from me to join and mingle with something of theirs until the levels were equal and tranquillity came".[39] These occasions gave him "moments of supreme happiness in equality". He also claimed that he had no desire to change the class system.[40]

At first Christopher found the war to be exciting but soon reality set in when he saw his first corpse lying dead beside the road with his head "broken and spilled like an egg that had been dropped on the floor".[41] There were many such instances, leading him to recognise the horror of war with its two components of "revulsion and fear".[42] In his memoir, he summarises what he believes to be the three stages soldiers go through in war. First, the soldiers begin with confidence, looking forward to the adventures. In the second stage, they develop a stoop, eyes down, looking for somewhere to hide, for cover. Lastly, they decide not to "bother. It wasn't worth it. If you're going to hit me, do it now for Heaven's sake, and get it over …".[43] His description of this process, especially the final stage, is reminiscent of what is likely to have happened to him at boarding school and so he recognised it in the soldiers around him.

He began preparatory school full of hope that it would be a place of adventures, as many children do when they start their boarding school experience, mainly because they have been told so or they have read it in books. Then they realise it is not so and they try to stay out of trouble, both with teachers and with fellow students. Finally, they develop a shell of protection, a Strategic Survival Personality.[44] At school, Christopher adopted the personality of one who didn't care, who couldn't be touched, of not being disturbed if he was teased about Christopher Robin. He had hunkered down as soldiers do, trying to avoid being targeted.

He also considered that his boarding school days helped him to cope with the strict daily regime of army life, with each day beginning and ending with a bell. He was proud that he belonged to the large group of men who wore the Black Cat on their sleeve (56th Division insignia), providing him with "a foundation stone, strong and lasting, on which to build" an adult life.[45] Yet there was also a part of himself that felt like he was a fraud and he stated that "for all his attempts to look like a soldier, yet remained a faintly ludicrous figure".[46] He had started in the ranks, spent many years overseas, commanded a Section in a Divisional Field Company, was wounded and had seen much of the world. However, in his mind his group weren't worthy to be infantry and didn't suffer what infantry suffered. It was Stowe headmaster John Roxburgh's speech on Armistice Sunday 1934 that cast a long dark shadow across time and place, allowing Christopher to denigrate himself in this way. His memory of Roxburgh's words showed how significant it was for him: "In war ... it is always the best who die".[47]

Christopher Milne managed the difficult periods of adolescence and young adulthood much more successfully than I did. He branched out on his own, rejecting the path that his father wanted for him. In contrast, I foreclosed on my parents' aspirations and turned away from an offer to travel overseas. I wonder if Christopher had more resilience because Olive, his nanny, had been with him until he was ten while I had gone to boarding school as soon as I turned seven? Cora Diaz de Chumaceiro, in her analysis of the loss of nannies in Frances Hodgson Burnett's book *The Secret Garden* (1911),[48] draws on trauma research which supports her view about Mary Lennox, the key character in the book. Mary's neglectful parents died in India when she was a child and, aged ten, she was sent to live with an equally disengaged uncle, Archibald Craven. There she meets Craven's sickly rejected son Colin and finds the secret garden. She entices Colin from his sick bed out into the garden, bringing it back to life with the help of a local Yorkshire boy. It is a transformative process and the two abandoned children come back to life again. However, Cora Diaz de Chumaceiro argues that Mary could only engage in this healing because: "*She had to have been loved by someone first*".[49] She concludes that the person who provided her with this foundational love was her ayah (her nanny) who cared for her in India.[50]

I believe I experienced love from my parents in my childhood and that the reverend mother at my preparatory school cared for us. However, it was not sufficient to give me the resilience I needed to maintain a sense of self when I was sent away at seven years of age. In contrast, Christopher (and Mary Lennox) had been deeply loved by his nanny until he was almost ten and had an additional four years in her care, allowing him to successfully work through Erikson's middle childhood stage of industry versus inferiority.

In his first memoir, which he dedicates to Olive, Christopher admitted that she was not a particularly good teacher but notes that what made her special was that she was "a very good and very loving person".[51] His comment about her teaching capacity illustrates Gathorne-Hardy's findings that most nannies were of working-class origins and uneducated.[52] Christopher's identification with the working classes was likely to have been influenced by her. However, Olive had an intuitive understanding of the needs of the child which it is likely she gained from being cared for herself by a responsive parent. In his first memoir, *The Enchanted Places*, Christopher includes a story that illustrates her capacity.

He begins the story by contrasting his nanny with the one in a poem, "Brownie", written by his father, in which the nanny brushes off the child's conversation without taking it at all seriously. Christopher's real story is about being highly disturbed one night in bed and calling out to Olive. She comes and he tells her that he is worried that God might be "cross" with him. Olive takes the time to explore what has led him to think this way. He shares that he feels guilty about the fact that he owns two Bibles, rather than one, and that God might not like it. On discovering his concern, Olive tries to reassure him that God would not be annoyed but he is not comforted and tells her he wants to give one of them away. He asks her to think to whom they might give the extra Bible. Olive comes up with the idea of sending it to a girls' school that had been writing to him for a number of years because of his association with Christopher Robin. They both agree and she suggests that, as the intended Bible has his name inside, she could just write "from" in front of it. She does so, returns to show it to him, assuring him that if God had been cross with him he would "have forgiven" him now and that they would post it tomorrow. Christopher is immediately at peace and goes to sleep. The next day as usual he takes the Bible to school and it is all forgotten. The Bible was never sent and he admits that the "from" looked a little strange before his name but he "left it there". This story ends with a final paragraph that begins with these words: "The next year I went to boarding school and Nanny departed".[53] He kept the Bible and I believe it is a treasured memento for him, a linking object, taking him back to the depth of her love. Those extra four years he gained before being sent to boarding school, in comparison with myself who left home just after I turned seven, had been enough to give him some resilience to negotiate the tricky waters of young adulthood and allow him to cast off into a life course of his own.

Olive was a responsive, loving surrogate parent until Christopher was almost ten. This stands in contrast to the young child at boarding school, especially when I was there, who did not have adults who were empathic to the worries of a small child. They would have been busy settling 20 or so children down to sleep for the night and that would have been their primary concern. For many children as for me, they did not feel they could turn to their teachers, especially at night, to voice such concerns and so they had to learn to deal with their worries and fears on their own. Joy Schaverien writes that the boarding school child "lives communally but feels no longer intimately known by their parents". She concludes that the outcome of this way of living may be: "An unconscious but deep and permanent lack of trust of loving relationships".[54]

References

1 Berk, L. (2007) *Development Through the Lifespan*, Boston, MA: Allyn & Bacon, p. 330.
2 Milne, C. (1974) *The Enchanted Places: A Childhood Memoir*, London: Pan Books, pp. 34–35.

3 Erikson, E. H. (1950) *Childhood and Society*, New York: Norton, p. 251.
4 Erikson, E. H. (1968) *Identity, Youth and Crisis*, New York: Norton, p. 87.
5 Ickes, W., Park, A., & Johnson, A. (2012) "Linking identity status to strength of sense of self: Theory and validation", *Self and Identity* 11 (4), pp. 532–540.
6 Marcia, J. E. (1966) "Development and validation of ego-identity status", *Journal of Personality and Social Psychology* 3 (5), pp. 551–558.
7 Berk (2007), op. cit., p. 402.
8 Milne (1974), op. cit., p. 130.
9 Dreyer, F. (1978) "The genesis of Burke's reflections", *The Journal of Modern History* 50 (3), p. 462.
10 Milne (1974), op. cit., p. 130.
11 Ibid.
12 Annan, N. G. (1965) *Roxburgh of Stowe: The Life of J. F. Roxburgh and His Influence in the Public Schools*, London: Longman, p. 56.
13 Roxburgh, J., cited in Annan (1965), op. cit., p. 58.
14 Milne, C. (1982) *The Hollow on the Hill: The Search for a Personal Philosophy*, London: Eyre Methuen, pp. 60–62.
15 Ibid.
16 Ibid.
17 Hardy, T. (1886, 2016) *The Mayor of Casterbridge*, New York: Vintage Classics.
18 Belenky, M. F., Clinchy, B. McV., Goldberger, N. R., & Tarule, J. M. (1986) *Women's Ways of Knowing: The Development of Self, Voice and Mind*, New York: Basic Books, p. 15.
19 Hardin, H. T. & Hardin, D. H. (2000) "On the vicissitudes of early primary surrogate mothering II: Loss of the surrogate and arrest of mourning", *Journal of the American Psychoanalytic Association* 48 (4), p. 1249.
20 Ibid.
21 Thwaite, A. (1990) *A. A. Milne: His Life*, London: Bello Pan Macmillan, p. 183.
22 Ibid., p. 183.
23 Ibid., p. 184.
24 Delamont, S. (1989) *Knowledgeable Women: Structuralism and the Reproduction of the Elites*, Abingdon: Routledge, p. 144.
25 Herman, J. L. (1992, 2001) *Trauma and Recovery: From Domestic Abuse to Political Terror*, London: Pandora, p. 105.
26 Erikson (1950), op. cit., p. 255.
27 Herman (1992), op. cit., p. 111.
28 Schaverien, J. (2002) *The Dying Patient in Psychoanalysis: Desire, Dreams and Individuation*, New York: Palgrave Macmillan, p. 32.
29 Herman (1992), op. cit., p. 102.
30 Milne (1982), op. cit., p. 18.
31 Ibid.
32 Milne, C. (1979) *The Path through the Trees*, London: Eyre Methuen, pp. 39–41.
33 Ibid., p. 30.
34 Ibid., pp. 30–31.
35 Milne (1982), op. cit., p. 19.
36 Milne (1979), op. cit., p. 56.
37 Ibid., pp. 32–34.
38 Ibid., pp. 46–47.
39 Milne (1982), op. cit., pp. 19–20.
40 Ibid.
41 Milne (1979), op. cit., p. 81.
42 Ibid.

43 Ibid., p. 88.
44 Duffell, N. & Basset, T. (2016) *Trauma, Abandonment and Privilege: A Guide to Therapeutic Work with Boarding School Survivors*, Abingdon: Routledge, pp. 7, 21.
45 Milne (1979), op. cit., p. 70.
46 Ibid., p. 90.
47 Ibid., pp. 103–104.
48 Burnett, F. H. (1911) *The Secret Garden*, London: Heinemann.
49 Díaz de Chumaceiro, C. L. (2003) "'*The Secret Garden*': On the loss of nannies in fiction and life", *Journal of Poetry Therapy* 16 (1), p. 51.
50 Ibid.
51 Milne (1974), op. cit., p. 26.
52 Gathorne-Hardy, J. (1972) *The Rise and Fall of the British Nanny*, London: Faber & Faber, p. 72.
53 Milne (1974), op. cit., pp. 27–28.
54 Schaverien, J. (2015) *Boarding School Syndrome: The Psychological Trauma of the "Privileged" Child*, Abingdon: Routledge, p. 141.

Chapter 13

Confrontation and captivity

Christopher was at war in his early 20s. He saw an opportunity to break away from the confines of his early life and make his own way. He took one path; I took another, turning back to security rather than forging my own identity. In my Bachelor's undergraduate study I studied history, psychology, fine arts and biblical studies. I also did two years of education subjects, which included educational and developmental psychology as well as comparative and historical education. I particularly remember studying what was then termed "special education", which included the study of people at either end of the intelligence spectrum—gifted or with an intellectual disability. A lecturer in the subject referred to what was, at the time, recent research in which it had been found that many highly intelligent students had been placed in the lowest of classes.[1] My memory of this study suggests that I may have seen some aspect of myself reflected back in the research.

I became interested in Aboriginal education, as those years (1968–1970) were important ones for the rights of the traditional custodians of Australia. It was only in 1962 that they were given the right to vote and in 1967 a national referendum resulted in 90.77 per cent of non-indigenous Australians agreeing for them to be counted in the census so that federal laws applied to them as they did to all other citizens.[2] As university students we were aware of the newly established Aboriginal Legal Service and Medical Service in the next suburb. The University paper, *Honi Soit*, often included articles about Aboriginal rights. I read them with interest. It was also a time of student protests and marches against the Vietnam War, which was particularly significant for people our age as there was a ballot system for calling young men up to serve in the army and fight in Vietnam. I didn't join in the marches but I watched on in admiration for those who felt so strongly about such matters.

When I look back, I see myself as a "watcher", always on the sideline trying to understand what was going on but never fully involved. I could see that there was a world "out there" but was not about to participate. James Marcia's research indicates that the path to identity involves a stage of Moratorium.[3] Young people in this stage are not definite about their beliefs and commitments and are in a process of "exploring—gathering information and trying out activities with the desire to find values and goals to guide their life".[4] I watched, while Christopher did more exploring in his first year at university.

In his one year studying mathematics at Cambridge before the army, he joined the Socialist Club for a period but drifted away. He then hired a wireless and began to listen to classical concerts as often as he could, fostering his love of music. A key memory involved attending a concert given by the Women's Symphony Orchestra. He was positioned so he could see the conductor, especially her face, as she conducted the Coriolan Overture and Beethoven's Eighth Symphony. What he particularly noticed was her "expression ... at each occurrence of the main theme". He doesn't elucidate, so I must provide a label—an experience of seeing a person with passion which reflected back the absence of it in his life. This small incident, coupled with the beauty of the Sussex countryside and the threat of German bombers, crystallised thoughts so that he could announce publicly what had previously been a private thought: "I am not going back to Cambridge next year ... I want to join the army".[5] It was a brave decision, given his father's hopes for him. His observation of the passion in the conductor echoes my experience of watching the students who participated in the anti-Vietnam war marches. Both of us saw passion in others and wanted it for ourselves. Christopher felt able to branch out on his own path while I foreclosed, using Marcia's term relating to those who take on the beliefs and values of authority figures around them.

When I finished university I took a secure path by immediately marrying and becoming a teacher at the school where I had completed my secondary education—another "safe" choice. However, I did enjoy providing challenging history and art history lessons for the lower grades and seeing them rise to the expectations I set them. The job lasted a year because I quickly fell pregnant, having my first son at the beginning of the following year. In my mind, I would not work again, as bringing up a family would now occupy me.

Three months after my son was born I fell pregnant again and, when I miscarried, I went to see a woman doctor who was a friend of my family, She had words of wisdom to offer me. *Go and get yourself a career! I see too many women who give their lives to bringing up a family and when they leave they have nothing left.* I realised she was right and within six months I had found a part-time position teaching art history at a private Catholic girls' high school. When I taught English and History in the first year after I left university I had quite liked teaching but, when I went back to it the second time, I fell in love with the job. I enjoyed the experience of successfully teaching students, particularly when it expanded their view of the world and often their view of themselves as learners.

I joined the school six months into the teaching year and was offered a full-time permanent position at the end of the year and I accepted. Meanwhile, a university friend was teaching art at the nearby Catholic Teachers College and told me that a job was being advertised in the Education faculty. It involved teaching Aboriginal Education. While I was studying Education at university we were given some lectures about an international philanthropic project focussed on improving the English of Aboriginal preschool children which involved teaching the mother as well. So, armed with this paltry amount of knowledge, I applied. It was a small institution headed by a male principal whose wife worked as his secretary. My friend had told me that they were a conservative religious couple, so I imagined that he would want to employ someone who personified Catholic womanhood. My application led to an interview and, in dressing for it, I carefully chose the robes of a modest Catholic woman: a pleated tartan woollen skirt, with a sleeveless mohair vest over a cream silky blouse that buttoned right up to the top of my neck.[6]

The memory of what I wore has been clear in my mind for over 40 years, leading me to ask myself two questions: *Why have you remembered all these years later what you wore to the interview and why did you go to such lengths to get the position?* After all, I had been offered and accepted a perfectly good job at the school. I also knew that reneging on my acceptance of the school teaching position would not be good for my reputation. I have no memory of thinking about the respective salaries and I don't think they would have been very different, so something else was motivating me. I first put this question to myself in 2017, which led me to write my first paper on boarding school trauma.[7]

When I trawled through my memories, I wanted to find what historians refer to as a "grand narrative" such as "wanting to make a difference". I do think there was something of that in my motivation. However, my conscience would not let me get away with such a limited or righteous explanation for why I wanted the job so much. A memory from the six months I spent teaching art history at the school kept pushing its way up and, for a period, I rejected it until it would no longer be silenced. My refusal to tell the story was because I knew it would lead to the telling of other more difficult memories that show the shadow side of why I went into Education as a career.[8]

Another art teacher had been employed at the school at the same time as me. She was a practising artist as well as being a knowledgeable and impressive person, so I was rather in awe of her. One day, as soon as I came to work, she told me that the principal of the school, a nun, had fired the library teacher. In her opinion, the principal had taken a personal dislike to the librarian and had no proper basis for her decision. The woman was also a single mother and my colleague pointed out to me that it had serious implications for her. At lunchtime, my colleague sat at the long table with the other teachers, with me beside her, when she suddenly· said: *What are we going to do about what has happened to ...?* There was a deathly silence, so she spoke again: *What are we going to do to support her?* More silence. Then the other teachers turned back to each other and took up their small talk again. I was so impressed by the courage of my colleague but was too young and ill-informed to offer her anything except silent approval. Later, when I reflected on what had happened to the librarian, I realised it could happen to me. I could be fired at the whim of the principal and I remember my mind flitting back briefly to the nun who had put me into solitary confinement. My experience at boarding school contributed to my desire to remove myself from such a powerless position.[9] My decision reveals the power of traumatic events to unconsciously shape future actions.

The period leading up to my employment at the college, the 1970s, was a time in Australia when many of us thought that everything would change for the better for all people. The election of a Labor government in 1972 under the leadership of Gough Whitlam ended 23 years of conservative government in Australia. "It's Time" was the catch cry of the Labor Party in the election, with its embedded message of "time for change" from the long reign of the conservatives. The year I was employed at the college, 1975, was also International Women's Year (and decade) and, to mark the event, the Federal government released the *Girls, School and Society Report*.[10] I can still see its yellow and black cover with a single pink rose and I can feel the excitement I felt at its release. Leading feminists such as Anne Summers, Eva Cox, Clare Burton and Elizabeth Reid contributed to it.

The report documented the under-achievement of girls, tracing the way in which schools passed on differing expectations to girls and boys—the "hidden curriculum" in which inequality was produced through the curriculum, the culture and the organisation of the school.[11] A goal of the Commonwealth Schools Commission was to open up to girls the same life choices and careers that were available to boys. I located myself amongst those whose education they were seeking to rectify but I was also clear that education was essential for women. I could see that it gave us the financial freedom to make decisions about our lives. Perhaps my recognition built upon the brief insight I had into the plight of women when I had read Thomas Hardy's *The Mayor of Casterbridge*.

Australian women had many public mentors to guide us but one stood out to me at the time: Germaine Greer, who wrote *The Female Eunuch*.[12] It was first published in 1970 and I read it when I was at university. She encouraged us to reject the traditional role of home maker, to break out of the prison of the female role that society expected, to challenge men in positions of power and to explore our sexuality. For some women the effect of reading the book might have been dramatic, but for me it was more of a slow simmer. Looking back, I suspect that the changing opportunities for girls' education, the public discussions of feminists on television and in the newspapers, as well as reading Greer's book, provided the fertile ground that allowed me to accept the advice of a woman doctor to *go and get a career*.

Six months after I started at the college I fell pregnant again. My immediate and rather desperate thought was that I would have to give up working again, but I was encouraged to stay on by some of the other women who had returned to work quickly after they gave birth. I was part of an exponential increase in the number of women who chose to go back to work after having children. Research by the Australian Institute of Family Studies indicates that mothers going into paid work was one of the most significant social trends of the twentieth century. The proportion of mothers who were in either full or part-time work with dependent children increased from 43 per cent in 1981 to 63 per cent in 2009. Even in 1987 the proportion of preschool-age children in formal childcare was still low at 29 per cent, increasing to 45 per cent in 2002.[13] However, in 1976 it was less the norm and I found that I did come under criticism. Sara Delamont writes that in the nineteenth century parents wanted their daughters to be educated "but did not expect them to work for wages all their lives".[14] Yet she argues that it was different in 1989 when she wrote the book and that the elite were happy for their daughters to work in the professions but not in business.[15] That was not my experience in 1976 in Australia. I think what gave me courage to go back to work, six weeks after my second child was born, was the community of female colleagues and also feminist writing about women having choices.

I enrolled in a Master of Arts degree at Sydney University, which involved completing a number of education subjects as well as doing a minor thesis. I wrote mine on innovations in Aboriginal education, including the use of Aboriginal teaching assistants in school, bilingual education and approaches to teaching reading. Two years after starting at the college I was promoted to lecturer level and began lecturing in the fields of child development, educational history and behaviour management, another steep learning curve.

The teaching I was doing slowly led me to realise what had happened to me when I had been sent away to boarding school. One insight came from teaching Aboriginal Education, the other from Developmental Psychology. I worked as a tutor in a team teaching child development. When it came to teaching about the importance of attachment in the early life of the child, we used a UK film on the impact of removing a young child from the care of its parents while the mother was in hospital having a baby. The film is called *Young Children in Brief Separation: John*.[16] Made in 1969, it is one of a series of five films made by James and Joyce Robertson, stimulated by the work James Robertson did in attachment theory when he joined John Bowlby at the Tavistock Clinic in London in 1948.

John is 17 months old and, while his mother is having her second baby, he spends nine days in a state-run institution where some of the other young orphaned children have spent considerable time. He has a secure attachment to his mother and at first tries to attach himself to a nurse, but she is busy attending to the needs of the group. He struggles to cope with the new food, routines and the occasional rough behaviour of the other children who are used to fending for themselves. His father visits and on one occasion he runs after him, crying pitifully at the door when he leaves. His distress eventually turns into hopeless apathy and he flops down on a large teddy, giving up attempts to seek reassurance and connection as he had when he first arrived. When he is reunited with his mother he rejects her in fury, crying and pulling away from her, and they struggle over the subsequent period to re-establish their bond. We used this film many times and each time I saw it I thought about what had happened to me at boarding school. I saw myself in the pain of John who unsuccessfully tries to attach himself to one of the caregivers and I also saw myself when he gives up trying to seek comfort from them. I also saw the boarding school culture reflected in the way the orphaned children had developed a toughness in the way they interacted with each other, taking the toys they want from him and others.

Another aspect of my work that led me to reflect on my early life was teaching Aboriginal Education. At that time, teachers did not choose where they were sent to teach. If you went to the college, you were tied to the Catholic system for two years after you graduated and your teaching position could be anywhere in New South Wales. As a result, a young student might grow up and go to school in a well-to-do city suburb but, after graduating, they might be sent to teach for two years in an isolated outback school with Indigenous students. When this happened, most of the new graduates spent the first six months crying and the next 18 months crossing the days off the calendar until they could leave and return to the city. It was not a happy situation for the teachers or students. It was hoped that a subject in Aboriginal Education would better prepare those who went out to teach in these settings.

The curriculum covered traditional Aboriginal culture and history, as well as teaching approaches used in the field at the time. I have to admit that I was on as steep a learning curve as the students, but it was interesting and I felt committed to the cause. The history I taught included the forced removal of Aboriginal children from their families and being placed in institutions where, if they were girls, they were trained as domestic servants. Most never saw their families again and they are now referred to as "The Stolen Generation". When I taught this part of the history I always thought to myself: *That is what happened to me!* Of course, I did see my family again but, as boarding school researchers have found, many of those who are sent away never really come home again.

The person who has experienced trauma may continue functioning in a normal way for years and may be a successful professional.[17] Those who have experienced childhood trauma may seek to "camouflage" a sense of "inner badness" by becoming "a superb performer". They may become an "empathic caretaker for her parents, an efficient housekeeper, an academic achiever, a model of social conformity", bringing to "all these tasks a perfectionist zeal".[18] However, the legacy of experiencing childhood abuse becomes "increasingly burdensome" in adulthood and eventually the defensive structures start to break down,[19] with the traumatic memories flooding into consciousness.[20] This happened for Christopher and myself at approximately the same age.

Christopher had coped with the fictional Christopher Robin by "not bother-ing" both at home and at school, feeling "no resentment" so that his relation-ship with his father was "quite unaffected".[21] In 1947, all this changed. When he graduated with an Arts degree, after he returned from the army, he strug-gled to find meaningful work. It led him to consider himself to be "the wrong person in the wrong place with the wrong qualifications nobody wanted".[22] He was 27 when his resentment exploded and he described it as "the worst period" of his life.[23] It led him into taking a series of jobs that were not suit-able for him, until he finally found the woman who would become his wife and they set out in a new direction.

The resentment towards my parents surfaced at the same age. Although my teaching led to some recognition of what happened to me when sent away to board as a child, I had not voiced the experience to anyone. My first expres-sion of it came physically. I now had two children and my husband and I had joined a local Catholic Church. A family weekend was organised by the parish and the venue was my old preparatory boarding school, now a retreat centre. I hadn't been back since I had taken my husband there to introduce him to the reverend mother and she had apologised for what she had done to me. I felt quite pleased about the idea of going there and taking my family, so we set off late on a Friday afternoon. On arriving, we were put in a family bedroom which was the original parlour where I had been asked over 20 years ago if I wanted to go to the school. I began to feel sick. Then I started to vomit and couldn't stop. I went to bed and assumed that I had the flu, although I had no temperature. The vomiting continued the next day, so I remained in bed. At some stage there was a knock at the door and two nuns entered, one of whom was the reverend mother who had been the school principal when I was at the school. She peered over me, asking various questions about my illness, then left.

On the Sunday, when we were packing up to leave, the reverend mother found me and took me out on to the veranda. There she took my hand and wrapped both her hands around mine. Then she said to me: *Christine. I want you to say this to yourself every day: God loves me just as I am.* I was stunned but simply agreed to her request and we left. Later, I realised that she knew something well before I was prepared to admit it to myself—that my years as a young child at boarding school had done me great harm.

A year later my anger erupted and I believed I could no longer continue in my marriage. We had been having problems, largely due to our difficulties in communicating at a self-disclosing level, and so I left. I realised that I had to take responsibility for my part in the break-up and so put myself into counsel-ling where the focus of my attention was my childhood. I cried out my deep resentment towards my parents for sending me away to boarding school and told my counsellor that it felt like I had become an orphan in the process. At boarding school I was on my own, having to care for myself with no one to turn to for help.

I turned on my parents, demanding to know why they had sent me away and kept my sisters at home. At first my mother told me I had wanted to go to boarding school, no doubt remembering my agreement in the parlour when we had visited the preparatory school the year before I went there. Then she told me she had been influenced by her sister who had sent her daughter to the secondary convent as a boarder. Finally, some months later, she asked me: *Do you really want to know why?* Of course, I said yes. Then she told me that, when I was young, her marriage was in trouble, as mine was at that time. She decided that either my father had to go or I had to go; and she chose me. Her chilling words stunned me into silence and joined us together in the chaotic space of a troubled marriage in which decision making is fraught with peril, especially in regards to the children.

When I left my marriage I firmly believed I was throwing off all the shackles of my early life. I was beginning to think for myself. My parents had wanted me to marry my husband and I had acquiesced. Now I was having none of it! Looking back, I can see that when I did my first degree I had progressed through Mary Belenky and her colleagues' early stages, moving from my childhood and adolescent "Silence" (seeing myself as mindless and voiceless) into "Received Knowledge" (seeing myself as capable of receiving and reproducing knowledge although not creating it). Now I had moved into the stage of "Subjective Knowledge" in which I saw truth as being "personal, private, and subjectively known or intuited".[24] It is a stage of "moving from passivity to action, from self as static to self as becoming, from silence to a protesting inner voice and infallible gut".[25]

The researchers found that most of the women who fell into this category came from disadvantaged, permissive and chaotic backgrounds. However, they also found that a smaller group of women were from middle- and upper-middle-class backgrounds, like mine. The family structures of this group followed traditional gender patterns with "remote" and "admired fathers" and mothers whose central concern was caring for the family. The women in this group went into tertiary education "only to find themselves confronted on all sides by alternative viewpoints and life-styles that opened up a Pandora's box of possibilities".[26] This slow process began when I was at university and speeded up when I started teaching at a teacher's college.

Women in the subjective stage of knowing turn to themselves and other women for "first-hand experience" as being the ultimate source of knowledge and they act on "what feels right for them".[27] They also "distrust logic, analysis, abstraction and even language itself", seeing this as "alien territory belonging to men".[28] They find "a new and fascinating object for study: the self" and many, like me, focus on analysing their past and current relationships.[29] There was a lot for me to discover, notably my childhood experience, including a new set of feelings ranging from intense joy to resentment and deep despair.

It was 1978 when I separated from my husband and the widespread culture of self-actualisation and the "me-generation" of the 1970s provided a supporting context for women to pursue an agenda of self-exploration. This was the journey I, and many of my friends, went on at this time as we sought to delve into our subconscious to understand who we were, observing ways in which we had, as women, been caught in a web of cultural expectations. We were angry with what we discovered and we were thrilled that we could now reject the constraints forced upon us. We were going to have none of what had been traditionally expected of us. We were not going to be like our mothers caught in marriages which were not fulfilling. We were not going to be denied the independence achieved through having a career. Yet we wanted all of it. We wanted to be mothers, we wanted to be attractive women, we wanted careers and we wanted to have a fulfilling relationship.

I suddenly saw that all my life I had been put in situations that I had not chosen. The danger embedded in my insight led me to think I could throw all of it away and lead my own life, paying no attention to the advice of older, wiser people. Indeed, I often said to myself at that time that I felt like I was opening up Pandora's Box, which for me was not just about possibilities but also about what had happened in my early life. Nick Duffell believes that "rage" for boarding school survivors is "healthy for a specific reason: *it is the natural and congruent response to the breaking of the natural law*, such as the abandoning of a child".[30]

It is certainly what I felt at that stage of my life and I directed it towards my parents. However, I have only recently realised that focussing my attention on my parents and my deep anger towards them was also a form of avoidant behaviour. It was so much easier to direct anger outwards than to actually revisit and explore my childhood experience. It is common behaviour for the traumatised person who cannot cope with revisiting the actual experience. It is easier to tell tales of "victimization and revenge—than to notice, feel, and put into words the reality of their internal experience".[31]

Belenky and her colleagues found that over half the women in the stage of subjective knowing ended their relationships with their partners, "pushing for freedom … from parental and community influences". Their drive paralleled the adolescent drive for independence. Like me, instead of exploring the world and its possibilities in late adolescence, they had foreclosed on traditional expectations of marriage and motherhood. Now they insisted on "going it alone", isolating themselves from those who might offer them more nuanced views about how to proceed.[32]

I was almost 30 and, although I tried to forge a new path for myself, I had no resilience to weather the challenges before me. My parents and sisters could not understand what was happening for me and I started to unravel. One Christmas period when I was on my own without the support of my family and my children were with their father, I had a psychotic episode. I hadn't slept for days and I began to hallucinate. Finally, I went to emergency in hospital and my father came to watch over me (how moved I am to remember his coming, although of course at the time I had no such feelings). Later I discovered that it was recommended that I go into a psychiatric hospital, but instead my father organised for me to see a psychiatrist. I remember the doctor asking me if I felt as though I had broken through some kind of barrier. It was a good question, as it was exactly how I felt, and in retrospect I realise that he knew what was happening for me—a seismic shift in how I understood my life or perhaps a separation from reality or perhaps both.

I saw the psychiatrist a few more times and I promised myself that I would never let myself get into such a state again. It was a warning to me that I didn't have the resilience I thought I had. I returned to my original counsellor but, by the time I was 31, I decided that I needed to pack away thinking about what happened to me as a child. Joy Schaverien has found that many ex-boarders who seek counselling leave before they have really confronted the traumatic experience. Some break off only to return later.[33] It explains what I did in my 30s, ending counselling too early, but also foreshadows what I did later in my life when I returned to complete the process.

So three years after I separated from my first husband, I met a new man who had full responsibility for his two children aged ten and seven. The marriage had broken down some years earlier and they had not seen their mother since. The children were in great need of care. In retrospect, I believe I saw myself as the lost child in them. Six months later we were married and I took on two more children. It has only been recently that I have realised that I recreated in my home what I had suffered in childhood—a boarding school. It is a recognised pattern that traumatised people often re-enact "some aspect of the trauma scene in disguised form, without realising what they are doing".[34] That was what I did and it had significant ramifications, not only for me but also for my own two children. They had suffered the separation of their parents, moved homes and now two very needy children and their father had moved in with us. This meant they suffered a further loss, the full attention of their mother, as well as having to deal with children they didn't know sharing their bedrooms. I also struggled unsuccessfully to meet the needs of my two step-children.

I have known over the past few years that I had created a boarding school in my home and that I had put myself back into an institution, in this case "marriage", but a further insight came to me when reading Judith Herman's book. I often use the time we spend on long car trips reading while my partner drives. On this occasion I had taken the book with me and was reading it when suddenly the whole of the area around my rib cage and across my back went into spasm. I thought I might be having a heart attack but the pain, which was spread out and more of a severe muscle spasm, led me to put that diagnosis aside. I asked my partner to keep driving to see what happened. After a few minutes the spasm stopped and I began to suspect that it had been caused by something from the book. I re-opened the book and found that I had been reading the chapter on "Captivity". Judith Herman writes that people who experienced being captured may "continue to carry out their captor's destructive purposes with their own hands".[35] I turned to my partner and said: *When I married my second husband I put myself back into captivity!* My recognition provided me with insight into my interest in the women in Hardy's book, *The Mayor of Casterbridge*. First, I had been put into "captivity" in boarding school as a child, then I had put myself back into it in adulthood. I had followed a trajectory first chosen by my parents then, like the book character Susan, I had chosen the "male" social construction of marriage as the best place for women.

References

1 Kellmer Pringle, M. L. (1970) *Able Misfits: A Study of Educational and Behaviour Difficulties of 103 Very Intelligent Children*, London: Longman.
2 The State Library of Victoria (2019) "The 1967 Referendum", available at: http://ergo.slv.vic.gov.au/explore-history/fight-rights/indigenous-rights/1967-referendum (accessed 1 October 2019).
3 Marcia, J. E. (1980) "Identity in adolescence", *Handbook of Adolescent Psychology* 9 (11), pp. 159–187.
4 Berk, L. (2007) *Development Through the Lifespan*, Boston, MA: Allyn & Bacon, p. 402.
5 Milne, C. (1979) *The Path through the Trees*, London: Eyre Methuen, pp. 25–26.
6 Trimingham Jack, C. (2018) "Lucky or privileged: Working with memory and reflexivity", *History of Education Review* 47 (2), pp. 208–216.
7 Ibid.
8 Ibid.
9 Ibid.
10 Committee on Social Change and the Education of Women, Study Group (1975) *Girls, School and Society: Report by a Study Group to the Schools Commission*, Woden, ACT: Schools Commission.
11 Ibid.
12 Greer, G. (1971) *The Female Eunuch*, New York: McGraw-Hill Book Co.
13 Australian Institute of Family Studies (2010) "The modern family: Look how we've changed", available at: https://aifs.gov.au/media-releases/modern-family-look-how-weve-changed (accessed 13 April 2019).
14 Delamont, S. (1989) *Knowledgeable Women: Structuralism and the Reproduction of the Elites*, Abingdon: Routledge, p. 63.
15 Ibid.
16 *Young Children in Brief Separation: John* (1971) five-film series produced by James and Joyce Robertson.
17 Nijenhuis, E., Van der Hart, O., & Steele, K. (2004) "Trauma-related structural dissociation of the personality", Trauma Information Pages website, January, available at: www.trauma-pages.com/a/nijenhuis-2004-php (accessed 14 January 2019).
18 Herman, J. L. (1992, 2001) *Trauma and Recovery: From Domestic Abuse to Political Terror*, London: Pandora, p. 105.
19 Ibid., p. 114.
20 Fisher, J. (2017) *Healing the Fragmented Selves of Trauma Survivors: Overcoming Internal Self-Alienation*, Abingdon: Routledge, p. 27.

21 Milne, C. (1974) *The Enchanted Places: A Childhood Memoir*, London: Pan Books, p. 145.
22 Ibid.
23 Ibid., pp. 145–146.
24 Belenky, M. F., Clinchy, B. McV., Goldberger, N. R., & Tarule, J. M. (1986) *Women's Ways of Knowing: The Development of Self, Voice and Mind*, New York: Basic Books, p. 15.
25 Ibid.
26 Ibid., pp. 54–56.
27 Ibid., p. 61.
28 Ibid., p. 71.
29 Ibid., pp. 84–86.
30 Duffell, N. (2000) *The Making of Them: The British Attitude to Children and the Boarding School System*, London: Lone Arrow Press, p. 279.
31 Van der Kolk, B. (2015) "Foreword", in P. A. Levine, *Trauma and Memory: Brain and Body in a Search for the Living Past*, Berkeley, CA: North Atlantic Books, p. 47.
32 Belenky et al. (1986), op. cit., p. 77.
33 Schaverien, J. (2015) *Boarding School Syndrome: The Psychological Trauma of the "Privileged" Child*, Abingdon: Routledge, p. 702.
34 Herman (1992), op. cit., p. 40.
35 Ibid., p. 95.

Chapter 14

Restoration

In 1948 Christopher married his first cousin Lesley de Sélincourt. Like him, she had been a solitary child who was sent away to boarding school. They discovered that they "liked doing nothing much together", especially in the country where they had both spent their childhood. It was a match made in heaven: "Together we were yet separate, touching, yet silent; she and I each engaged in our own thoughts—yet lost and lonely now without the presence of the other".[1] They set out to find a way of earning a living, finally deciding on opening a bookshop. The story of the decision is multi-layered.

When Christopher graduated from Cambridge in 1945, he rejected his father's suggestion that he go into publishing because it would lead him back into the world of the fictional Christopher Robin. Yet here he was, five or so years later, facing the two things from which he had sought to escape: his father's fame and his fictional nemesis. Later he would ask himself: "Was it that I was deliberately turning to face the dragon that had been pursuing me?"[2] The couple chose Dartmouth, although many warned that it was not a good place to earn a living. The predictions left the couple despondent. Then they rallied, imagining themselves as the town's "saviours". The Harbour Bookshop opened in 1951. When Enid Blyton heard about it, she sent Christopher a catalogue of her books and a picture of herself to put in the window.[3] She was still in his orbit, but not for much longer.

A first reading of how they chose Dartmouth seems partly logical (they worked systematically through possible locations for their requirements) and partly lucky (the property they bought was the only suitable one available in the area and it happened to be in Dartmouth). However, Christopher believed there was something else at work. After he graduated from Cambridge, he wrote a novel (not published) about a murder designed to look like an accident, with the victim being pushed over a cliff. The plot required the person to fall in an attempt to dig up a rare wildflower growing on the cliff edge. He also needed a name for the murderer, choosing "Prout" after checking that the name wasn't in the London phone book. Research into plants led him to choose the rare white rockrose as the enticing flower.

Not long after they arrived in Dartmouth, he discovered that the white rock-rose actually grew on the cliffs there *and* that the town was full of people called Prout. He concluded that: "It was almost as if Dartmouth had known all along that we were coming".[4] Jung would recast the statement, seeing it as Christopher intuitively knowing all along that he was going there because the unconscious is "no mere depository of the past, but is also full of germs of future psychic situations and ideas".[5] Christopher first saw Dartmouth "sparkling in the sun" when he crossed the river towards it in a ferry. "A dead town?" he thought to himself "... it could hardly look more inviting".[6] The luminosity affirmed it was the right place for them.

In 1956 their only child Clare was born. She had cerebral palsy. They cared for her at home until it was time for her to go to school when five. Then they were faced with choosing a school and, because it had to be a specialised school for someone with a disability, it meant sending her away to boarding school. The decision left him feeling guilty and wondering if he could have made a different choice with an implicit reference to the fact that maybe they could have kept her at home educating her themselves.[7] His response to his questions seems to have come from an acceptance that both he and Lesley went to boarding school and so it would be the pattern for Clare as well: "But we do only what by our nature we are able to do". Is it an implicit acknowledgement of intergenerational patterning? Then in 1959 something happened that changed "everything".[8] It was an invitation to set up a book display at a forthcoming conference for teachers to be held at Dartington Hall. The school falls into the category of what became known as The New Education. In Australia it was called the Progressive Education Movement.

Proponents of The New Education turned their backs on the hallmarks of traditional education, the kind that both Christopher and myself were subjected to at school. They rejected the authoritarian, punitive role of the teacher, no longer seeing themselves as the keepers of all knowledge imparted through a lot of didactic "teacher talk", with students expected to repeat it back through drill and in examinations. The strict separation of subjects, mainly the "3Rs" (reading, writing and arithmetic) taught throughout the day with a formal timetable, was also rejected. Students were now seen as "active learners", discovering knowledge for themselves, often using a project approach that integrated all aspects of the curriculum: history, geography, reading, mathematics, science, writing and the arts. Classrooms became more democratic in developing classroom rules and often students were involved in decision-making about what they learnt. Teachers sought to understand the inner life of the students, their interests and individual capacities, developing learning activities based on their observations.

Although children had received "art" lessons in the past, they usually consisted of still life drawing/painting that demanded an exact representation. Now the abstract expressiveness of "child art" was valued. Children wrote and produced their own plays, which might also include dance. Classrooms opened out to include the local community, studying various aspects of what they found there, learning through experiences and inviting people into the school to share their expertise.[9] Creative writing became a widespread practice in schools, opening up the child's emotional life.[10] This sat alongside a change in the literature children read in primary schools. In the past, formal "readers" were used to teach reading; now children's literature found its way into classrooms.

Christopher and Lesley had been trying unsuccessfully to expand their business by selling to schools. Now they had an opportunity. A few months later he realised that what he was being offered was far more and meant "lining up for another Great Advance", as he had done in the army on D Day. This time the advance was towards The New Education and his part was to be "unique" because he "was the only bookseller in the convoy". The books initially required were books that provided the children with information they could use in doing individual projects, such as learning about forms of transport or the mining industry.[11]

What appealed to him about the movement was that it turned "old ideas inside out, upside down" because previously students had to sit at their desks, arranged in rows, silently doing the same thing at the same time as both Christopher and I had when we were children. In contrast, the new approach fostered movement in the classroom with children working on individual projects.[12] He writes that "where once they learned with tears, now they learned with pleasure". He saw the attitude of schools change towards being involved in their immediate world rather than being "inward-looking" which resulted in them being removed from the real world. He used the metaphor of giving up "high windows" with "a view only of the sky" to replace them with "low windows with a view to the neighbourhood".[13] This is exactly what appealed to me when I first learnt about Progressive Education when I was at university.

Christopher was delighted to discover that textbooks were to be replaced by children's literature. Previously, teachers relied on "readers" rather than children's story books to teach reading. Now, home and school were to be "integrated" with books the children would enjoy reading in either setting. The teachers who were committed to the new approach "welcomed" him "as one of themselves, a fellow revolutionary, and then trusted" him, sending him out as "a missionary, to convert others". He believed they welcomed him because for them the "Bible was the Book and the Book was mine". He saw what it meant to the children when he delivered books and they surrounded him in the school playground. "Miss! He's brought us some books. Miss! When can we have them?"[14]

He considered the whole venture to be "one of the most important episodes" in his life. What impressed him was that The New Education didn't come as "an edict from above but rather as a forest fire that is spread by the wind and sets light only to what is combustible".[15] Some teachers and schools welcomed it while others rejected it. He found out which books were the most valuable in classrooms by seeking out expert teachers in each subject area and learning from them so he could recommend the books with confidence to others.

He began to be asked to give small talks about the various books.

> To a group of French teachers visiting Devon the subject was the history of children's books in England. To a week-end course for playgroup teachers it was story-telling. At a course for teachers of backward readers I ventured my own theories on the subject. At a conference of school librarians I talked about book selection. To parents I talked about books in school and books at home.[16]

He summarised the experience as a one and only "hilltop" that gave him a great "sense of pride, happiness and achievement".[17] It seems as though Christopher, who had thought that he could never be a public speaker, who could not "trust his voice", who stammered, had finally found his voice and, once found, it could not be stopped.

He never saw a class being taught but he educated himself by observing, talking to others, especially teachers, and by reading all that was available on the subject. Two books he noted in his second memoir were Sybil Marshall's *An Experiment in Education* (1963) and David Holbrook's *English for the Rejected* (1964).[18] Sybil Marshall's book is "a blend of autobiography and teacher's handbook" on her 18 years in a small village school in Cambridge-shire, with the central theme being child-centred and integrated teaching.[19]

David Holbrook draws on the work of Melanie Klein who, like Virginia Axline, saw children's play as their primary mode of emotional communication. It led him to argue that teachers need to access "the mind of the child", penetrating their "imaginative, phantasy world and sharing their view of life". He considered it essential for the teachers to develop a close personal relationship with struggling students.[20] I believe that these two books assisted Christopher to begin to analyse his own childhood inner life with all the emotional content. It was what I did when I studied and taught child development.

When Christopher and Lesley expanded the children's section in their book-shop, their first decision was to get "rid" of all the Enid Blyton (and Biggles) books. He acknowledged that, while Blyton's books may be thought of as "immoral", "shallow" and their "language feeble", they gave a great deal of pleasure to children, including himself (and me), over many years. However, he believed "a diet of nothing but cream cakes leaves out too much that is beneficial" and that it was best not to have them in their bookshop. Instead, he wanted books written "*about*" children, not "*for*" children.[21] Books that accessed the mind of the child, looking at the world from their perspective. Finally he achieved what he had tried to do as a child in his encounter with the young Enid Blyton—to use his dragon's breath and blow her away!

In the same period the couple became advocates for Dartmouth, motivated by their concern that new roads through the town were destroying the townscape. Christopher wrote a plan for the town based on the notion of retaining its historical background.[22] The words he uses to describe saving the town are reminiscent of the heroic St George and the Dragon legend: "Into battle!"

It was not the first time he had set himself the agenda of being a hero. During the war, he had "no doubts" they were engaged in "a crusade against the forces of Evil". He knew he could be brave but if that involved public speaking then that was beyond him. Still, when he put together some thoughts about what he wanted to achieve in the process, the first thing he wrote was that he wanted "to do something as heroic as possible".[23]

Like Enid Blyton, I too was fascinated with the story of what happened when she met him in childhood. Later, when I read his memoirs, I could see that the heroic St George and the Dragon legend was an organising trope throughout his life. It led me to look back at my early life, analysing my interest in the Lascaux Caves. It was also Christopher's story about how he came to open a bookshop, leading to his involvement in education and its place in beginning to understand the perspective of the child, that led me to think about the impact of being involved in education beyond opening up insight into childhood trauma. Christopher married Lesley when he was 28. He had managed to cope with his anger about his childhood while at the same time finding a soulmate to marry. In contrast, I had tried to direct my own life only to put myself back into a form of captivity.

My following 13 years were ones dedicated to home and work. In 1986 I had another child who would eventually be diagnosed with autism and schizophrenia. My two step children were very difficult, mainly because they had no contact with their mother from the ages of seven and three respectively. The four older children, two from one family and two from another, did not "blend" as the literature tells you they should. My husband spent a good deal of time away from home. However, while I was "captive" to the family, I was also free outside it, especially in my work, and I used the time well.

I took on a second Master's degree which required an honours thesis. In so doing, I moved into Belenky's fourth stage of "procedural knowledge". Women in this stage fall into one of two categories in their epistemological perspective for viewing the world: "separate knowing" or "connected knowing". Those in the first category (separate knowing) are usually university graduates and are interested in critical thinking and in learning the methods of their discipline. They are also suspicious about all knowledge, including their own, and work to develop sound arguments for their beliefs. These women's voices are "specialized" and they exercise their capacity for independent thought only when called upon by those in authority.[24] This well describes me in my 30s. I was now a lecturer and I was good at bringing together ideas and information, thinking them through critically and delivering thoughtful lectures to my students that I could defend if necessary. However, I was still not confident about creating and publishing my own knowledge.

Completing an honours Master's degree added significantly to my procedural knowledge: learning how to develop a hypothesis, test it and defend the findings. I really wanted to write a thesis with a focus on educational history, perhaps some aspect of progressive education, but at the time educational psychology was highly valued in teacher training institutions. Once again, I allowed my personal preferences to be submerged under a tide of popular discourse, but I did learn a great deal in the process. My research project was a longitudinal study of the primary students at the college where I was working.[25] The theory on which I chose to focus my research, that of American feminist psychologist Jane Loevinger (1976), was powerful in assisting me to understand myself and how I viewed the world.

Loevinger began her career as a research assistant to Erik Erikson at the University of California, Berkeley, and, like Mary Belenky and her colleagues, she moved into researching women's experience. Her theory of "ego development" is built on Freud's view of the ego as the "master trait", but she recasts it as "the organiser of experience". It gives meaning to all experiences whatever their origins—"physical, physiological, instinctual and social".[26] It is a stage theory, with each level having its own inner logic covering all aspects of the way in which the person views and interacts in the world, incorporating interpersonal relations, moral development, impulse control, cognitive complexity and conscious preoccupations. The lower levels of ego development relate to the simplistic thinking of childhood. Physical maturation and exposure to a more complex environment assist movement into higher levels. The more mature levels are marked by recognition of one's own inner life and that of others, with the complexity of emotions, needs, motivations and patterns leading to increased empathy. The capacity for self-evaluated goals and ideals, responsibility and enhanced cognitive complexity allows the person to be appreciative of psychological causality and development. Life is approached with a broad view, a high tolerance of ambiguity, freedom to express impulses, tightly controlled at lower levels and a valuing of social ideals such as justice providing the guiding force for life.[27] In summary, it is about movement through predictable stages, with a growing capacity for autonomy (for the person to be self-directing in their decision-making) and growth in consciousness (awareness of one's inner life and that of others).[28]

Working with Loevinger's theory was important, not only for my career but also for my own psychological and cognitive growth. She argues that development of the person through the various stages is dependent on the social environment, that is, the context in which one lives. The people and ideas one is exposed to may act as a "pacer" to push the person to a higher level.[29] Working so closely with this theory, testing students and rating their responses, and thinking deeply about it for three years, acted as a pacer, mentoring me to think in a more complex way about my own development. When I now combine working with Loevinger's theory with reading Belenky and her colleagues' *Women's Ways of Knowing* in the same period, I can see that I was quietly drawing on these theories to be self-reflective about the way I thought and interacted in the world. The theories offered me something to aspire towards, especially because they gave me an understanding of what "being mature" actually meant! Researchers who work in the field of education are very interested in how education changes students, but they usually give little thought to how researching in a field changes them. I believe it is a rich field that needs exploration.

Another, different form of learning was also happening for me at this time. Belenky and her colleagues found that, by contrast with the women who were busy learning the method of their discipline (Separate Knowing), some women learn through their interactions with others (Connected Knowing). These women acquire knowledge through empathy with others. They "learn to get out from behind their own eyes and use a different lens ... the lens of another person". They particularly enjoy learning in groups.[30] While I was engaged in learning the skills of academic research, I had also become interested in human relationship skills. The therapist I had in my late 20s, when my grief about being sent away to boarding school erupted, worked for an organisation that ran seminars on human relationship skills. I joined a number as a participant. It led me to value the importance of listening with an open disposition to the experience of others and being able to reflect back to them what I had heard, including their feelings—the hallmark of empathy. At the college where I was teaching we had begun teaching these skills to students and so I became a part of a team working in the field. I did this for a number of years and it led me to reflect deeply on the way in which I had learnt to communicate in my family of origin. I believed that in our family we subscribed to an unrecognised personal rule: *Thou shall not be vulnerable!* It is similar to the Strategic Survival Personality adopted in boarding school in which children keep their emotions and vulnerability to themselves. This personality might help the person to survive in childhood, but it becomes problematic in relating to others, especially in intimate relationships later in life.

Christopher went on a similar journey, illustrating that what was lost in childhood can be restored in adulthood. When he was in Italy during the war, he met and fell in love with an Italian girl, Hedda. She was his first girlfriend and it was a totally new experience, bringing up feelings that he had not experienced previously.[31] It was also the first time he "needed to understand the feelings and emotions that governed the life of another person". It was a powerful realisation. He started to study the interactions between Hedda and himself, forming what he referred to as a "working model" of the relationship.[32] He was developing what is loosely referred to in the cognitive sciences as a "theory of mind": the capacity to "ascribe mental states to other persons and how we use the states to explain and predict the actions of those other persons".[33] People on the autism spectrum have great difficulty in their social relationships, especially in understanding the inner life of another person. I wonder if this was the case for Christopher? It may explain his father's anxious "hovering"[34] when he went away to boarding school, as well as the isolation Christopher seemed to experience in the various school settings. If he was on the autism spectrum continuum, it would have made his school life even more problematic.[35]

Christopher's admission about his lack of experience in thinking about the feelings of others provides insight into how intense was his ability to live in his own world. He must have swung between an outer world in which he allowed others to make all the decisions (his nanny, mother and father, teachers), working hard to do what pleased them, then retiring into his unshared inner world, with little connection between the two. It is similar to how I lived my life well into adulthood, as so well described in boarding school trauma literature. It is a lonely way of living. When the inner world is not disclosed to another, we miss the opportunity to understand how we view the world in comparison with others, leading to insight both into ourselves and other people.

Loevinger also acknowledges that, while the "ego functions as a whole, some memories or experiences are retained by the person outside that frame of reference".[36] Now, when I read her words again, although I didn't recognise it at the time, I can see that bringing new traumatic memories into consciousness and working with them must lead to a new view of the world and the self. It is the central work of narrative trauma therapy.

During my 30s I turned to writing poetry and I kept some of it across the years. One example from that time, while not a good piece of writing, does exemplify that unconsciously I knew that there was much I still had to face from my early life.

One day
I will speak
about the mess
acknowledge
the confusion
honour
the rage
One day
I will allow
the drooling hags
to walk above ground
reactivating frozen land
one day
I will come of age.

When I read those lines again almost 30 years later, especially in relation-ship to "the drooling hags", my mind is immediately taken back to the nuns at the secondary boarding school, although it isn't an individual image that comes to mind. It is a collective image of a group of people that had so much control over my life, who made me feel so afraid. As a young child at my preparatory school, I appreciated that the women were not trying to hurt me but I knew they could totally decide what happened to me. I felt differently about secondary boarding school because of the woman who had inflicted solitary confinement on me.

During these years I heard that she had experienced a breakdown, as many of the religious did after Vatican Two (1962–1965). In this period the religious congregations opened out to the world, including going to university, which led to more independent and informed ways of thinking. Many religious struggled with the changes. Some left their congregations, while others worked through it, experiencing a confronting "break-up" of a world view in which they had been enmeshed for so long. Engaging with new ways of understanding may have led her to realise what she had done, leading to experiencing what has recently been termed "moral injury". It arises from engaging in actions that "transgress deeply held moral beliefs and expectations".[37] For her, it may have been a recognition that her actions transgressed the duty of care she owed each student. Such a realisation can lead the person to suffer from a great deal of psychological discord, which can be particularly difficult for those who operate from a religious orientation.[38]

She was now living at the retreat centre, formerly my preparatory school. I decided to go and see her and talk about the difficulties I was experiencing in my marriage. I rang and made an appointment with her and, driving there, I decided I would confront her in some way about what she had done to me. I spent a day there, both talking to her and sitting quietly in the gardens. I told her generally about my life, including that I had married again and taken on two motherless children. Her summary of what I was doing was confronting: *You are doing social work in your marriage.* Of course, I knew she was right but I was not prepared to look directly at what I was doing. She also told me I was exhausted and asked me to come and live at the retreat centre, saying: *I will look after you.* I responded that I had a small child. She was not deterred: *Bring him with you. I will look after both of you.* I realised that she was trying to make amends for what she had done, but I also knew I would not take up her offer. At the end of the day, just before we parted, I said to her: *I have very bad memories of you.* Her response was immediate: *And you would have very good reason.* At the time, it was enough for me. I had confronted her and I drove away feeling satisfied, believing that it was all behind me. What I failed to realise was that I had not faced the *actual* traumatic event of being placed in solitary confinement. It would take me another 30 years to do so and has been a part of the process of writing this book.

In the early 1990s the Colleges of Advanced Education (my small teachers college had amalgamated with three others to form one of these institutions) were transformed into universities. This brought a new demand for teaching staff to undertake doctoral studies. It was something I was both keen, and needed, to do. It also came at a time when I was realising that I needed to regain my freedom from a relationship that was not life enhancing. Two things finally led me to free myself. One was some couples counselling that supported my growing realisation that we were not a couple and were unlikely to become one. The second impetus came from the AIDS epidemic. Three of my male colleagues died of AIDS and, after I attended the funeral of the final of the three, I decided that I needed to "choose life". I left the marriage and enrolled in doctoral studies.

I decided that if I was going to do a doctorate it was going to be in a field totally of my own choosing—educational history. I took leave from work for 18 months to write the thesis just after I moved cities from Sydney to Canberra. Four of my five children (two of my own children and two step-children) were now living away from home and my youngest child came with me. He was nine and all attempts to find a school for him in Sydney had failed. I had been educating him at home for the past year, teaching him in the morning, lecturing at the university in the afternoon and doing my doctoral studies in the evening. I had formed a wonderfully liberating and loving relationship with one of my colleagues who lived in Canberra. He was prepared to take on supporting me through the doctoral process, as well as co-parenting my difficult child, hence my move to Canberra to be with him. We found a school that would take my son for four hours in the morning and so I used that time to write, picking him up at lunch time and sharing the caring of him for the rest of the day.

I began by writing 25,000 words and felt rather pleased with it until I sent it off to my supervisor. Then I began to doubt myself. In 1995 we weren't using email and so I printed a hard copy and mailed it to Sydney. I waited to hear what he thought of my work and the answer came in a telephone call. *Yes*, he was happy with what I had done and had nothing to criticise. We spent the rest of the phone call chatting briefly but, just as we were about to end the conversation, he said in a tentative voice: *Christine. Just one thought. I could be wrong but it seems to me that somehow in your writing you might have lost your own voice.* I knew immediately that he was absolutely right. I took what I had written and threw it in the bin.

The next day I began again. I found that deep place within myself out of which I love to write, a dive into the unconscious, and I found a subject that I wanted to write about: the religious iconography that was contained in a painting that dominated the small preparatory school vestibule. Comprising a critical analysis of sacred symbols, the writing required courage, something I wrote about in the narrative, beginning my movement into reflexivity.[39] I believe the writing I started to do at that time, and which I continued to do, has a connection back to my childhood interest in the Lascaux Caves. As Lewis-Williams argues, the person who goes down into the cave experiences an altered state and returns from the symbolic death "resurrected with a new persona and social role".[40]

At times, when I write from that deep space within myself, constructing a new way of thinking about something, then I too am changed, coming back with an altered consciousness because what I write is intimately connected to how I view the world. My writing draws upon conscious and unconscious (the inner cave), bringing together knowledge I have acquired through reading what others have written, often linking seemingly diverse material, ideas that have surfaced in meditation and dreams or through paying attention to thoughts that are running through my mind behind those at the forefront, such as lines from a poem, a song, or an image. It is how I have approached this book and, in so doing, I have been changed in how I view myself and my life—my very persona. My name for this part of myself is "cave diver".

When I retired from university life in 2008, I gave away most of my library. *Women's Ways of Knowing* was one of the few books I kept. It sat in the tiny unused study underneath our house (another cave?) until I went down and found it ten years later, reading it again in relationship to writing this memoir. The pages are yellow and it smells old—an artefact from another time. I re-read most of the book but decided not to read the section that outlined the last stage, Constructed Knowing. I had read that part of the book in my 30s and realised at the time that I had not arrived at this final stage. Instead, I wanted to wait until I had finished writing to see if there was any relationship between my understanding of how I now approach knowledge and that final stage. Finally, on the day on which I wrote this chapter, ending with my process of writing, I allowed myself to read those pages.

In the final stage, the person knows that "All knowledge is constructed, and the knower is an intimate part of the known".[41] At this stage, the person appreciates experts, but for them "true experts must reveal an appreciation for complexity and a sense of humility about their knowledge". The work they are doing is about "charting new territory" by bringing together "thousands of pieces of new information and weaving this new theoretical base", becoming a "passionate knower".[42] Let me use the words of Belenky and her colleagues to sum up women at this level:

> Constructivists seek to stretch the outer boundaries of their consciousness— by making the unconscious conscious, by consulting and listening to the self, by voicing the unsaid, by listening to others and staying alert to all currents and undercurrents of life about them, by imagining themselves inside the new poem or person or idea that they want to come to know and understand.[43]

For me, the work of this book has involved listening carefully to Christopher's story and allowing it to speak to my story. It has involved trying to bring into consciousness the unconscious of all characters involved, as sources of knowledge for understanding the nature and longstanding implications of boarding school trauma. I believe it offers new ways of thinking about Christopher and, to some degree, his parents. It has certainly offered new understandings about my life. However, there will be insights I have missed or perhaps misread—all knowledge is partial and open to new interpretations. It is just one journey amongst many into understanding a life, including my own.

References

1   Milne, C. (1979) *The Path through the Trees*, London: Eyre Methuen, p. 135.
2   Ibid., p. 139.
3   Ibid., p. 148.
4   Ibid., pp. 140–141.
5   Jung, C. (1964) "Approaching the unconscious", in C. Jung (ed.) *Man and His Symbols*, New York: Dell Books, p. 25.
6   Milne (1979), op. cit., p. 143.
7   Ibid., p. 218.
8   Ibid., p. 183.
9   Cunningham, P. (1988) *Curriculum Change in Primary School, 1945–85*, London: Falmer Press.
10 Steedman, C. (1999) "State-sponsored autobiography" in F. M. Conekin & C. Waters (eds) *Moments of Modernity: Reconstructing Britain: 1945–1964*, London: Rivers Oram, pp. 41–54.
11 Milne (1979), op. cit., pp. 186–187.
12 Ibid., p. 189.
13 Ibid.
14 Ibid., p. 190.
15 Ibid., p. 188.
16 Ibid., p. 193.
17 Ibid.
18 Ibid., p. 190.
19 Cunningham (1988), op. cit., p. 18.
20 Holbrook, D. (1964) *English for the Rejected: Training Literacy in the Lower Streams of the Secondary School*, Cambridge: Cambridge University Press, pp. 16–22.
21 Milne (1979), op. cit., p. 201.
22 Ibid., pp. 225–237.
23 Ibid., p. 47.
24 Belenky, M. F., Clinchy, B. McV., Goldberger, N. R., & Tarule, J. M. (1986) *Women's Ways of Knowing: The Development of Self, Voice and Mind*, New York: Basic Books, pp. 103–112.
25 Trimingham, C. (1989) "Female primary trainee teachers: Maturing ego development, academic performance and practice teaching". A thesis submitted to the University of Sydney in partial fulfilment of the requirements for a Masters of Education Honours Degree.
26 Loevinger, J. (1976) *Ego Development: Conceptions and Theories*, San Francisco, CA: Jossey-Bass, p. 339.
27 Ibid., pp. 23–26.
28 Ibid., p. 41.
29 Ibid., p. 431.
30 Belenky et al. (1986), op. cit., p. 115.
31 Milne (1979), op. cit., p. 110.
32 Ibid., p. 112.
33 Marraffa, M. (n.d.) "Theory of mind", in *Internet Encyclopedia of Philosophy: A Peer-Reviewed Academic Resource*, available at: www.iep.utm.edu/theomind/ (accessed 2 November 2018).
34 Milne, C. (1974) *The Enchanted Places: A Childhood Memoir*, London: Pan Books, p. 87.
35 As I read Christopher's memoir and thought about him, it seemed to me that he was on the autism spectrum. At no point is there any mention of forming friendships and he continually stressed that he was a lonely child, which I have

reinterpreted as an "isolated" child. Still, I was reluctant to suggest he was on the autism spectrum because I hadn't met anyone who knew him. Then, fortuitously, I did meet and interview a man who sold Christopher books twice in 1965. He found him to be "a strange man", who "looked down the whole time" making no eye contact, who showed "no enthusiasm" and did not engage in any way including "banter" as was usual in the interactions he had with most bookshop owners.

36 Loevinger (1976), op. cit., p. 384.
37 Litz, B. T., Stein, N., Delaney, E., Lebowitz, L., Nash, W. P., & Silva, C. (2009) cited in Kopacz, M. S., Connery, A. L., Bishop, T. M., Bryan, C. J., & Drescher, K. D. (2016) "Moral injury: A new challenge for complementary and alternative medicine", *Complementary Therapies in Medicine* 24, p. 29. This research is currently being applied to the military but it seems to me that it is equally applicable in this situation.
38 Kopacz, M. S., Connery, A. L., Bishop, T. M., Bryan, C. J., & Drescher, K. D. (2016), op. cit., p. 30.
39 Trimingham Jack, C. (1998) "Sacred symbols, school ideology and the construction of subjectivity", *Paedagogica Historica: International Journal of the History of Education* 34 (3), pp. 771–794.
40 Lewis-Williams, D. (2002) *The Mind in the Cave: Consciousness and the Origins of Art*, London: Thames & Hudson, pp. 264–265.
41 Belenky et al. (1986), op. cit., pp. 137–139.
42 Ibid.
43 Ibid., p. 141.

Conclusion

There are claims that contemporary boarding schools are now different yet, as Alex Renton writes in response to these assertions—"No"—"a lot has changed, but not everything. They are still boarding schools".[1] The practice of sending children away to board is still embraced in the UK and Australia. It continues to flourish in the face of growing evidence that societies are more likely to "prosper" if its citizens are "securely attached and empathic … citizens".[2] French sociologist Pierre Bourdieu argues that elite schools, a category to which most boarding schools belong, are based on a desire for social success and the development of "a *consecrated* elite … that is not only distinct and separate, but also recognized by others and by itself as worthy of being so".[3]

I began this book by stating that it is partly memoir and biography as well as educational history. It certainly falls into all the genres making a "claim on history even … if it seems to align more with fluidity of imagination and memory".[4] For me, it is also a "*testimonio*", defined by John Beverley as "a narrative … told in the first person by a narrator who is also the real protagonist or witness of the events he or she recounts".[5] *Testimonio* is a Spanish term referring to a "witness account", particularly used in narrative research methodology by those undertaking Latin American history. In this context, it is defined as "a first-person account by the person (narrator) who has faced instances of social and political inequality, oppression, or any specific form of marginalization".[6]

Giving testimony is a political and oppositional act, "insofar as those who have witnessed violence are authorised to speak truth to power".[7] It differs from a personal account that locates "the cause, experience and end of suffering within the framework of the individual", implicitly charging the person with the responsibility of overcoming and redeeming their suffering.[8] Leigh Gilmore, in her analysis of what leads women's testimony to be doubted, argues that memoir has the capacity to be "anticonfessional" if the writer presents "herself as a subject coming to terms more with the mystery of her agency than her injury".[9]

I offer this book as a witness account of the trauma of sending children away to boarding school. Indeed, I consider that my outsider position as a teacher educator and historian carries with it a responsibility to use my insider experience to bear witness and contribute to a "relentless tide" (drawing on Winston Churchill's reference to the tradition of sending children away to board) of historical and psychological evidence that boarding schools are inherently problematic. It is one of a long line of testimonies, as outlined in the introduction, going back to the eighteenth century and forward in time with the recent research into the damaging long-term impact on the developing person.

The previous chapter of this book, with its celebratory understanding of my arrival at Belenky's stage of Constructed Knowing, may seem to place me in the category of "resilient survivor", but this isn't so. There are psychological scars arising from my boarding school experience that I must carry for the rest of my life. In particular, the sadness I feel for the damage that, as a result of it, I have unwittingly inflicted on those I love. There is also the fact, as Jung points out, that "whether consciously or unconsciously, individuation continues to the end of life".[10] It is also tempting to think that, once I arrived at an understanding of my relationship with knowledge and my journey to use it to its full capacity, the project is finished, but that is not the case. Janina Fisher has found that "shame and self-loathing often interfere with clients' ability to feel connected even to strengths they are aware they possess".[11] This has become stronger for me as I have grown older, which surprises me. Shame in association with using my intellect wasn't something I experienced when I was in my 30s and 40s, or perhaps I simply didn't recognise it as such. My first reading of it is that by giving testimony I have moved out of the group. It is a dangerous place to be because with it comes a fear of rejection and abandonment, especially given the self-disclosing nature of this book. A second reading, based on the work of Alice Miller, offers a deeper understanding.

In her clinical practice she found that often her gifted patients are "admired for their talents and achievements" and success in whatever they do.[12] Yet they are also "plagued by anxiety or deep feelings of guilt and shame". The reason for this is that from childhood they have lived up to their parents' expectations to be clever, while sacrificing an understanding of their "childhood vicissitudes" and their "true needs—beyond the need for achievements".[13] These children were not able to experience and express feelings of "jealousy, envy, anger, loneliness, impotence, anxiety" and to find comfort and acceptance from their primary caretakers when they did so.[14] This well describes me, as I outlined in the Prelude. Knowledge was a highly valued currency in the family and culture in which I grew up. Additionally, people of that generation did not express their inner feelings nor disclose their vulnerability. The suppression of needs and emotions was also the currency of boarding school. It has been a powerful combination in my life.

Miller found that facing the true feelings and aspects of oneself, especially the shabby, shameful, needy, angry, impotent, inadequate, frightened parts, and treating them with compassion is what is required if true reconciliation is to occur.[15] This offers another way of thinking about the "drooling hags" of my poem—that they are the cut off and vulnerable aspects of myself. It has also led me to think more deeply about the hot air balloon and Jung's warning that I was in danger of floating away. Going back and admitting the "shameful" story of what happened in the infirmary before I left boarding school for the last time put me on a path to reconnection with these cast off aspects of myself. It protected me from "floating away" into a false belief that I had come through it as the "strong survivor" and also from the attraction of living only in the intellect. It brought me back to parts of myself that I wanted to shy away from, to ignore and to de-value.

It has taken many years to get to know these cast off aspects of myself. Expressing them publicly in the pages of this book has been confronting. At times I have wondered if I can bear such exposure. The depth of my trauma became clear to me in a therapy session just after I had finished the book and it had been accepted for publication. I went into the session pleased to be able to tell my therapist the good news. Then I started to dissociate, wanting to go to sleep and unable to see clearly. I acknowledged what was happening, locating the feeling as one of fear. Immediately I was taken back to the 14-year-old girl who had been put into solitary confinement. I realised I was afraid of speaking out, of writing about what had happened to me, of being punished. It was a scary, powerless place to be and it took some time to reassure me that what I was experiencing was a part of "me" in the past, not me in the present. The event reveals that reclaiming the rejected traumatic aspects of myself, in this case the scared girl, is still a work in progress. Indeed, establishing a deep connection to these aspects of myself has been the central business of my lifetime work of getting to know myself. Now each day, especially when I meditate, I search for and welcome them home.

It took Christopher Milne many years to reconnect with his young self. In his first memoir, *The Enchanted Places* (1974), he revisited himself as a child imagining that he was writing for those who were admirers of his father's books, especially about Winnie-the-Pooh, and who wanted to read about that long ago and ostensibly happy period of his life. The first draft of the book ended with this audience in mind. Then he added The Epilogue, fashioned for a different audience, in which he wrote about later and more painful aspects of his life.[16] It is in that section that we read about the impact on him of the fictional Christopher Robin and the problems it caused him in boyhood, including the "cursed" boarding school event involving the recording of *Vespers*, and on into young adulthood. He claims that his major problem was jealousy, wanting to be as successful as the other schoolboys were, especially at sport. In writing his first memoir, he tried to keep the impact of the fictional Christopher Robin at bay but, in the end, needed to provide a balance to the view he had constructed as the happy child of the famous author—a legacy that seemed at first to be like a "blessing" but was in fact "somewhat of a curse".[17] It was the beginning of deeper truth-telling.

In his second memoir, written only a few years later, *The Path Through the Trees* (1979), he admits (again in The Epilogue) that he wrote his first book as a reaction to his mother destroying all her husband's personal possessions after he died in 1956. He was furious with her and decided to write a memoir for his father's "sake", to record what he knew about him, later realising that he needed to write something for his "own sake too".[18] When he began, he could find no clear direction and thought he might write an introduction to a new version of the Pooh books. Then something happened.

> It was at this point that I began to see, not the Christopher Robin I had intended to write about, but another small boy. And as I looked at him he grew clearer and I saw to my surprise that he was beckoning to me. I took a few hesitant steps towards him and he came to meet me. He took me by the hand and led me back.[19]

Finally, he is able to take the child's perspective of himself in the writing. It is what he learnt to value when he was involved in the New Education which he saw as contributing so much to the development of children's literature.[20] It was not an easy process and his description of writing autobiography resonates with my experience in writing this book: that "each session at one's typewriter is like a session on the analyst's couch". For him, the outcome from his insights and how positively it was received by readers when he wrote it, "combined to lift me from under the shadow of my father and Christopher Robin, and to my surprise and pleasure I found myself standing beside them in the sunshine, able to look them both in the eye".[21]

To my mind, what he is writing about is the long process of recovering from trauma. The process of recalling the events, experiencing the associated emotions, placing them into a wider perspective of understanding and, finally, integrating them into autobiographical memory. It is also the process of individuation—"a slow, imperceptible process of psychic growth"—leading to the maturation of the person.[22] It is "the unique task of self-realisation" which may include many problems shared by others, but is characterised by "the fact that each person has to do something different, something that is uniquely his own".[23] Christopher had something to do that was experienced only by him and, when he wrote his first memoir, he stated that "it is the story of the effect on someone's life of an unusual event that occurred when he was a child".[24] In this late stage of his life he was able to face the dragon and name it for what it was—something idiosyncratic that happened to a child that had a significant impact on the trajectory of that life. As for all people who must deal with trauma in their lives, it is a heroic journey.

There is an innate drive for us to tell stories about our lives, one that can be traced back through human history to first expressions by our ancestors in cave art—where I began at the Lascaux Caves. That urge is still strong. It is why we read books, watch movies, value art, join churches; it is our desire to provide explanation for our lives, with the embedded hope that they matter. Remembering is a voyage of discovery—a process of working out who we are. It is why we carry stories about our experiences across our lives, telling and re-telling them. As Michaela Maftei expresses it, our memories slowly "construct" our lives, creating "a channel through which we view the world".[25] Yet when we engage in such "tellings" we often fail to be reflective about why they are important to us. In so doing, we author our lives as a series of discrete short stories rather than as a complex novel. There are good reasons for avoiding the project.

Remembering can be time-consuming, complex and painful. It requires supportive companionship in which we feel safe to make ourselves vulnerable. However, the cost of avoidance is that we remain small, limited, often captured in the shadowy web of fear and suppressed emotions. We miss the opportunity to know the unique journey of our lives. We fail, as Jung calls it, to individuate, reconnecting the conscious with the unconscious mind, restoring aspects of ourselves that have been "missing for a long time, that give purpose to and thus enrich human life".[26]

Narratives are never free of discourse. We tell stories according to the ideas available to us at the time. It has been the writing and research of other ex-boarders and those psychotherapists who work with them that have given me the language to bring forth the story of my life—to finally face the "drooling hags" of memory that had cast a spell over my life. Yet as I went about doing this work, charting each stage of my life, it was heartening to see the drive that I had to heal myself. There were periods when I had re-created the restrictions of my childhood, causing suffering to those around me, while at the same time I was struggling to free myself from my hauntings.

I was initially unaware that the theories I intuitively chose to work with as a researcher were feeding back into my life, providing guidance into a more mature way of thinking and living. As I have argued, I believe this was also true for Christopher with the ideas he encountered through his involvement in the New Education/Progressive Education movement. However, it was our education that made our engagement possible and we both came from families who valued it. They wanted us to have the best education possible, even if they fell subject to the belief that boarding schools were the best way to provide it. It was our education, including tertiary studies, that allowed us to read, reflect and engage in analysing our lives. I had the additional advantage of working in the field of teacher education including teaching child development, undertaking two Master's degrees in education, studying for a doctorate in educational history and of being able to afford therapy. Our healing was facilitated by the resources available to us from being born into families who were financially well-off, educated and moved easily in the social world. I have also had the enormous benefit of the many informative conversations I have had with my partner who was also an academic in the field of education. It is a position of privilege.

The fact that I have been able to form a secure, loving attachment with him confirms American psychiatrist and author Dan Siegel's notion of "earned secure attachment". This refers to research indicating that "childhood attachment wounds can be modified through life experiences that 'grow' states of secure attachment, even in adulthood".[27] Nurturing friendships, rearing one's children, forming healthy intimate relationships "or creating secure attachment relationships" with parts of oneself that have been split off in memory "capitalises on the brain's ability to grow new neural networks", allowing the encoding of "new, pleasurable feeling states".[28] The outcome of these experiences changes the "ending of the story".[29]

The last stage of Erik Erikson's eight life stages is that of Ego Integrity versus Despair. The person, who is now moving towards the end of life, must come to accept "one's one and only life cycle, as something that had to be and that, by necessity, permitted no substitution".[30] It is based on a recognition that "an individual life is the accidental coincidence of but one life cycle with one segment of history". This understanding leads to a "different love of one's parents".[31] Christopher and I were the recipients of a particular aspect of British cultural patrimony in which, for the purposes of education, children lived a significant part of their young lives under the care of people who were not their parents. It had traumatic consequences for us and for many other children who were brought up under that system. Yet Erikson writes that even "under the most favourable conditions" of family life, "there is a sense of having been deprived, of having been divided, of having been abandoned", so that throughout life, the interaction between the self and the society in which one lives provides an arena in which the person must seek to resolve "this sense of inner division".[32] Erikson's final life stage is a time of bringing together all that has come before. In this stage, there is the possibility of an ultimate trust that one's life has meaning, an acceptance of it as it has been, and a sense of wisdom and peace versus despair about how one has lived one's life.[33]

A significant outcome of this cultural legacy for Christopher was that it disrupted the attachment he had to his mother, leading to estrangement from her in adulthood. He saw her only once after his father's death. Yet he continued across his adulthood to love being out in the countryside alone in the night, a replication of what he had begun with her in his childhood. He wrote that as an adult he found pleasure in all the night-time sounds of wind and animals, enjoyed passing the lit window of a house and longing to peer in to see their life. It was coming home that he particularly loved about these night-time walks: "to see the lights of my own house shining ... soon I will be home, part once more of the indoor world of light and warmth".[34]

Christopher had to accept that, even though he had not liked boarding school, he had to send his daughter away for most of her young life, but when she finally came home to live he devoted himself to her. The last paragraphs of his second memoir are about carrying her up to the highest point at the back of their home. There they sit together and he ponders about what might be done in the garden, but decides it can wait: "Small and slow is our world, and luckily that is how we like it".[35] Then it occurs to them that Lesley will be walking home from the shop and he suggests to Clare that they go out to meet up with her. He plans where they might intercept her walk, a mathematical problem of calculating time, although he admits he is rusty at working out such problems. Finally, he picks Clare up and with her arms around his neck they set out together "slowly, because the path is a little slippery, down through the trees".[36] To my mind, both his night walks and his final description of going to meet Lesley are an unconscious expression of a deep attachment to his mother which he could not express to himself, an unrecognised imprint on his psyche which he continued to act out in his life. It is an example of the long-term impact of children being brought up in ways that distance them from their parents, contributing to an intergenerational pattern of isolation, loss and a struggle to connect.

I have discovered that, like my friend Christopher, who became my psychological companion, who found a small boy waiting for him when he began to write, I too need to make a journey back across time. It is an essential part of the process in integrating the split off parts of traumatised selves by "welcoming them 'home' at long last, creating safety for them, and making them feel wanted, needed, and valued".[37] For me, this has involved visiting the young woman, wife and mother, who made so many mistakes, offering her words of consolation: *You did your best with what you had. It wasn't all up to you.* Then there is the girl in the infirmary and my words to her are: *When you found a place of safety, you were wise enough to put yourself there under the care of a protective person. You were right to seek rescue. I am here now. You are safe.* Finally, I have an answer for that young child who lay in a field at boarding school and wondered what her life would be about: *Your life has involved many rich experiences: being a mother, loving companionship with a dear partner, learning, teaching, writing and friendship; and it has been about you, Christine. It has, above all, been about finding my way back to you.*

References

1 Renton, A. (2017) *Stiff Upper Lip: Secrets, Crimes and the Schooling of a Ruling Class*, London: Weidenfeld & Nicolson, p. 378.
2 Duffell, N. & Basset, T. (2016) *Trauma, Abandonment and Privilege: A Guide to Therapeutic Work with Boarding School Survivors*, Abingdon: Routledge, p. 91.
3 Bourdieu, P. (1996) *The State Nobility: Elite Schools in the Field of Power*, translated by L. C. Clough, Cambridge: Polity Press, p. 102.
4 Gilmore, L. (2018) *Tainted Witness: Why We Doubt What Women Say About Their Lives*, New York: Columbia University Press, p. 81.
5 Beverley, J. (1993), cited in Gilmore (2017), op. cit., pp. 59–60.
6 Mora, R. A. (2015) "Testimonio", *Key Concepts in Intercultural Dialogue*, No. 45, available at: https://centerforinterculturaldialogue.files.wordpress.com/2015/01/kc45-testimonio.pdf (accessed 20 August 2019).

7 Gilmore (2017), op. cit., p. 81.
8 Ibid., p. 101.
9 Ibid., p. 95.
10 Schaverien, J. (2002) *The Dying Patient in Psychoanalysis: Desire, Dreams and Individuation*, New York: Palgrave Macmillan, p. 125.
11 Fisher, J. (2017) *Healing the Fragmented Selves of Trauma Survivors: Overcoming Internal Self-Alienation*, Abingdon: Routledge, p. 15.
12 Miller, A. (1981) *Prisoners of Childhood: The Drama of the Gifted Child and the Search for the True Self*, translated by R. Ward, New York: Basic Books, p. 6.
13 Ibid.
14 Ibid., p. 9.
15 Ibid., p. 26.
16 Milne, C. (1974) *The Enchanted Places: A Childhood Memoir*, London: Pan Books, pp. 2–3.
17 Ibid., pp. 144–150.
18 Milne, C. (1979) *The Path through the Trees*, London: Eyre Methuen, p. 280.
19 Ibid., p. 281.
20 Ibid., pp. 198–201.
21 Ibid., p. 285.
22 Von Franz, M. L. (1964) "The process of individuation", in C. Jung (ed.) *Man and His Symbols*, New York: Dell Books, p. 161.
23 Ibid., p. 167.
24 Milne (1974), op. cit., p. 3.
25 Maftei, M. (2013) *The Fiction of Autobiography: Reading and Writing Identity*, London: Bloomsbury Publishing, p. 152.
26 Jung, C. (1964) "Approaching the unconscious", in C. Jung (ed.) *Man and His Symbols*, New York: Dell Books, p. 89.
27 Fisher, op. cit., p. 17.
28 Ibid.
29 Ibid.
30 Erikson, E. H. (1950) *Childhood and Society*, New York: Norton, p. 260.
31 Ibid.
32 Ibid., p. 241.
33 Ibid., pp. 260–261.
34 Milne (1979), op. cit., pp. 31–32.
35 Ibid., p. 286.
36 Ibid., p. 287.
37 Fisher (2017), op. cit., p. 21.

Index

Vespers: poem 19, 96–7, 133, 175
Volkan, Vamink 68
Von Franz, Marie-Louise 112

Walton, Frank 86
Wells, H. G. 138
White, Antonia 59
Whitlam, Gough 151

Women's Ways of Knowing: stages 13, 127, 139, 155–6, 164, 166, 170, 174; *see also* Belenky
Würmster, Lèon 113, 115
Wyndham Scheme 99–100, 123

Young Children in Brief Separation: *John* (film) 152

Printed in Great Britain
by Amazon